SHOOTING PADDLERS

PHOTOGRAPHIC ADVENTURES

WITH

CANOEISTS, KAYAKERS and RAFTERS

toni harting

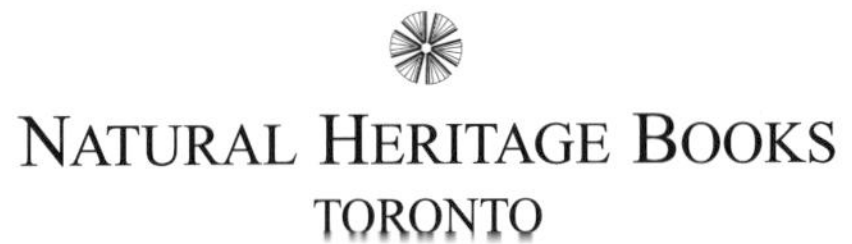

NATURAL HERITAGE BOOKS
TORONTO

Published by Natural Heritage/Natural History Inc.
P.O. Box 95, Station O, Toronto, Ontario M4A 2M8

Design by Toni Harting
Edited by Jane Gibson
Cover design by Blanche Hamill
Production by Norton Hamill Design
Printed and bound in Canada by Hignell Printing Limited

Canadian Cataloguing in Publication Data

Harting, Toni, 1927–
Shooting paddlers : photographic adventures with canoeists, kayakers and rafters

Includes index.
ISBN 1-896219-62-4

1. Action photography. 2. Photography of sports. 3. Photography, Artistic.
4. Canoes and canoeing–Pictorial works. I. Title

TR821.H37 2000   778.9'9797122   C00-931288-9

The Canada Council | Le Conseil des Arts
for the arts | du Canada
since 1957 | depuis 1957

Natural Heritage/Natural History Inc. acknowledges the support received for its publishing program from the Canada Council Block Grant Program and the assistance of the Association for the Export of Canadian Books, Ottawa. Natural Heritage also acknowledges the support of the Ontario Council for the Arts for its publishing program.

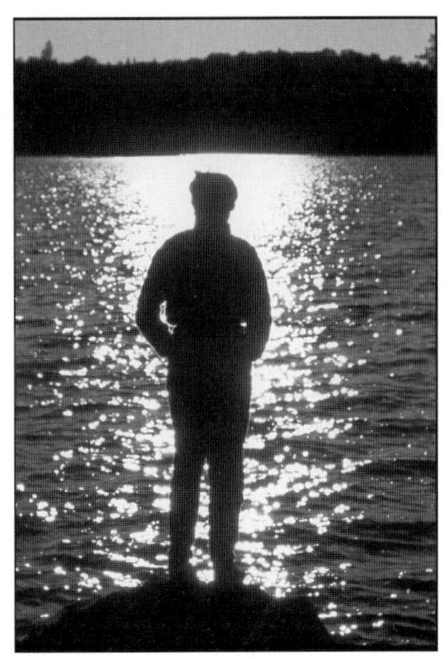

for my Ria

ACKNOWLEDGMENTS

Without paddling, my life would have taken a completely different direction, and without the Wilderness Canoe Association there would have been much less real paddling for me. Many thanks to all the members of the WCA.

Roger and Sandy Harris have given so freely of their time and knowledge of paddling, photography, art, computers and language that I feel very grateful indeed. I thank Sandy Richardson for granting permission to use the three sea kayaking photos on pages 22 and 23, and Harry Litz for letting me discuss his photo presented on page 37.

Most of all, I want to thank my wife and indispensable partner, Ria, for the patience and support she has given me when, over many years of photographing paddlers, I was making the pictures used in this book. She has also become quite skilled at shooting paddlers herself, as shown by the photos made by her and reproduced on pages 35, 75, 76(bottom), 77, 80, 138(top), 139, 160(bottom), 166, 167 and 171. Her dedicated assistance, criticism and confidence in the project during the creation of this book have been of crucial importance.

Finally, many fond thanks are due to our incomparable house cat, Hasselblad F-stop Harting, without whose persistent interference this book would have been finished not only much earlier but also at a lower quality.

CONTENTS

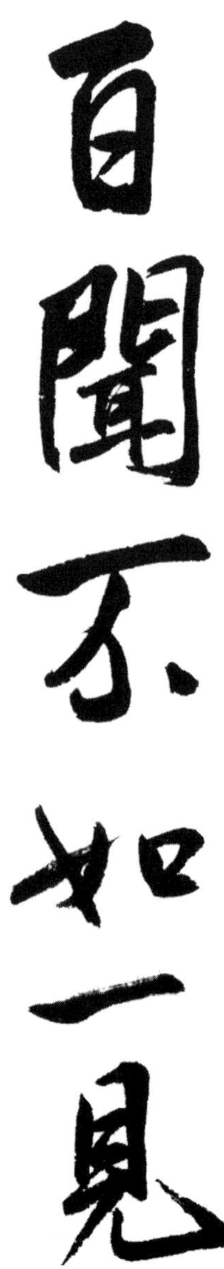

one picture is worth a thousand words

INTRODUCTION

Millions of people all over the world are united by a passion for paddling. They feel a powerful need to hear again and again the seductive swishing sound generated when paddle meets water in an elegantly choreographed dance. Every spring, summer, fall and even winter, these devoted lovers of the outdoors take their paddlecraft to favourite waters and enjoy the peace, freedom and excitement of doing what they all love: paddling.

They are the accomplished wilderness canoeists exploring the wild and lonely waters of the far North. They are the whitewater enthusiasts who go on excitement-filled weekends playing in rapids and even plunging down falls. They are the sea kayakers searching for magical islands and bays in coastal waters. They are the racing fanatics, both marathon and sprint, spending numerous hours on the water in canoes and kayaks enjoying their demanding sport. They are the people who use inflatable rafts to run challenging rapids and visit wilderness rivers far and wide. They are the cottagers, who use the beloved family canoe only for some quiet puttering about on the placid neighbourhood lake. And they are the kids in summer camp, for whom paddling is often central to their activities.

What many of these diverse people share, besides a sincere love of paddling, is the desire to bring home a memento of their times on and near the water, something that will always inspire fond memories of the moments they had outdoors and the joy they discovered there. They want to add illustrations to the stories of their adventures, of the challenges they met, of their demanding races and of the people they befriended.

There is no better way to do that than through photography, the easiest but also most effective method of building a fine collection of visual souvenirs. Nothing, not even the spoken word or moving pictures, beats still photography as a medium to capture memories. Verbal descriptions of events are easily forgotten, but photographs, be these simple snapshots or venerated masterpieces, will be retained because these provide unsurpassed intimacy with the subject. No wonder photography has become essential to our society.

Everybody can discover the language of photography; it is just a matter of learning how to express your vision through technology. So, if you consistently want to make good photographs under a variety of conditions, you have to start by understanding a few basic techniques and by acquiring a minimal grasp of the equipment and the processes involved. Of course, the better you understand the technical side of photography, the more opportunities you have for making good photographs through allowing the camera to gradually become an extension of your senses. Do not let technique take over and rule you, though; it is no more than a tool to help record the pictures you see.

Because paddling photography takes place around water, a deadly enemy of delicate equipment, the photographer often needs a special approach to successfully shoot paddlers. Once a reasonable level of knowledge of photographic equipment and techniques, as well as some understanding of the demanding water environment, has been reached, paddlers soon discover that this particular kind of outdoor photography gives immense satisfaction. Now the paddlers themselves can produce a wealth of images of their various paddling activities.

Shooting Paddlers aims to help paddlers strengthen their ability to see, recognize and record meaningful images encountered when using canoes, kayaks or rafts. It is intended for both amateur (amateur comes from the Latin *amare*, love) and professional photographers, presenting an original approach to the study of photography and providing a wealth of specialized information that is difficult if not impossible to find elsewhere. The book discusses what is most important in paddling photography: subject, lighting and composition; and also explains how the photos in the publication were made and why. Emphasis is concentrated on specific possibilities and problems unique to the paddling environment, rather than on the technical basics of general photography.

The reader is taken along on a series of educational and exciting 'adventures' in the varied world of paddling, and is shown how to create fine pictures in any situation. The photographs presented in the book have been selected on the basis of their effectiveness as tools for instruction. Their purpose is to give useful information to the reader about many aspects of paddling photography, including things that can go wrong. Together with the numerous 'good' photos offered for study are several mediocre and even bad ones to strengthen the reader's analytic ability.

Most of the 238 black-and-white and colour photographs are discussed through the presentation of one or several pictures on a page, each accompanied by an analysis that includes explanations, tips, recommendations and other useful instructions. Some pertinent suggestions on technical photographic aspects complete the support material, but are held to a minimum.

The majority of the pictures were made in Ontario; several were shot in Quebec and West Virginia. Where the pictures were taken is really not important, though; the photography of paddlers is the same everywhere.

Once your photos have been taken and processed, you can collect them in albums or slide shows, creating absorbing capsules of images frozen in time, memories you can relive over and over again. Such personal recollections become priceless documents of important and unique events in your life, forming a link between the viewer and your experiences. What you will show in those collections is limited only by your own creativity and the strength of your desire to express yourself through photography. By bringing back some good evocative pictures that excite, educate and inspire, you will be able to tell fascinating stories supported by the images you discovered in the wonderfully diverse world of paddling. There is no limit to what you can achieve if you are dedicated.

May this book be an inspiration to all who share the joy of paddling and photography.

RECREATIONAL PADDLING

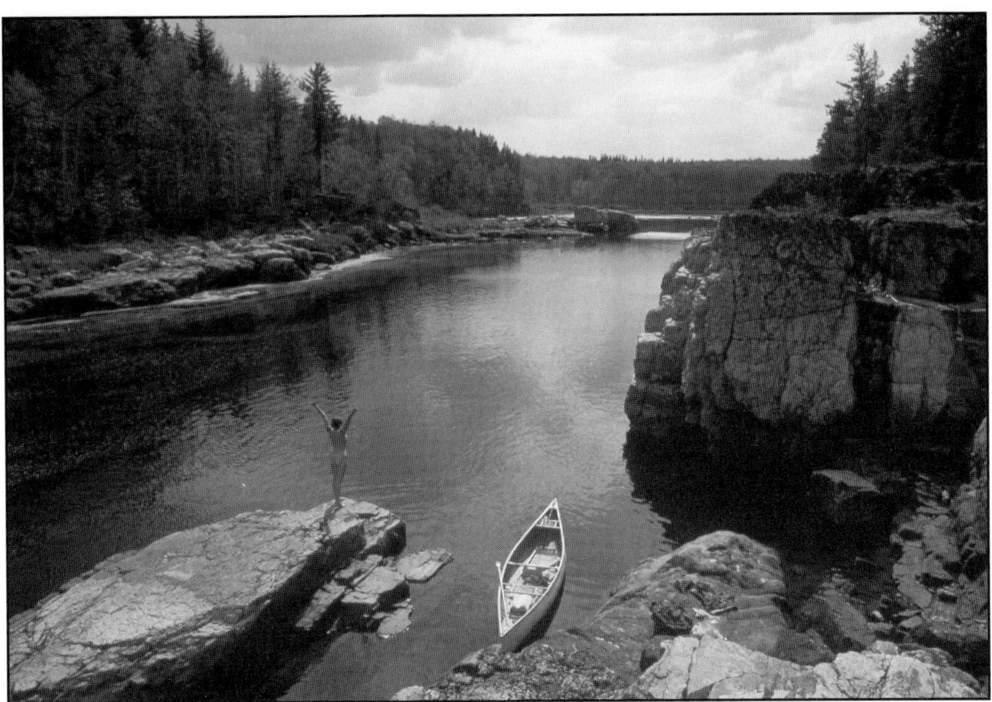

Somewhere a miraculous place full of wonder exists, alive with lakes, rivers, rapids and waterfalls. A place where the night sky is singing with the light of stars and the forest can be dark and mysterious. A place where life and death are an indivisible part of each other, where survival is central. That place is called canoe country.

People go there to find the beauty of nature, the stillness of far-away places and the freedom of independence. But above all, they go there to find themselves. These adventurous trippers pack their canoes with supplies and disappear into the wild country for days or weeks or even months. And when they come back, tired but refreshed, they have changed, they have seen something special out there, they are wiser. Indeed, they have tasted the captivating magic of wilderness canoeing.

One of the many rivers these people travel in search of such profound experiences is the fabulous Missinaibi, which winds its 560 kilometres down a twisting channel from Lake Missinaibi to James Bay, creating the old trade route used first by the Native peoples and then, from the 17th century, by fur traders from the west. The woman in this picture, raising her arms in a joyous embrace of this enchanting river as it flows serenely below the turbulent Thunder House Falls complex, expresses her feelings of oneness with the river in a pure primary gesture.

The composition of the photograph has some interesting elements: the diagonal line of the river; the backlit woman looking in the distance; the cloud-filled sky in the background reflected in the water surface; the hard bedrock framing the picture on three sides, embracing and protecting the vulnerable human form. If the light-coloured canoe, which is the dominant element in the picture, were taken out, the image would become quite different, without any reference to canoeing, just to nature.

Little or No Current—Recreational Paddling

The remarkable S-shape of this section of the Barron River in eastern Algonquin Park, flowing southeast between the majestic 100-metre-high gneiss walls of the Barron Canyon, can only be seen from above. The high point of view provided by this picture enables the smoothly curved line to take the eye from the bottom almost to the top, providing a strong feeling of depth. The way the various elements of the photo are arranged within the frame make for a dynamic, well-structured composition.

The Barron Canyon is a famous gorge of spectacular beauty, accessible by canoe on the river itself as well as by hiking up a twisting, often steep, trail leading to the top of the north side of the canyon wall. From the observation area one can look straight down into the

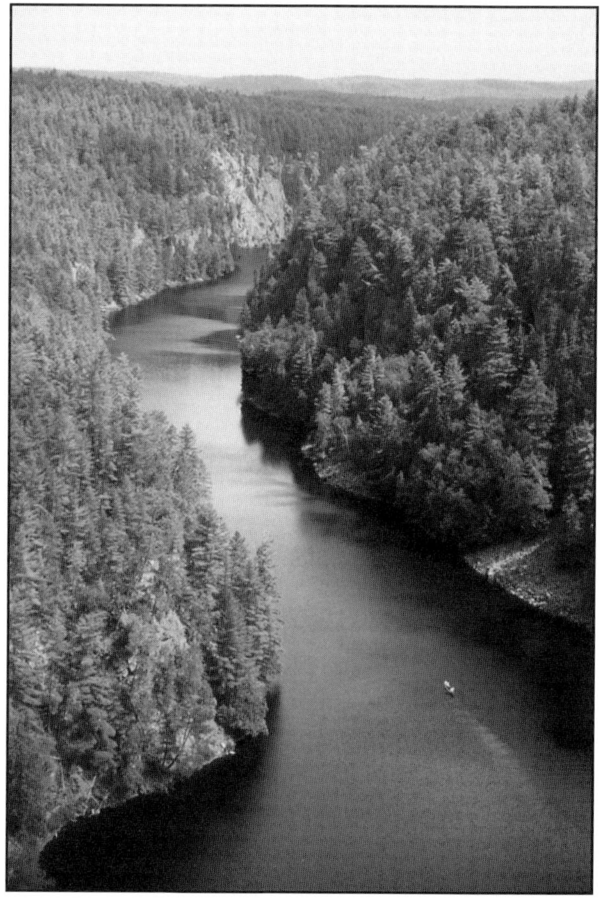

chasm, making it possible to create some striking and unusual photographs.

Although it is quite small, the canoe near the right-bottom corner of the picture is a good example of the importance of a centre of interest (an object that immediately attracts the attention of the viewer). Its presence at a position advised by the 'rule of thirds' is important to the image's appeal. Without it, there would be no sense of scale and the vertical depth depicted in the picture would be less impressive. It also adds a human element to the scene.

Because of its stunning topography and wild nature, the Barron Canyon is an ideal location to experience the change of light in the course of the day, from when the sun is just rising through to nightfall when the light gradually disappears. Dedicated photographers with a sense of adventure can spend many hours here, hunting for a diverse range of pictures created by the changes in light, weather and even their own perception. For instance, when early morning fog fills the whole canyon with thick rolls of dense white cotton, the views are absolutely breathtaking. Every moment spent in this photographic paradise, ready to take advantage of unexpected encounters with nature's bounty, will enrich you. By training your eye in places like the Barron Canyon and developing your personal vision, you will learn to see more than the average person in the same environment.

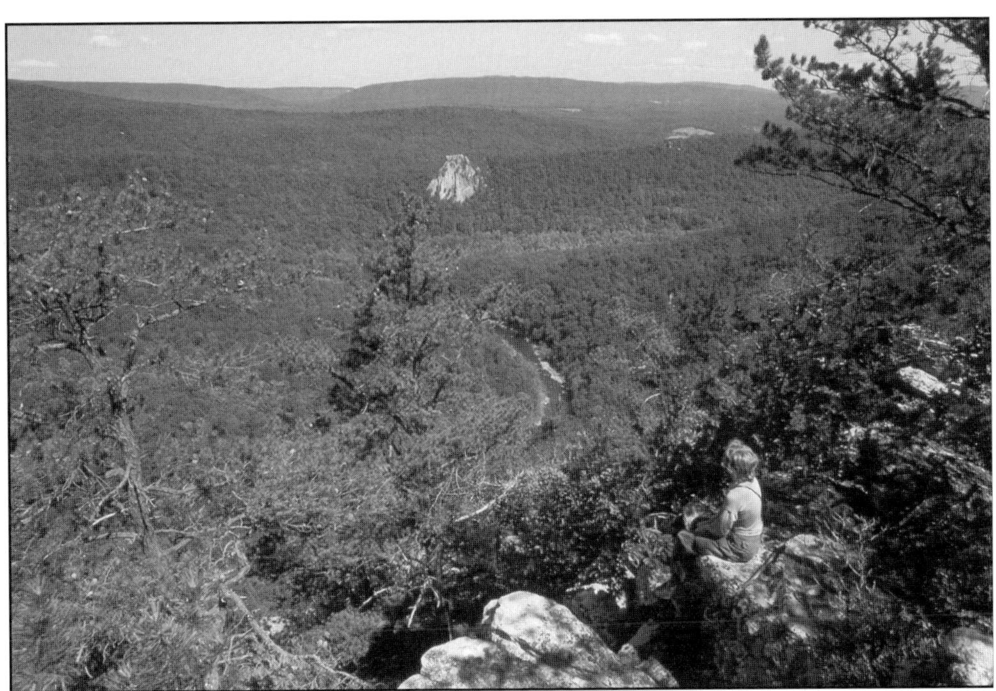

Having a bird's eye view of the route you are going to paddle is a great way to begin a trip. I always try to obtain aerial photos of places we have never visited, but if that is not possible and the area is mountainous enough, we climb up a hill at the start of the trip to survey the kind of terrain we will be traversing. That is what happened at the Cacapon River in West Virginia. A high rocky ridge behind an early campsite provided us with the opportunity to discover this view of the upper valley of the river, which itself showed up as a narrow ribbon below us. (It is hard to get a good impression of three-dimensional depth from a two-dimensional photograph.)

It may not always be appreciated by your paddling companions that you want to spend so much time and effort on making photos of the many locations your group is passing through. But rest assured, they will see that aggravation in a different light when they look at the results of your efforts at home. Having a fine collection of trip images will surely make everyone's day.

The Cacapon empties into the Potomac, a very different kind of river, which at times

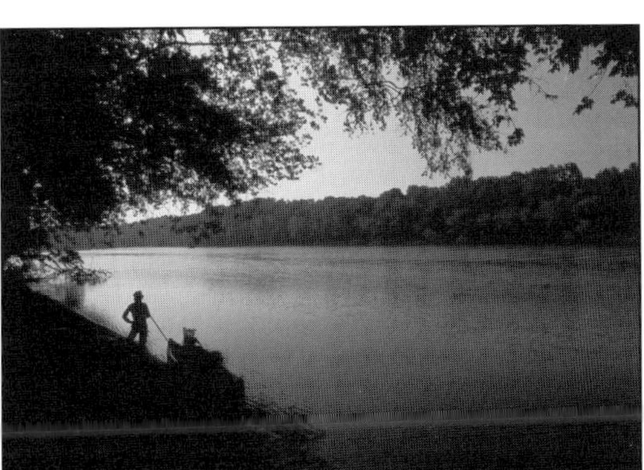

is wild and untamed, but can also be a wide and placid stream as in this photo. I placed the figure in the lightest spot of the image as a conspicuous silhouette, framed by shore, tree branches and the dark part of the river. There are few greys in the picture, making it rather gloomy. The overhanging branches conveniently cover the bright sky, which would otherwise have spoiled the dark feeling of the picture.

Little or No Current—Recreational Paddling

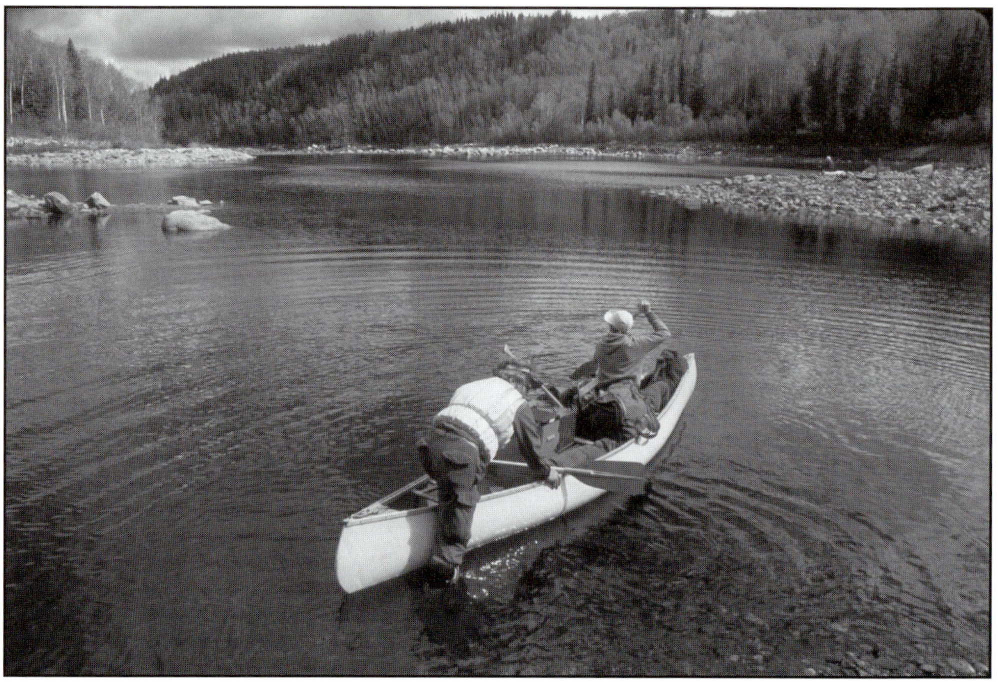

When telling the story of your canoe trip, it is important to include a wide variety of images depicting your many different experiences. In order to make photos of yourself on a one-canoe / two-people trip, it will be necessary to use a tripod or other support and a self-timer, or to ask somebody else to take the picture for you.

At the put-in point below the four-kilometre portage around Hell's Gate Canyon of the lower Missinaibi River, when we were just about ready to run Long Rapids, we luckily found another tripper willing to help make a shot of us leaving. I pre-set the camera controls so that the volunteer photographer only had to point and shoot. He did a fine job, producing a well-composed picture with the horizon level and high in the frame, the canoe nicely off-centre and the beginning of the rapids in the background. Before paddling off, you should, of course, thank the person and not forget to get your camera back. Also take notes, recording in your little notebook the where/what/when/who/why/how of the event, just as you do with everything worthwhile happening on the trip.

The small photo was taken by the owner of the place where we had camped overnight. We always try to have a record shot like this made at the start of each trip, showing all the gear we have with us; in this case enough (including 20 kilograms of photo gear) for a three-week trip down the upper Missinaibi River. We are very happy with this simple snapshot, and gladly forgive our friend the slightly crooked horizon as well as the fact that our heads almost disappear into the background.

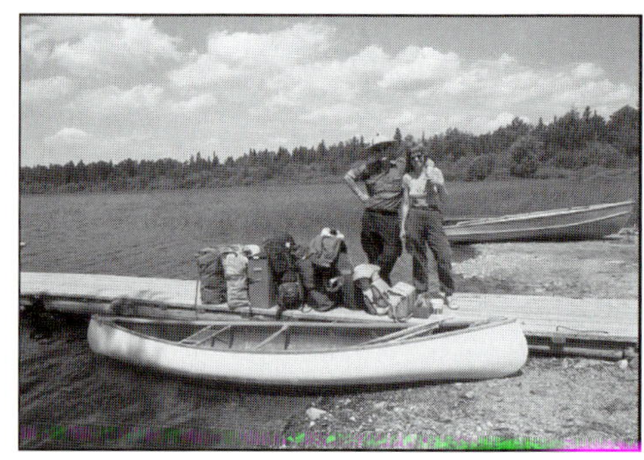

Little or No Current—Recreational Paddling

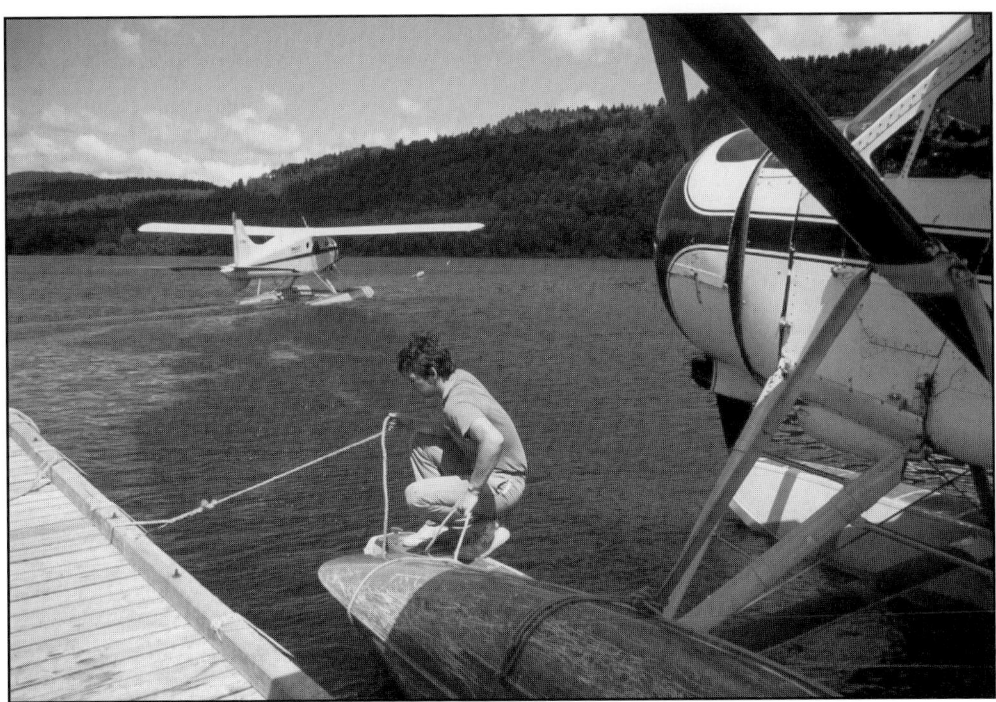

Another kind of record shot worth the taking is found at the start of a trip when you are going to fly to some remote and/or difficult-to-access destination from which to begin your adventure. For many people, actually flying in one of those sometimes quite old bush planes is an adventure in itself, something to talk about at home and include in your photo album or slide show. In the very far North (such as Nunavut, Labrador, Arctic), often the only way to get to many starting points is indeed by plane. More to the south there also are numerous canoe routes where flying-in is required.

This shot shows the Ottawa River at Rapides des Joachimes, where the pilot of the De Havilland Beaver is tying our canoe to one of the plane's floats. He absolutely did not want us to do that ourselves, and rightly so. I delayed making the photo until there was another plane in the background, neatly filling the empty left side of the frame.

After you have been dropped off at your destination (here, a rather far off-shore one in Lac Dumoine at the start of our trip down the Dumoine River) and have climbed into

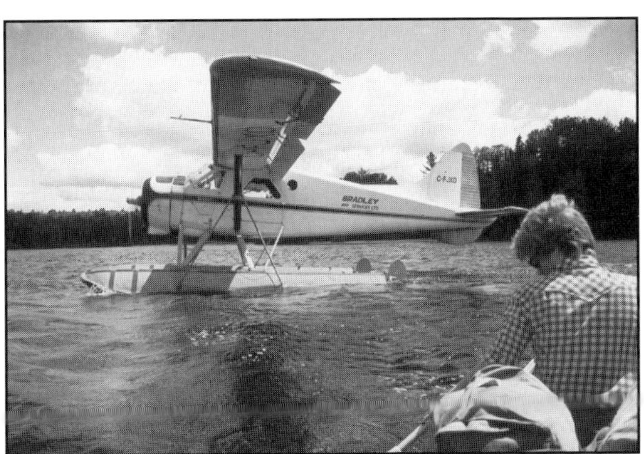

your now floating canoe, make some shots of the plane leaving. I was careful not to cut off the wing tip in the photo and to keep the horizon more or less level. I also ensured the security of the camera by carrying it on a strap around my neck. Dropping it in the water would have been an unfortunate start to the trip!

Little or No Current—Recreational Paddling

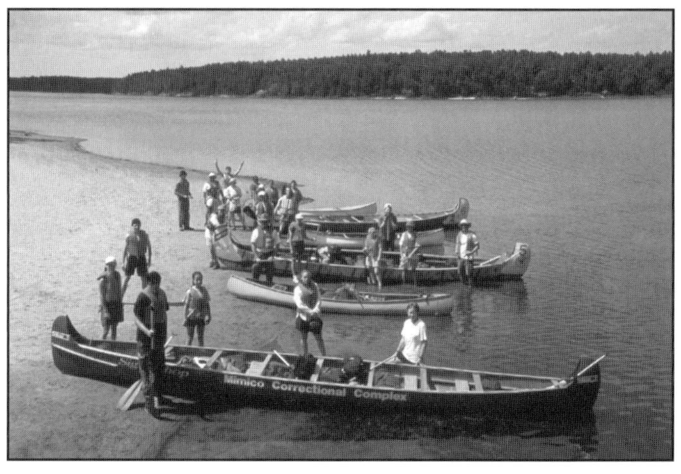

Many young people, when exposed for the first time to a canoe tripping adventure, are curious about these new experiences but, of course, also a bit apprehensive. When you have been asked to help guide such a group on an outing down a beautiful river, there is more to it for you than just to tell them where the campsites and the rapids are. Above all, you have to introduce them to the value of the place and teach them about its history and subtle magic. Also, because many of the new trippers are not (yet?) interested in photography or do not own a camera, it is part of your responsibility to make a visual document of this small but significant part of their history for them, making sure they get to see copies of the photos later. When they grow up, these pictures will be among their most appreciated memories. Remember to write down the people's names for future reference.

At the start of any group adventure trip it makes sense to find a good spot from which to take a photo of everybody involved. In the case of the shot above, I stood on a low bridge and recorded the whole group and all the canoes in one picture (except myself, of course; the photographer is always the one missing!). Everybody is distinct and the edges of the photo are clean, nothing sticks out of the picture. The noon sunlight was quite harsh, producing black shadows; that could not be avoided as the trip started at that time of the day.

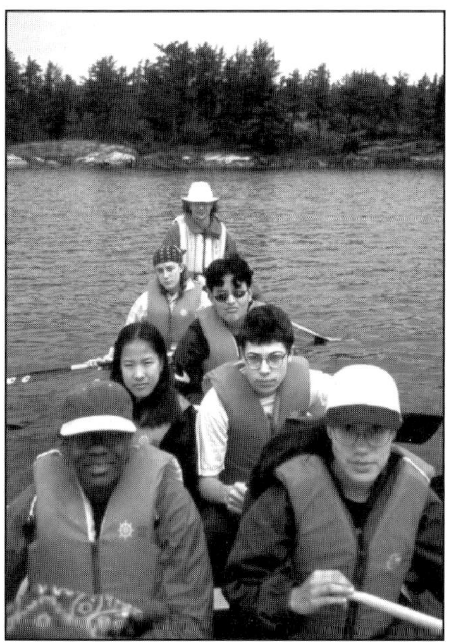

Also, once everyone is in the canoe and paddling, there are plenty of opportunities to make useful record shots. These young people sitting rather morosely in a North canoe do not seem to be enjoying themselves very much. (No wonder, it was still early in the trip and they did not really know if they could trust this guy with the camera.) However, such cloudy moments are also part of canoe tripping, and therefore worth a picture to help illustrate your story. This photo is a rather off-beat vertical, but it shows an interesting perspective, emphasizing the sense of depth. As the sunlight was diffuse, there are no harsh shadows in the picture; yet the eyes of the two women in the front are somewhat shaded by their caps.

Little or No Current—Recreational Paddling

Finally it is time to relax. Members of the canoe club have reached the point in their day outing that the canoes have been pulled ashore, the lunch parcels taken out and the serious business of sunning and swimming begun. Ah, the bliss of soaking tired muscles in cool water, the delight of doing absolutely nothing useful at all. Go, everybody; it is play time!

Except for the photographer, of course, the one who risks life and limb climbing that rock wall to get a nice high viewpoint of the club's lunchtime activities; the one who is always buzzing about with that camera, looking for a better picture, hunting for the most effective angle from which to shoot. But, boy, it will be so much fun next week at the clubhouse, looking at the results of his tireless efforts: all those crazy pictures of

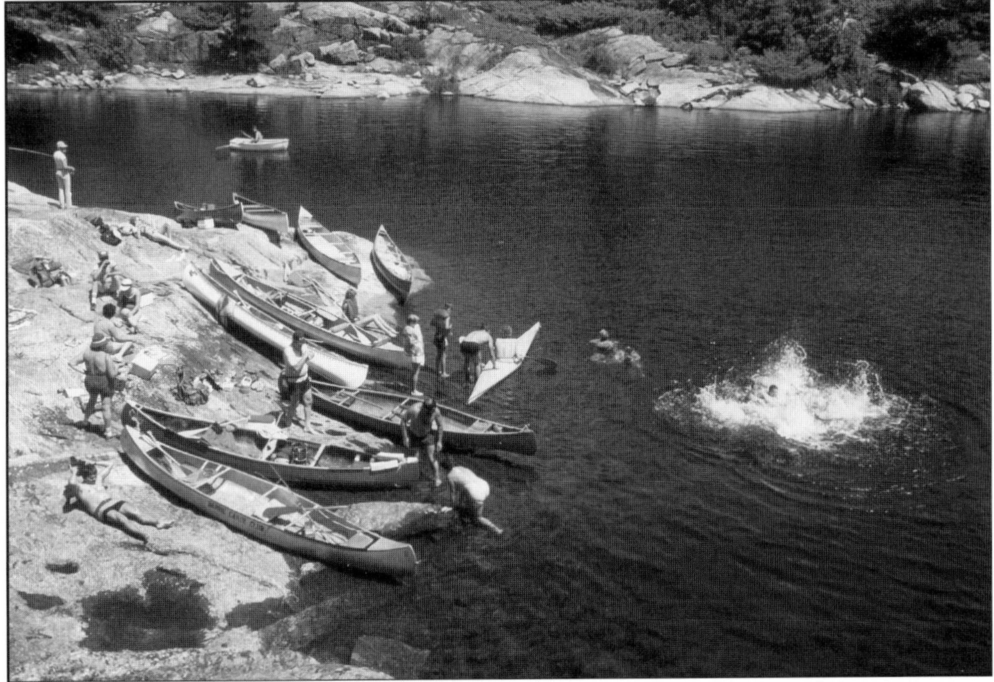

all those lazy people enjoying themselves on the rocks and in the water; all happy to have such a dedicated photographer around.

That is but one of the rewards if you use your photographic talents to record some of the club's activities. But do not take it all too seriously; you should relax and have fun too, like the rest of them. After all the searching and shooting, climb down, put your equipment in its case safely out of the sun, and jump in. Heaven!

This photo gives a fine rendition of such innocent fun-filled times. It is all about interaction between people and nature, something very much worth recording. The horizontal format makes good use of the available picture elements, while the splashing water creates a powerful centre of interest because the light spot in the dark water immediately attracts the eye. Having seen the swimmers make the splashes before, I asked them to do it again, just for the picture. They gladly co-operated, of course. A hand-held zoom lens was used to make the correct framing of the photograph from the fixed position on top of the rock wall.

Little or No Current—Recreational Paddling

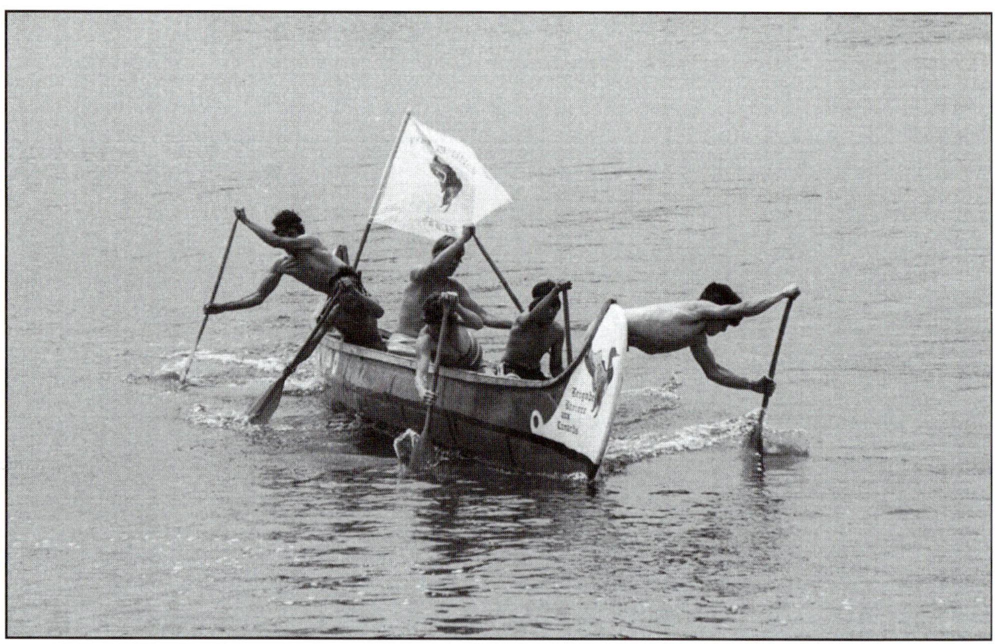

This arresting picture was taken at a canoe festival when six young men took a North canoe and started playing with it. Playing is the right word here; the paddlers were not trying to go fast or break any records. They only wanted to make the boat dance to their touch, perform an intricate mesmerizing ballet, filled with unexpected turns and smooth glides on the calm surface of the water.

I was transfixed by the spectacle. Putting my 75-300 mm zoom lens on the camera loaded with black-and-white ISO 400 film, I shot hand-held, following them in the viewfinder, reacting to what they were doing and anticipating the decisive moment of their actions. Of all the pictures made of those guys, this one shows their artistry the best, a moment of peak activity while the bow and stern paddlers are hanging far out to pull the boat around in a superbly co-ordinated effort. Granted, to get shots like this luck is needed, but luck only comes to those who are prepared to take advantage of it. Either one is ready to take the shot at the right moment, or it is gone forever.

Although the canoe is in dead centre of the picture, against the 'rule' of composition requiring the main subject to be away from the centre, here it works well because it isolates the canoe and its occupants from the surroundings, thus forcing the viewer to look only at the subject. This picture was cropped from a larger one, which contained the shoreline in the back and more water all around.

Canoe festivals are great places to indulge in your photography, to train your eyes to see photo opportunities, to look beyond the obvious and find the images that will delight the viewer. Take care to have your camera ready and loaded with film at all times. There is nothing worse than running out of film just when the action peaks. Do check the frame counter on your camera at regular intervals.

Searching for such photographs is very satisfying and a wonderful training ground for improving your split-second reaction to what you see happening on the water.

Little or No Current—Recreational Paddling

Rarely have I had as much fun making paddling pictures as with this giggling bunch of young ladies, eleven of them together in one canoe. Of course, this shot seems to break some important rules of paddling safety because there are far too many people in the boat, nobody is wearing a life jacket and it is not even known if each one of them can swim. But it was, in fact, a perfectly safe situation.

All took place in a conservation area near Toronto where several Canoe Ontario instructors were demonstrating various paddling techniques to anybody who would pay attention, including the many mothers and young children present. Seeing an opportunity for a unique picture, I first asked the mothers' permission and then got as many kids as I could to sit in the canoe and wave at the camera. There was no chance anything could go wrong with this happy crowd, since the canoe was in shallow water resting on the sandy lake bottom. I was only a few metres away standing on the beach, photographing the heartwarming scene. Although it was early afternoon, the shadows created by the sun were not too dark because of the light reflecting off the water surface onto the faces. I am quite pleased with the shot, still remembering the cheerful smiles these girls gave me.

In cases like this where you see an opportunity for something special, follow your instinct and make best use of the situation. I busily chatted with the girls and their mothers to relax everybody while arranging the young ones in the boat, keeping them enthusiastic and willing to do what I asked. Placing the canoe on a pleasing and frame-filling diagonal, I made several shots because, when a group of people are being photographed, there are always a few of them blinking their eyes or holding their arms in front of each other's faces. With some ingenuity and improvisation you can make delightfully off-beat photos like this one. And if you are willing to spend the time on it, mothers and daughters will be happy to receive a free print.

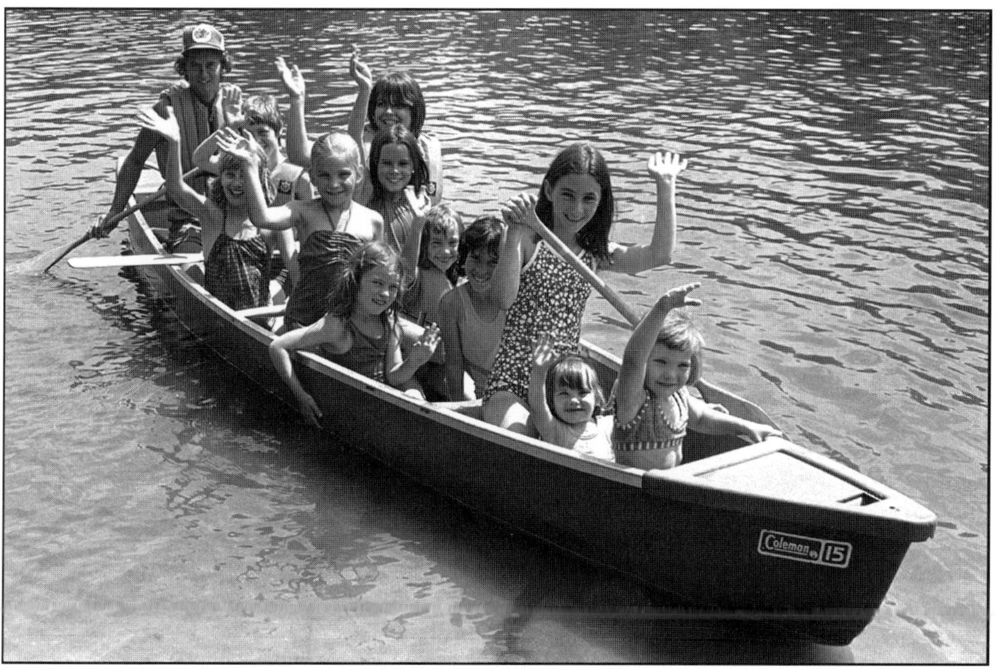

Little or No Current—Recreational Paddling

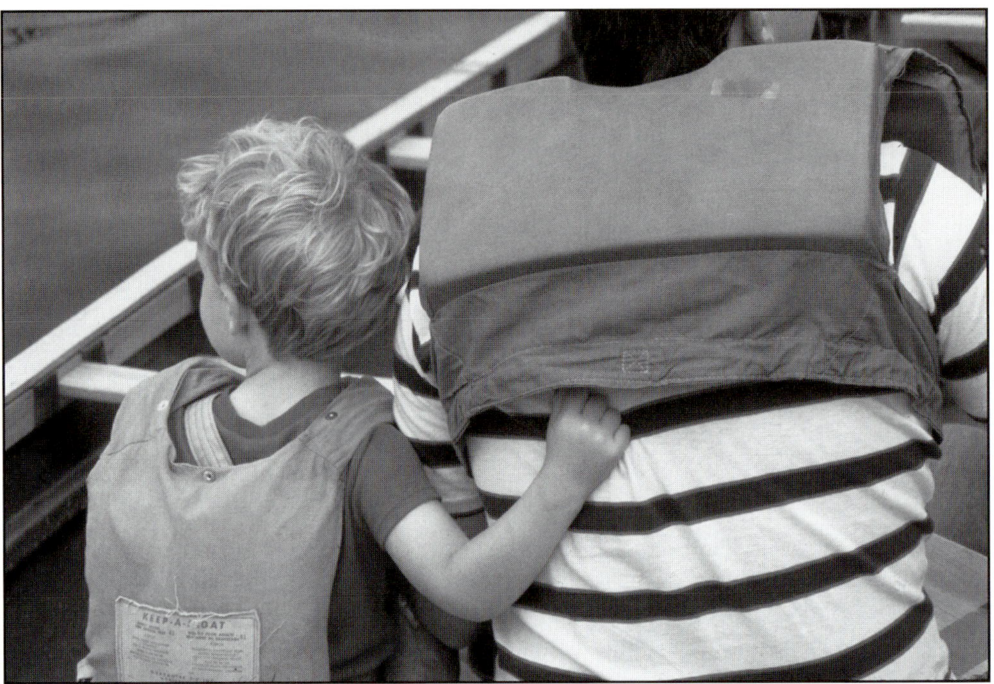

Parents (and grandparents!) know that nothing beats the power and impact pictures of young children can have. Everybody simply loves to see children enjoying themselves and, in canoe country, there are countless opportunities for making such prized photographs. All you have to do is follow children around, look at what they are doing, recognize the picture in the scene, point the camera and push the button.

The story of this little boy in the big canoe is obvious: he is on his first outing. Holding on to his dad gives him the necessary support to help overcome this frightening encounter with the fantastic world of paddling that is going to unfold on the lake he is looking at so timidly. The picture is defined by the little guy's hand touching his father's back and finding much-needed reassurance there. Without that arm establishing contact between them, this would be nothing but a snapshot of two people in a boat. With it, there is a story of a little boy on a big adventure. This is a great addition to the family album.

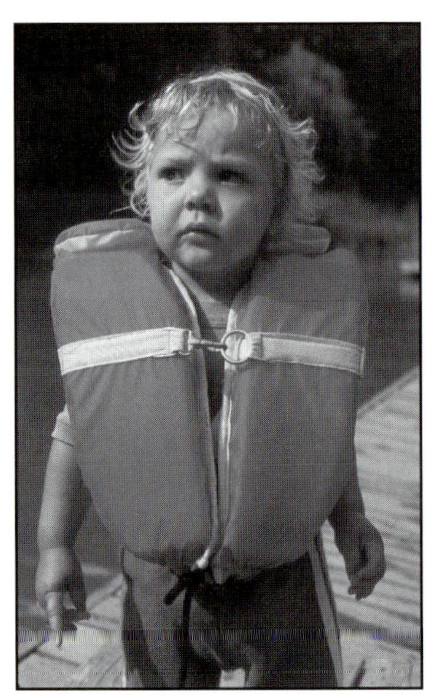

The photo of the little person to the right tells a different story, one of confidence and trust in the knowledge that the over-sized life jacket will keep her (or him?) afloat, no matter what. In such a tightly composed portrait, avoid cutting off part of the head and hands of the person you photograph. Keep the background free of clutter and see to it that there are no trees or other things growing out of the head. Remember, try to shoot at the child's eye level; do not point the camera down from where you are standing.

Children grow up so fast that every picture you make of them is a unique record of a moment in their lives. Their unpredictability and profound curiosity lead them into situations that create numerous occasions for fine pictures, so photograph them before it is too late. This little guy obviously loves to canoe. He appears to be training hard for his first solo and does not mind showing the photographer the finer points of paddle control. Here, both canoe and paddle are on diagonal lines, together forming an interesting cross shape. Even though the shadows created by the sunlight are rather harsh, it really is unimportant, provided the printing of this snapshot is not too dark.

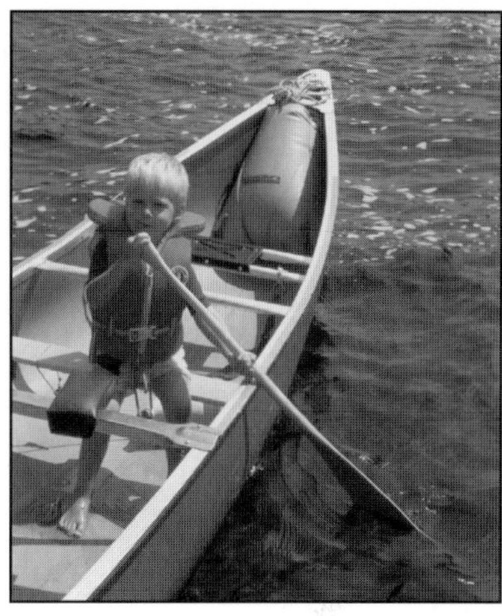

The 'pooped' person in the much-softer-lighted bottom photo is far away in slumber land, after what must have been a tough day portaging and paddling against the wind. Or maybe he also did not get enough rest last night because he and his tripping buddies were raising hell all the time. Who knows? All he wants to do now is sleep.

The combination of travel and photography can be a great experience for the whole family. Give the young ones their own cameras with which to experiment and, later at home, discuss the results with them so they (and you!) can learn from their successes and mistakes. Teach children the fascinating art of seeing and recording photographs, and they will soon start making their own visual memories of the family canoe trips. Never too young to learn.

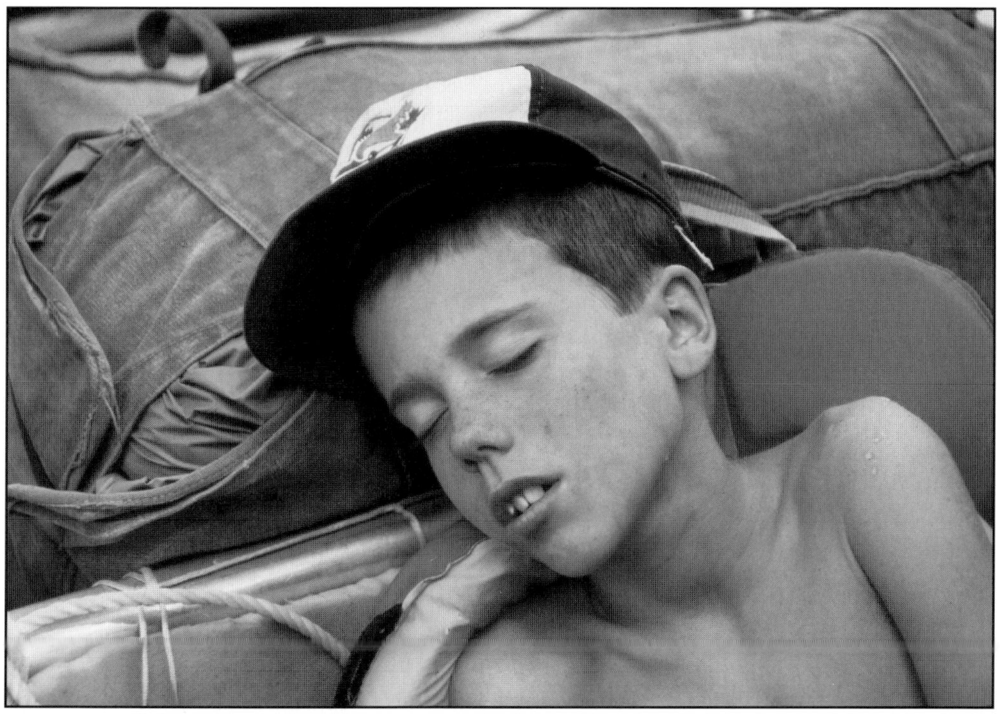

Little or No Current—Recreational Paddling

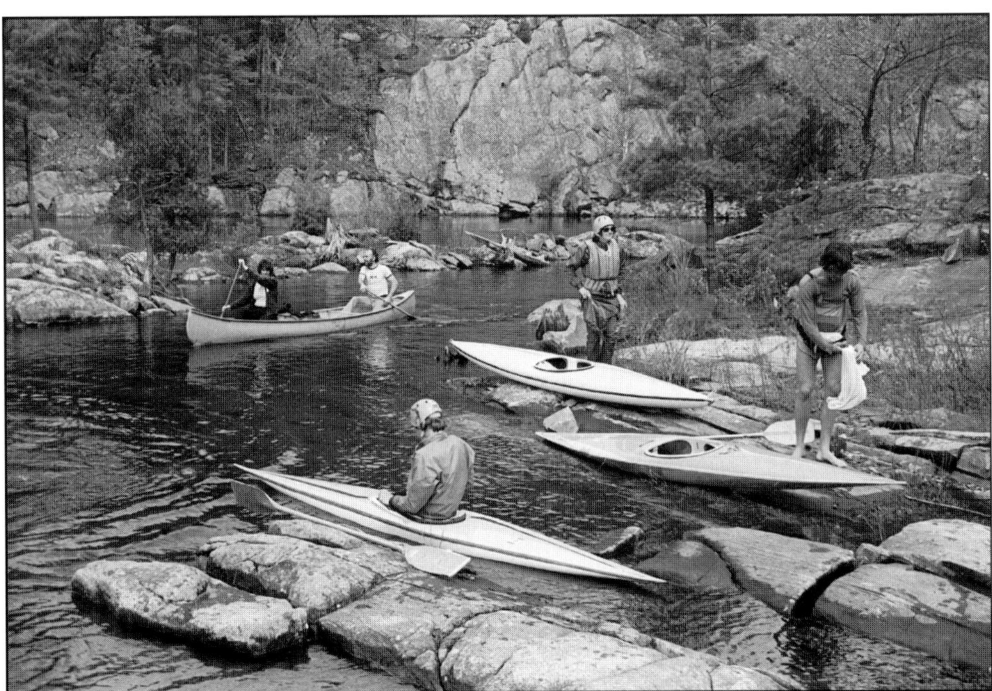

When people are tripping in a group, such as a canoe club outing, pictures of several of them together are always welcome. If the trip report produced by you or somebody else contains a few of these, it will be much appreciated by everybody. All you have to do as a photographer is keep your eyes open and the camera ready.

In this photo of a group of paddlers preparing to leave their lunch spot, there is no obvious dominant subject, but the somewhat diagonally placed kayaks all point to the open canoe, leading the viewer's eye to it. This is a spontaneous, natural shot; all people in the picture are busy doing something and nobody is aware of the camera, nobody is posing. The overcast sky makes for soft diffuse light, thus avoiding hard shadows.

The photo is set up in such a way that the immediate surrounding area is included; the rocks in the foreground present launching opportunities to the kayaks, and the cluttered background shows the vertical rock wall of the upper Moon River. Typically, there are only a few trees growing on these exposed Canadian Shield rocks. The shot, made with a zoom lens to allow proper framing, was taken from a fixed position on a large rock; it was not easy to move without the risk of stumbling and dropping the camera.

The good thing about making photographs at club outings is that most of the time the tripping pace is slow and relaxed. Hence, you can take your time and move around at your leisure, looking for pictures. Everybody knows each other; asking them to do something special for the camera is therefore quite acceptable. That gives you the opportunity to organize all kinds of activities to photograph, especially if there are young children in the group. In canoe country, one does not have to look far; interesting shots are everywhere, some perhaps better than others, but do keep looking until you find them, even in those places you think you know.

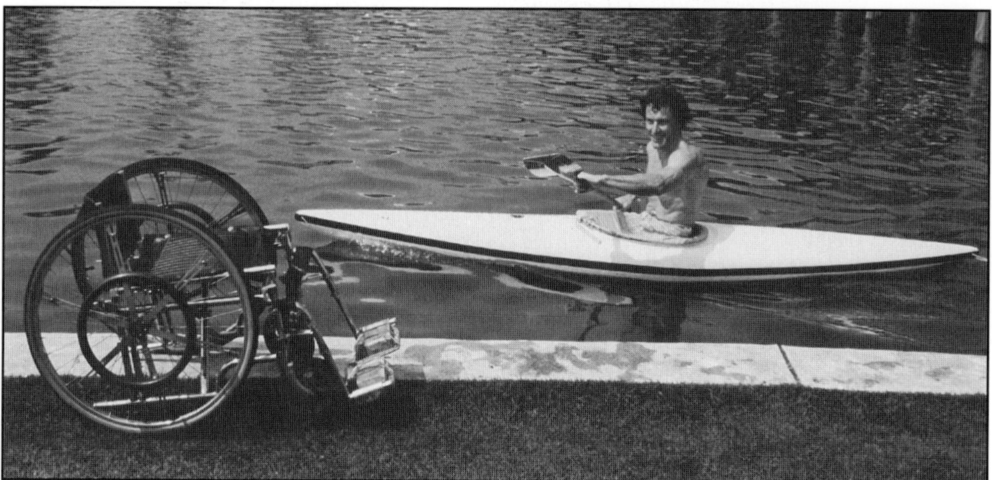

When looking for photographs, always keep your eyes open for the unusual, something you do not see every day, a picture that grabs your immediate attention because it is out of the ordinary. For instance, the obvious joy of this kayaker, who, after exchanging his wheelchair for the freedom of the water, is proving that paddling is for everybody, creates a great picture. By including the wheelchair in the photograph, you now have something special; your shot tells a story that anybody can understand. The omission of the chair would present the kayaker as just one of many.

The shot had to be made quickly because the kayaker would have partly disappeared behind the wheelchair if he had moved more to the left, making the composition less compelling. Because of a distracting bridge in the background, the picture has been cropped considerably, producing a much stronger image.

Another unusual photo is the one with the kayakers forming a star as part of their training in whitewater paddling. Through fun-filled games like these they learn to balance their kayaks while standing up in them; not something they will need very often on the water, but obviously a good way to improve balance control. If this were a 'talking' picture, you surely would be able to hear the group of kayakers excitedly yelling to each other.

Grab the photo opportunity when it presents itself, such as the pictures on this page. Keep your eyes open and capture the spirit of the moment you encounter. The more tricks of the trade you learn and the more you refine your photographic eye by trial and error, the better photographer you will become. An important realization is that, in order to *see* and then take the photo, you have got to *be there* in the first place.

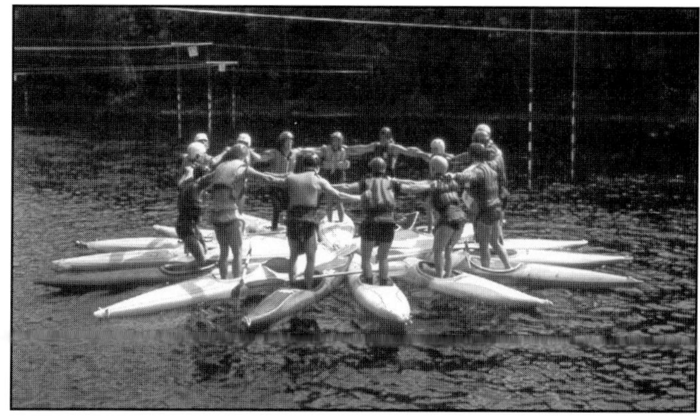

Little or No Current—Recreational Paddling

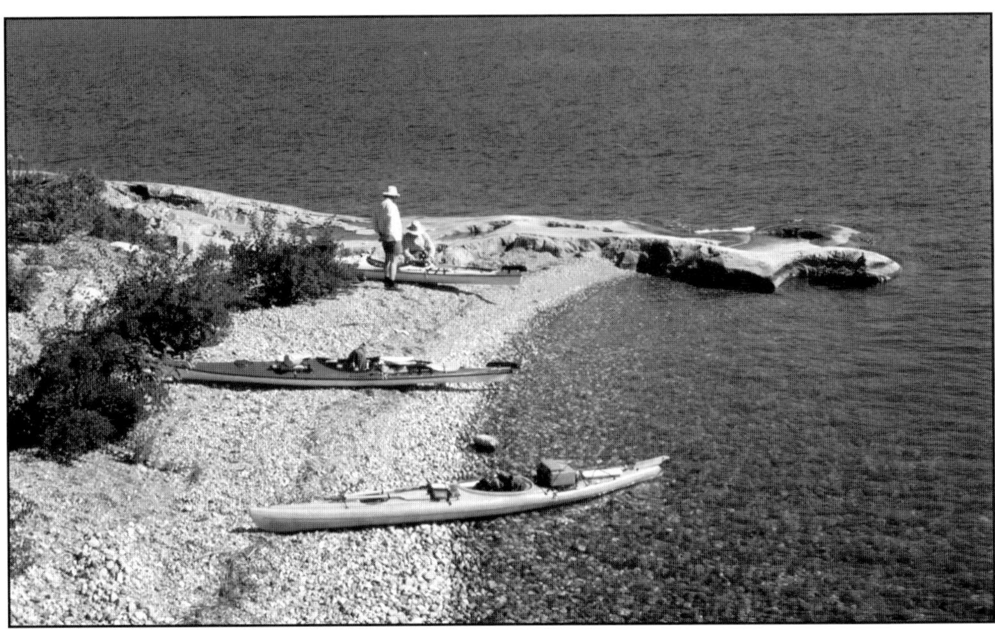

Sea kayaking, also called coastal kayaking, is a type of recreational paddling particularly suited for exploring coastal areas along seashores and the shores of large inland bodies of water such as the Great Lakes.

The long narrow shape of the sea kayak, a completely covered craft with access to the interior provided only by one or more waterproof hatches, makes packing photographic equipment a task that requires special attention, particularly if one decides to take large items along such as camera cases and tripods. Everything must be packed small enough to fit through the hatches.

When on the water, a major complication is the difficult access to the photo equipment. You can, of course, hang a waterproof camera around your neck from a strap. Another possibility is packing some photo gear in a hard waterproof case strapped to the deck in front of or just behind the cockpit. Remember that, when paddling, your hands are wet much of the time, so handling equipment must be done with great care.

When paddling on salt water, your equipment needs extra protection to keep it away from the very corrosive water. Unfortunately, when you dunk your camera in salt water, there is not much you can do to salvage it; see page 77. Also, when you regularly camp on sandy beaches, you should get used to having sand in everything, including your photo equipment. Keep camera and lenses meticulously clean!

For some unfortunate people, myself included, sea kayaks are regrettably not the way to go. Sitting with one's legs stretched out in front for long periods of time, without easy opportunities to change position and attend to sore muscles, is a major strain on a painful lower back. However, there are millions of dedicated sea kayakers all over the world who enjoy this beautiful craft tremendously and spend countless hours on the water in search of the special pleasures sea kayaking can give. I am most grateful to one of them, Sandy Richardson, for allowing me to include three of his photos on these two pages.

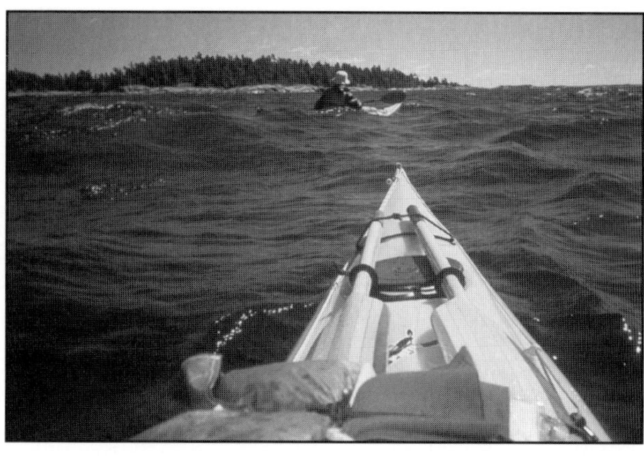

The photo on the previous page provides a nice overview of several beached sea kayaks, shot from a higher point of view, on an island in Georgian Bay. Such land-based photos are important if you want to tell a complete story of your trip. The small photo on this page illustrates the view from the paddler's cockpit. When shooting straight forward, it is hard to avoid including the front end of the kayak in the photo. Keeping the horizon level is also not easy from within these craft that are continually moving with the waves.

Below is an interesting example of the fine photos one can take from a sea kayak. The delicate sunlight illuminates the lighthouse beautifully from the side, and its reflection is cut into many slices by the gentle waves. The solo paddler is an important element in the picture, because the figure introduces a human touch to the scene and also creates a pleasant balance with the lighthouse and the clouds. There is nobody else visible in the wide expanse of the water surface; the picture therefore generates a feeling of loneliness. The photographer obviously paid attention to the horizon; it is perfectly horizontal, as it should be.

Sea kayaking is an experience all on its own, quite different from open canoeing. Making photographs when travelling in a sea kayak has its particular problems and possibilities. For those who have adapted to this environment and solved the problems, the results can be most satisfying.

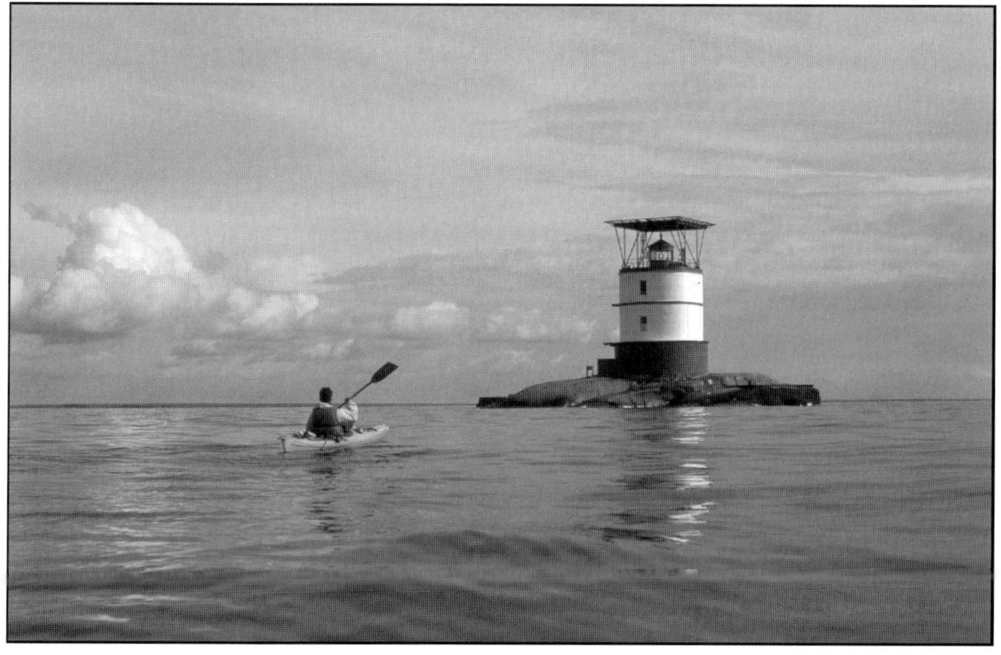

Little or No Current—Recreational Paddling

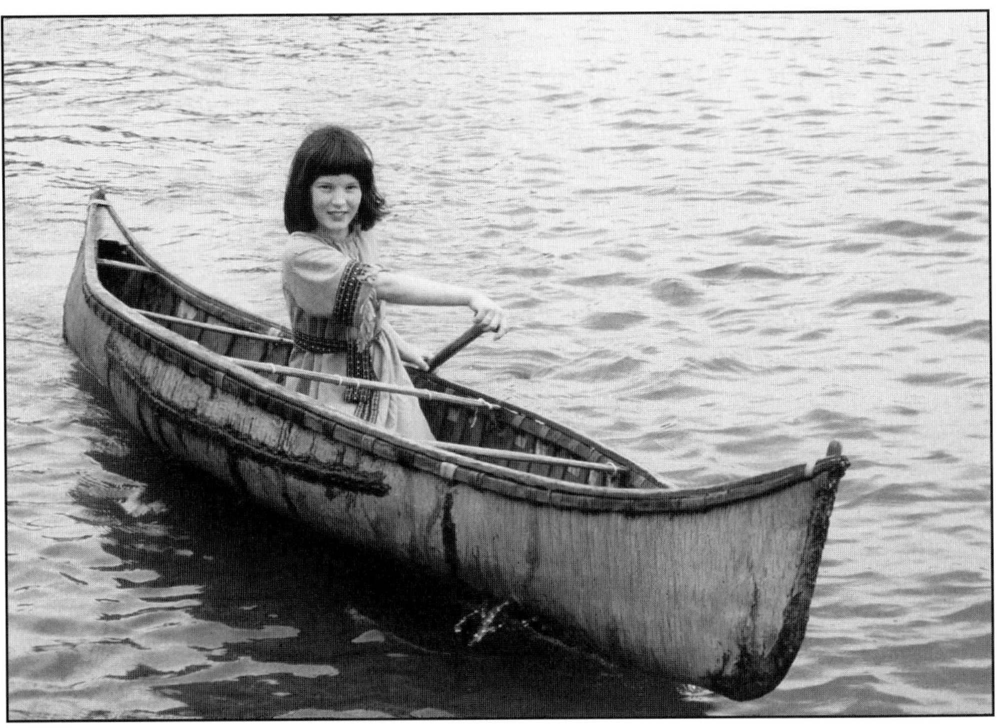

Modern canoeing started with the birchbark canoe, developed and perfected in the distant past by Aboriginal peoples of northern North America. This wonderful craft is the ancestor of all open canoes we paddle nowadays, and the natural material shaping its graceful lines delights the heart of each one touching it.

These days, the delicate handcrafted birchbark canoe is difficult to find because it is not as sturdy as modern boats and is relatively expensive. These canoes are, therefore, rarely used anymore for outdoor canoe tripping, and can usually be found only at some Native settlements or in museums and at demonstrations. The small birchbark canoe with the young female paddler was photographed at a canoe exhibition in Toronto. The beauty of the exquisitely textured bark shows up well in the picture, as does the black pitch applied all along the boat to make it watertight.

This broken old North canoe was discovered in Old Fort William, a historic fur-trade museum near Thunder Bay, Ontario. After several years of faithful service in the museum, it had died a dignified death and was now resting beside the walls of its place of birth, the canoe shop in the background.

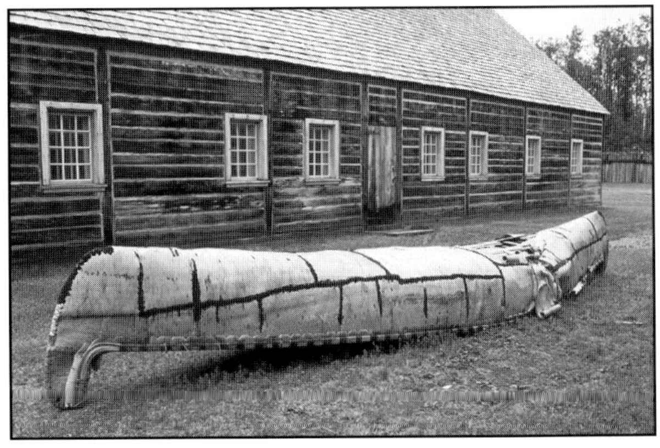

The cultural value of such historic objects is obvious. Always keep your mind receptive to unexpected photo opportunities like these.

On sheltered vertical rock faces all over canoe country, one can find intriguing pictographs, made hundreds of years ago by the Aboriginal peoples. Many of these signs from the past were created by applying a mixture of red ochre and grease to the surface of the rock. Several such treasures are visible at Fairy Point in Lake Missinaibi, where they adorn a slab of rock that can only be approached from the water.

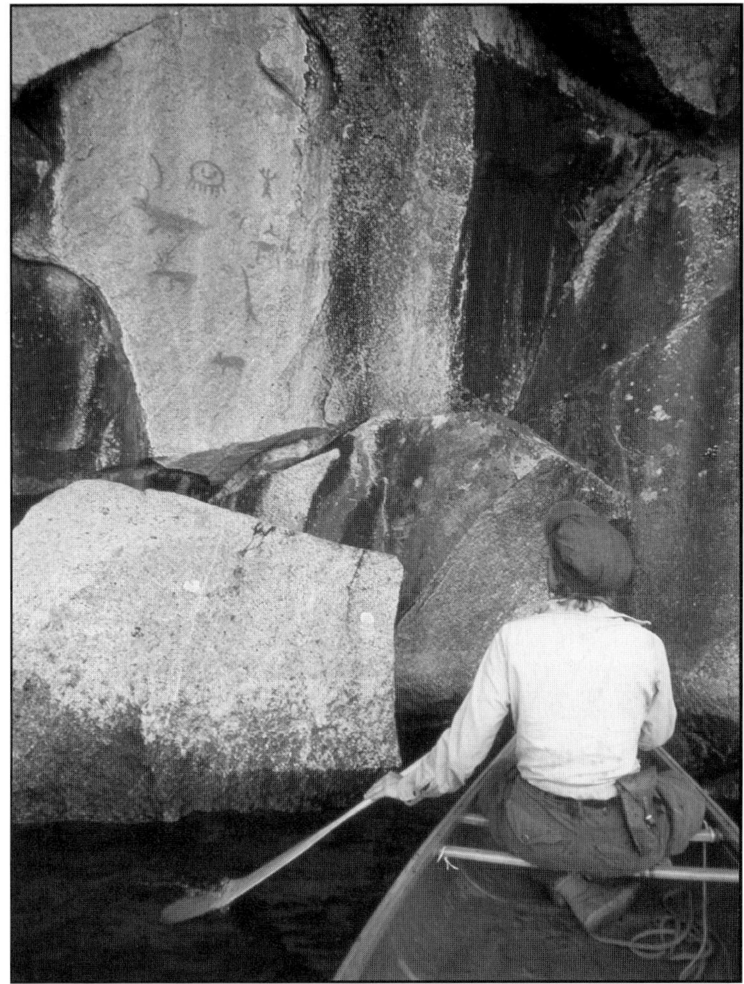

It is humbling to sit there in your canoe and look up at these symbols of another way of life, made by people who travelled these waters long before modern paddlers discovered this fascinating place. Just imagine the artist, possibly a shaman, crouching on the rock with the paint in his hand, after having come here in his birchbark canoe. You can only wonder why the painter had selected this spot for his message and what it all meant to him and his people. Truly this is a place that captures one's imagination.

By all means, study and photograph these rock paintings from a convenient distance, but never touch or damage them in any way. They are precious and irreplaceable messages from a past culture and should be protected from all outside influences but the weather.

In order to make a simple vertical record shot of the place, I carefully stood up in the stern of our canoe and made the photo (in fact, several of them) with a medium zoom lens on my hand-held camera loaded with ISO 100 slide film. Very carefully, indeed! This is not a place to drop your camera in the water; it is 70 metres straight down to the bottom. Without the figure in the foreground sitting in the canoe, this photo would not have been as informative; with the paddler's presence there is a sense of scale to indicate the size of the paintings.

Little or No Current—Recreational Paddling

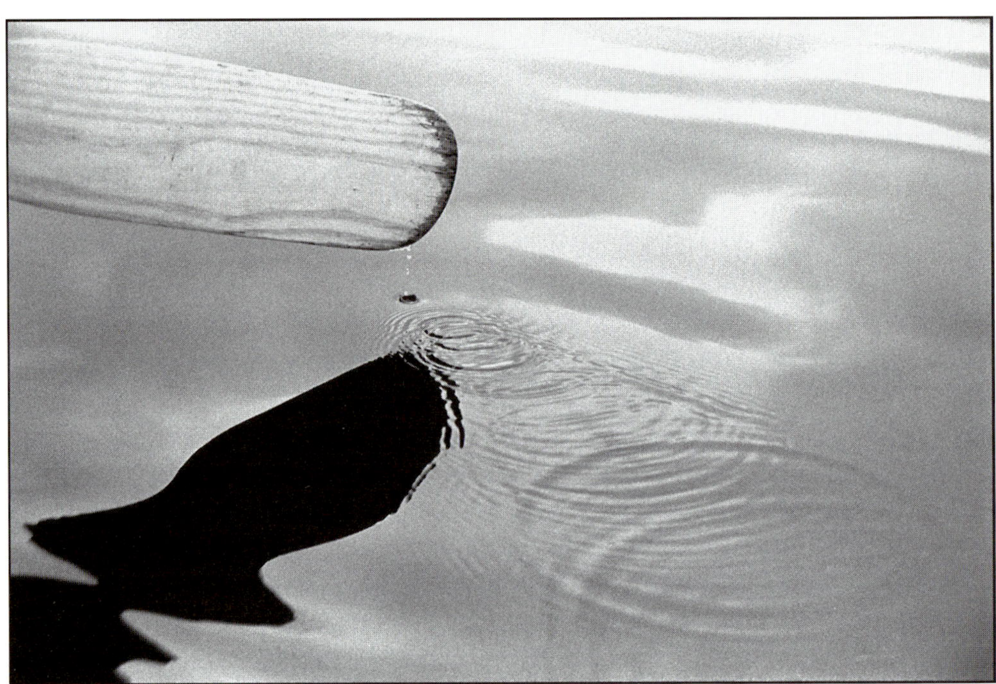

Your beloved paddle, the most important tool to take along with your canoe or kayak, deserves a few special photographs of its own. The simple beauty of the long straight and curved lines makes the paddle an excellent subject to be photographed while actually placed in its proper position at the water surface. Once you see the many possibilities, it requires relatively little effort, using almost any kind of camera, to take some fine photos that can be enlarged and hung on the wall or entered in competition.

This picture consists of four elements, three of which—the paddle, its reflection on the water and the ring-shaped ripples created on the surface by the droplets coming off the paddle—meet at the central point of interest, the falling drops. This is a good example of a powerful design assembled by using simple building blocks, such as lines and patterns. These elements are always around but must first be recognized before they can be appreciated and combined into a picture. The photo was made in black-and-white, which turns out to be the right choice, as colour would only have diminished the graphic impact of its composition.

The paddle used in this photo is a traditional wooden one that had already seen many a rough expedition. Its weathered tip gives the picture an extra touch of character and contributes some charming realism to the overall mood. In general, plastic or aluminum paddles are less suitable for such 'artistic' photos. They do not have the warm appeal of wooden ones.

There are countless opportunities to make beautiful photos of the many prosaic pieces of equipment besides your paddle: a dewdrop-covered tent glistening in the morning sun; wet canoeing boots and socks drying out on a rock; a lining rope rolled up in a neat coil; your favourite knife stuck in a fallen log; even your old and dearly loved greasy hat. Look around you, learn to *see* and you will discover many treasures waiting to be admired.

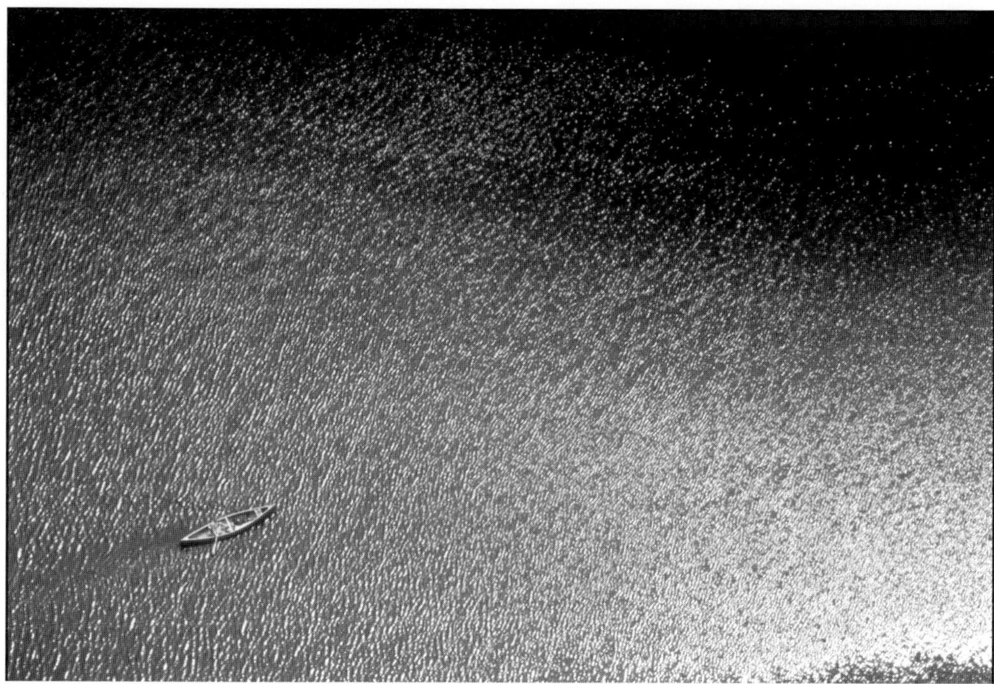

This is another one of those extraordinary photographs that can be discovered at the Barron Canyon. It was made looking almost straight down from the 100-metre-high rim and shows a tiny canoe floating in a pattern of small waves. Patterns are repetitions of lines, textures, shapes, curves or forms, that can help create appealing images. A variety of patterns exists all around us; you should train your ability to detect and recognize designs in nature and their photographic potential. In this peaceful photo, the canoe is placed in a dominant rule-of-thirds location and points to the centre of the image, strengthening the photo's feeling of unity. This frame-filling pattern image is successful also because the composition is very unpretentious and has an obvious centre of interest. The photo would have been even more attractive if, by zooming in somewhat, the small dark area in the right bottom corner had been eliminated. As it stands now, this area attracts attention away from the canoe.

The beautiful simplicity of the above photo is also present in this small one, but on another level. Here the canoe and its single occupant are presented as a horizontal form

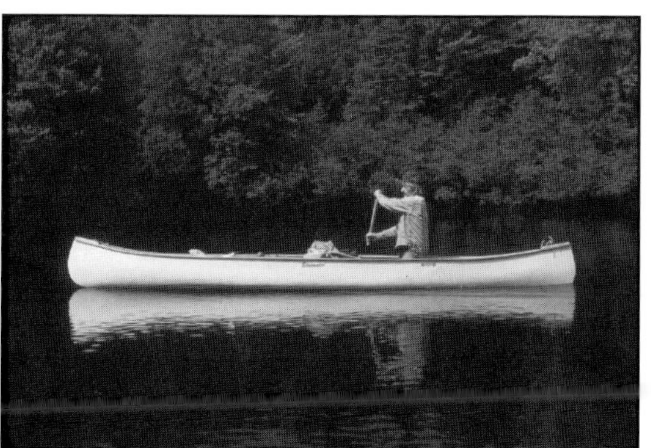

against a neutral background. It is not the canoe as a means of transportation that is depicted here, but the craft's lovely long sweeping lines, forming a perfect unit with the paddler, both reflected in the water surface. Notice that the line of the canoe is uninterrupted, because the paddle is held on the other side of the boat. Obviously, beauty can also be found in the familiar; it is just a matter of *seeing* it.

Little or No Current—Recreational Paddling

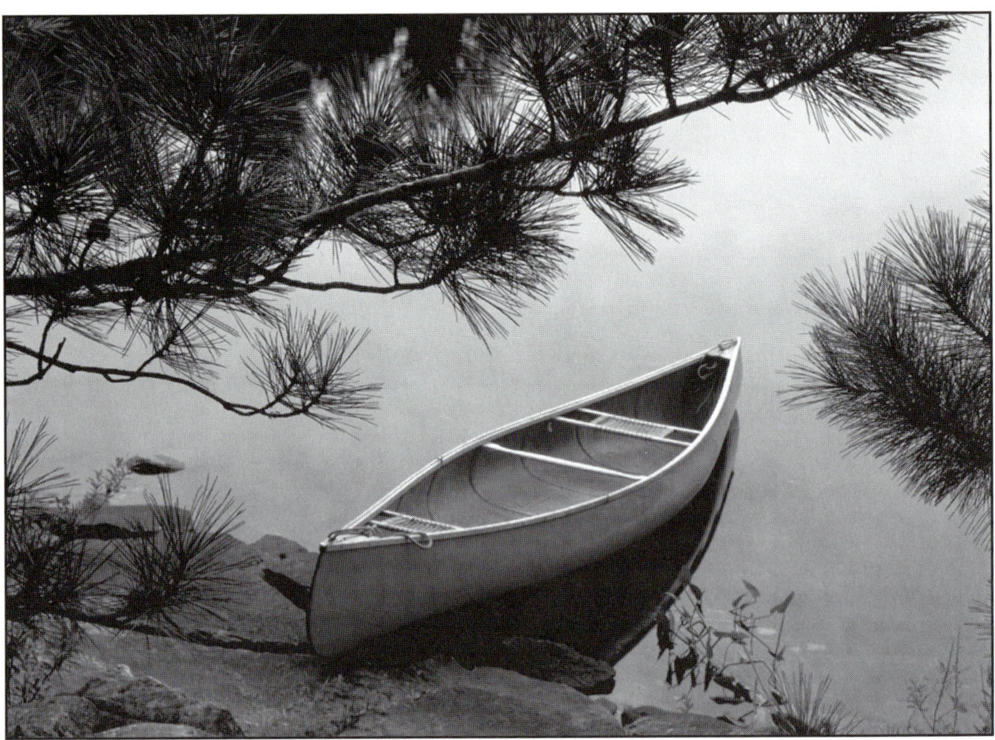

The canoe is often called "the most beautiful craft ever created." Indeed, the graceful, flowing lines of a well-designed canoe are immensely pleasing and never fail to touch the heart of the dedicated canoeist. Making photographs that do justice to its timeless beauty is an exciting challenge, requiring a keen eye for composition and attention to detail. But once you have taken the time to 'construct' a truly fine portrait of your beloved canoe from the various visual elements available to you, it will always have a treasured place in your collection.

To emphasize the elegance of its curves, the canoe in this photograph is placed in an attractive diagonal under the overhanging branches of a pine tree, creating striking contrasts between the finely detailed needles of the tree, the smooth canoe and the rough rocks. On the right-hand side, a branch is included to close the picture off there. The canoe is now framed on all sides.

The canoe is well separated from the featureless background (the water surface on which it is resting). Since there was no wind at all when the photo was set up, the water was smooth. Leaving the paddles in the boat would have created a distraction, so they were taken out, along with other items normally found there. Because of the diffuse light from the somewhat overcast sky, there are no harsh shadows. A tripod was used to provide an opportunity for easy experimentation with different compositions, vertical and horizontal, as well as with different exposures. Other possibilities were explored by throwing a small pebble in the water and photographing the scene while circular ripples moved over the surface.

If designing and photographing scenes like this become regular features of your activities, your appreciation of the surrounding beauty will surely be strengthened.

A photograph radically different from the previous one is shown here. The shape of the canoe has been deliberately distorted because I wanted to see beyond the canoe itself, and experiment with its pure form. There is no single correct way to make a photo of any object; numerous approaches are possible and should be pursued to help discover hidden treasures. Finding the ones that please you most is just a matter of personal view and interpretation.

Wanting to look at the canoe not from eye level but from a different perspective, I placed it on the beach so that distracting background elements such as trees and large rocks were eliminated. Only the clouds were allowed to fill the blue sky with their towering irregular shapes. The distortion of the canoe's bow was achieved by using a 20 mm wide-angle lens and putting the camera as close to the ground as possible, just in front of the bow. The very bright early afternoon sun made using a small aperture possible, assuring sufficient depth of field to get the whole canoe as well as the sky in sharp focus. Because I was lying flat on the ground, looking through the viewfinder was rather awkward, resulting in a somewhat tilted horizon, but fortunately not overly so.

Photographing canoes as objects of beauty for their own sake is an excellent way to train your eye to see shapes and how these can be manipulated photographically into

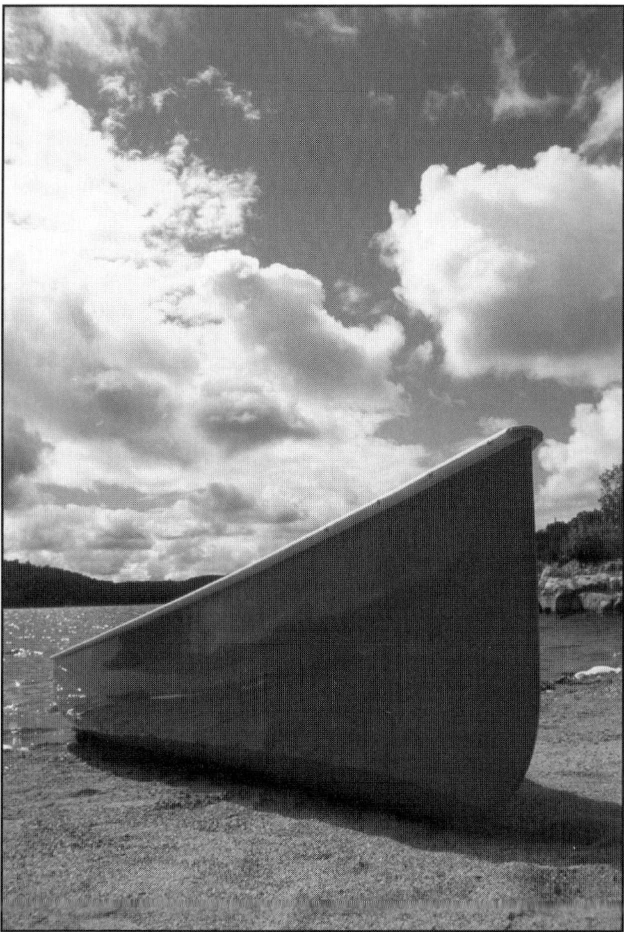

many different and unfamiliar forms by 'playing' with them. Be open to other approaches; really look at the canoe in new ways; do not always follow the same path. By spending hours observing and photographing its lines, shapes and colours under varying conditions of light and shadow, you will cultivate your visual imagination and camera control.

That afternoon on the beach, while trying to discover why the beautifully curved lines of the canoe provide so much visual pleasure, and by experimenting with other ways of looking at them, I came across many intriguing images. This photograph is just one. I look upon it as a paddler's still life, created from sun, sand, water, clouds and a single canoe.

Light is everything. Without some form of light there is no photography (a term which literally means "writing with light").

If the only thing you know about photography is how to handle light, you have already made a giant step in the right direction. Only when there is enough light to take a picture, can you begin to worry about shape, line, colour and texture. Dedicated photographers can spend their whole lives learning about the subtleties of light: about its colour and character; the effects of changing its direction; whether it is hard or soft or somewhere in-between; how it can harshly outline a subject or caress it with a tender touch; that using special illumination may also make the picture special.

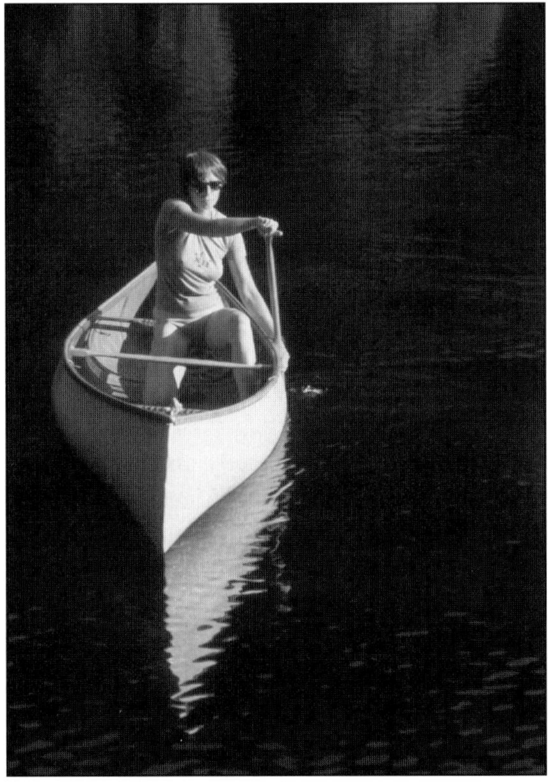

Light changes dramatically throughout a summer's day, from the subtle scarlet or pink light when the sun is still below the horizon early in the morning, gradually changing into the harder and whiter light shining almost straight down at noon, and on to the golden light embracing the world by the end of the day. Light also varies enormously in the course of the year with the passing of the seasons.

Learn to play with light, see its magnificent qualities, watch it coming from different directions to create frontlighting, sidelighting or backlighting. Recognize the best light for portraits or landscape scenics and relish the fading light as a storm cloud slowly obscures the sun. You will also realize that the human eye sees light differently than the film in the camera does, that there is no such thing as absolute photography truly representing the world as it *is*. Photographs are only interpretations of reality.

As a canoe tripper on the go, you often have no time to wait for the best light for photography, so you have to learn how to adapt to the existing situation and make appropriate use of the available light. However, if you keep your eye attuned to the quality of light around you, and *if you are lucky*, some real gems may offer themselves to be photographed by you.

This picture is a good example of how to use light to your advantage. The low evening sun illuminates the canoe like a floodlight skimming over the water surface, leaving the rest of the picture almost completely dark and making the canoe stand out against a surrounding area that has no distracting elements. The canoe seems to float on its own reflection and is placed somewhat left of centre in the frame, giving the vertical composition a pleasing asymmetry.

Little or No Current—Recreational Paddling

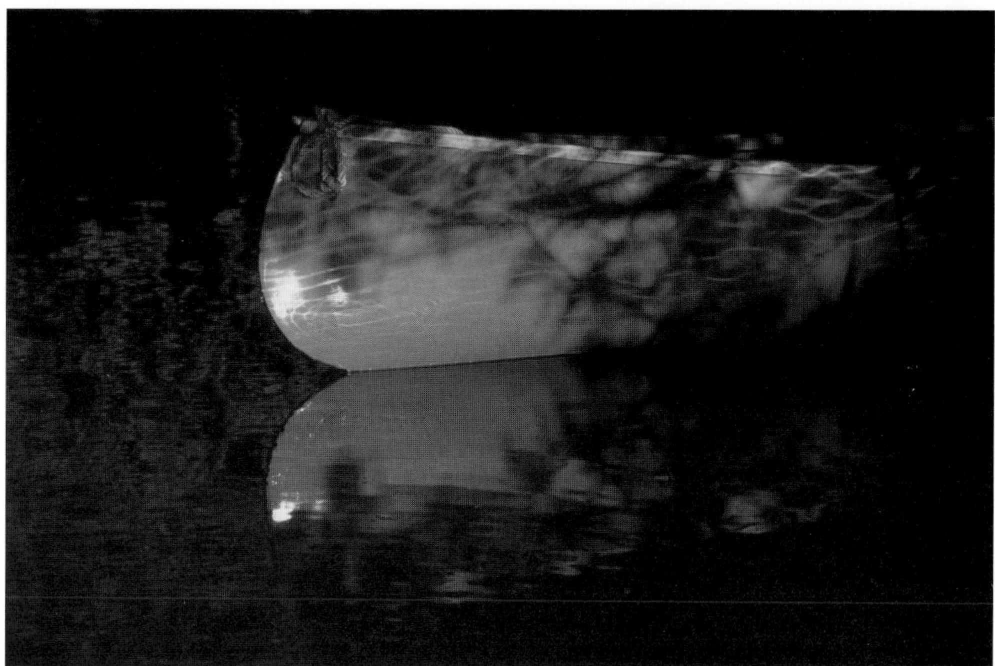

The pictures on this page are two more examples of gorgeous interplay between canoe and light. The top photo was taken under the same circumstances as the vertical photo of the same canoe presented in the section Colour. However, each of those images has a markedly different 'feel,' which shows the importance of carefully observing a situation and then making several different photographs of the same subject.

Although the above picture works quite well in black-and-white, the colour print mentioned clearly illustrates the significant difference colour can make. Both photos of the canoe's bow were taken late in the day while I was standing waist-deep in the calm water of a small bay, carefully selecting an unlit dark background so that the canoe would be isolated from the surroundings.

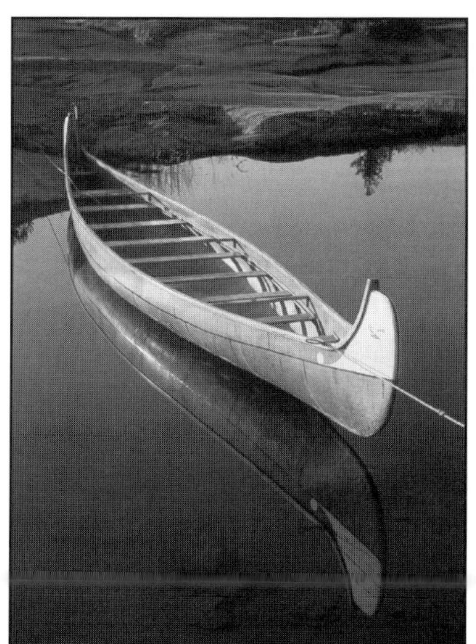

The photo on the left was also taken on a windless day, the smooth water surface reflecting the curved lines of the 11-metre-long Montreal canoe, resting from a day of tripping. This is a pleasant enough shot, but I find two details in it somewhat irritating: the black reflection of the small tree in the background, and the conspicuous light-coloured rope used to tie the boat to the shore. I am inclined to improve the picture by scanning the slide and then digitally removing those details in the computer. However, digitally altering pictures can be controversial and should be approached with care if the images are used for publication. If you use them only for yourself, you can, of course, do whatever you want.

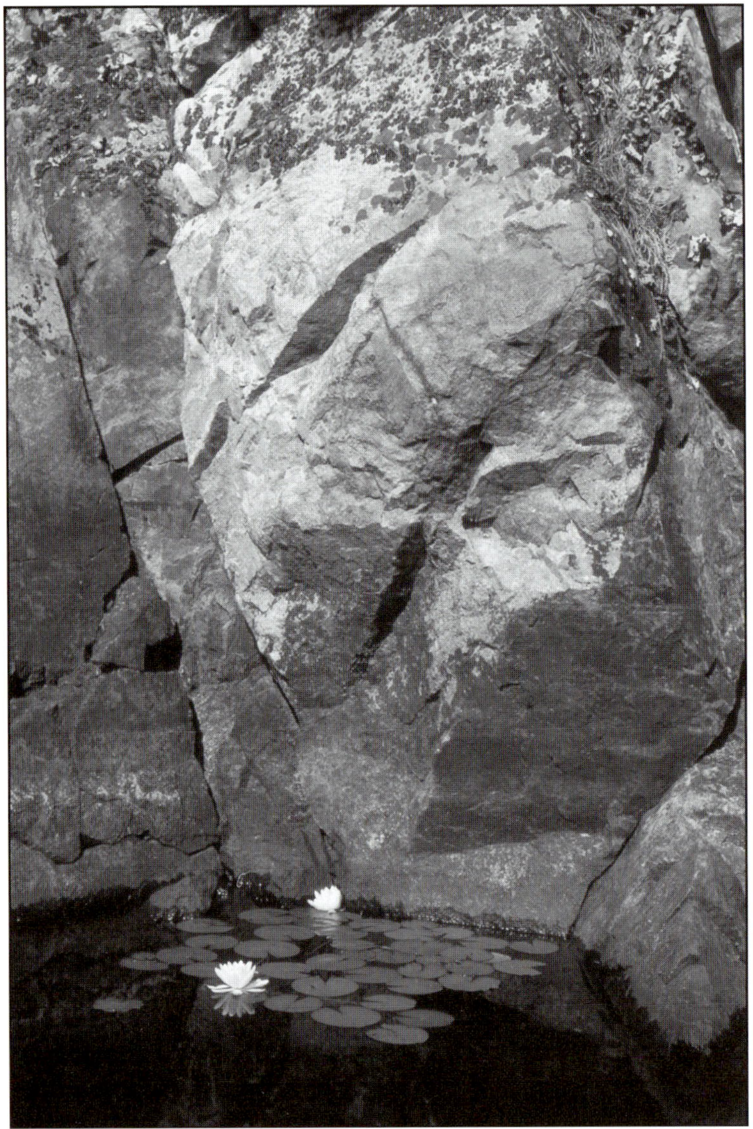

Canoes, of course, are not the only worthwhile subjects that can be studied by paddling photographers. Nature itself provides the keen-eyed observer with an infinite variety of material to be turned into personal souvenirs.

For instance, the ancient Precambrian bedrock of the Canadian Shield comes in many shapes and colours, and the canoeist with an eye for beauty has countless opportunities to discover attractive images of all kinds. This picture presents just such an image, revealing an intriguing contrast between the unyielding rock and the delicate flowers of the water lily. This can be made only from a canoe.

But there is something more in this photograph, something you can use to teach your kids the art of observation by getting them involved in a finding game. Ask them if they can recognize a large face in the rock wall, a face turned slightly on its side, complete with chin, mouth, nose, eyes and lichen-hair. They will be delighted by such a visual challenge and quickly point out the rock-face. Can you?

Little or No Current—Recreational Paddling

It is amazing how much even a tiny subject can change the look of an image.

Both these pictures have an obvious, but small centre of interest that immediately attracts the eye of the viewer. But both of them are also breaking some long-established visual 'rules.' In this small picture, taken at the Barron Canyon early in the morning with the mist rising from the river below, the tiny figure is located very close to the top-left corner, not at all in a position advised by the rule of thirds that would place it closer to the centre. And in the bottom picture, the silhouetted canoe is located smack in the middle of this high-contrast image, again defying accepted rules of composition.

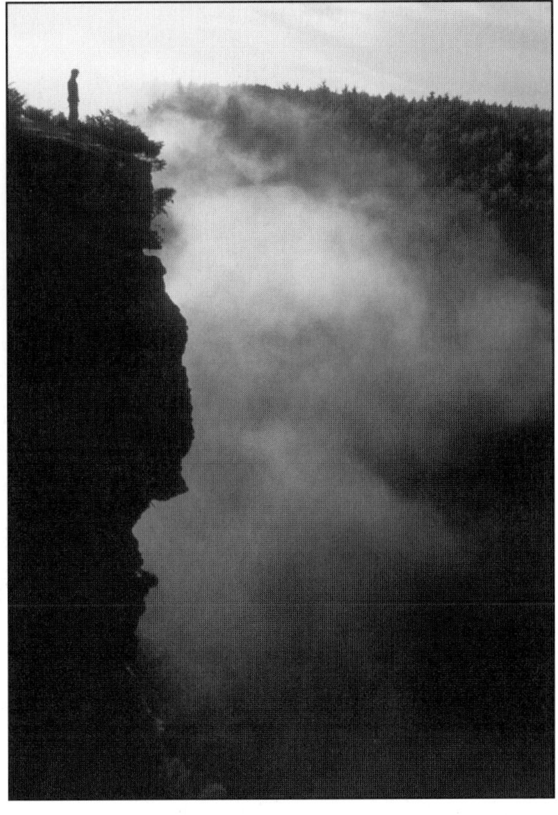

However, both these pictures have a compellingly graphic quality and are definitely 'good' photographs. This illustrates that following the rules can be a good thing, but occasionally breaking them can be even better.

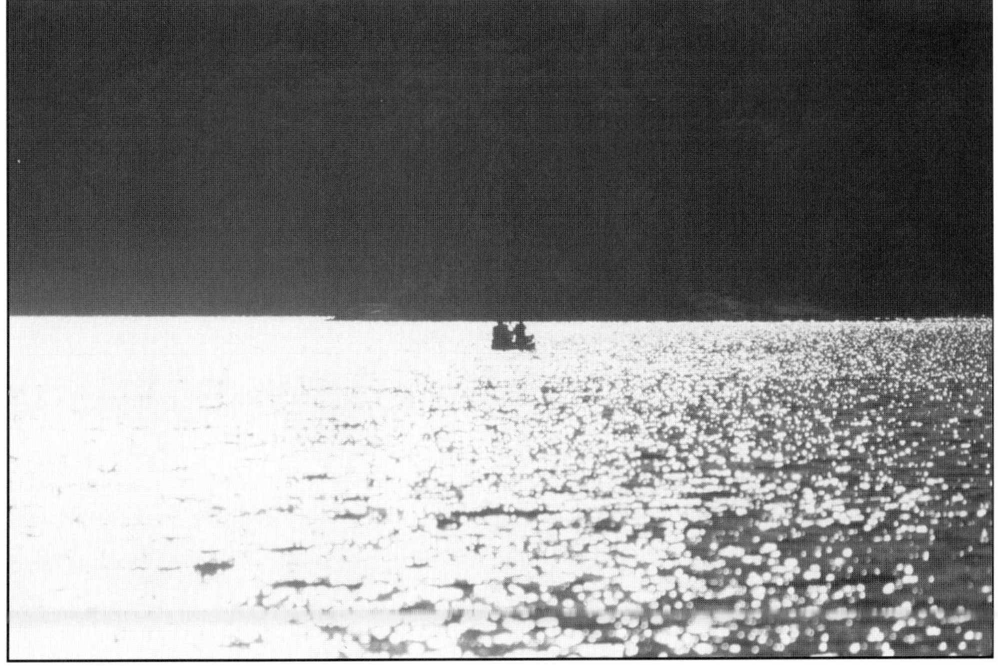

Little or No Current—Recreational Paddling

To the adventurous paddler, wetlands and beaver ponds are synonymous with heaven. They are filled with marvellous mysteries waiting to be discovered, and their peaceful solitude is balm to the soul. Also, the only way to get to most of them is by canoe, which makes them even more special to canoe trippers.

The beaver pond in this photo, created by a 20-metre-long dam built and maintained by a family of beavers living in the lodge shown in the picture, had caught our eyes a few days earlier. We decided to go back for a closer look. Because we had lots of time to explore, I got out of the canoe and walked around on the shore, looking for locations from which to shoot. By getting as high as possible and using the versatile zoom lens to get the best framing for pictures, I found a good place with a nice overview. This is one of the photos I took, showing the main part of the pond while eliminating most of the uninteresting sky. The slightly hazy clouds filtered the sunlight to a pleasant softness, while the canoe in the pond provides a convenient sense of scale.

This photo is a useful example of how the eye is immediately drawn to bright areas in a picture. In this case there are two such spots: the light-coloured rocks in the bottom-right corner and the rocky shoreline below the trees near the top-left corner. When composing your picture, pay attention to details and try to avoid such disturbing elements.

Pristine places like this pond are extremely delicate and vulnerable to human interference. Always remember to respect the places you visit; do not trample the vegetation, but do pick up your trash. Leave everything in the same condition you found it, the only exception being the removal of garbage left by others. Never, ever disturb beaver lodges. When paddling near them, be extra careful and keep your voice down. If you are lucky, you may even hear the beavers talking to each other in their home.

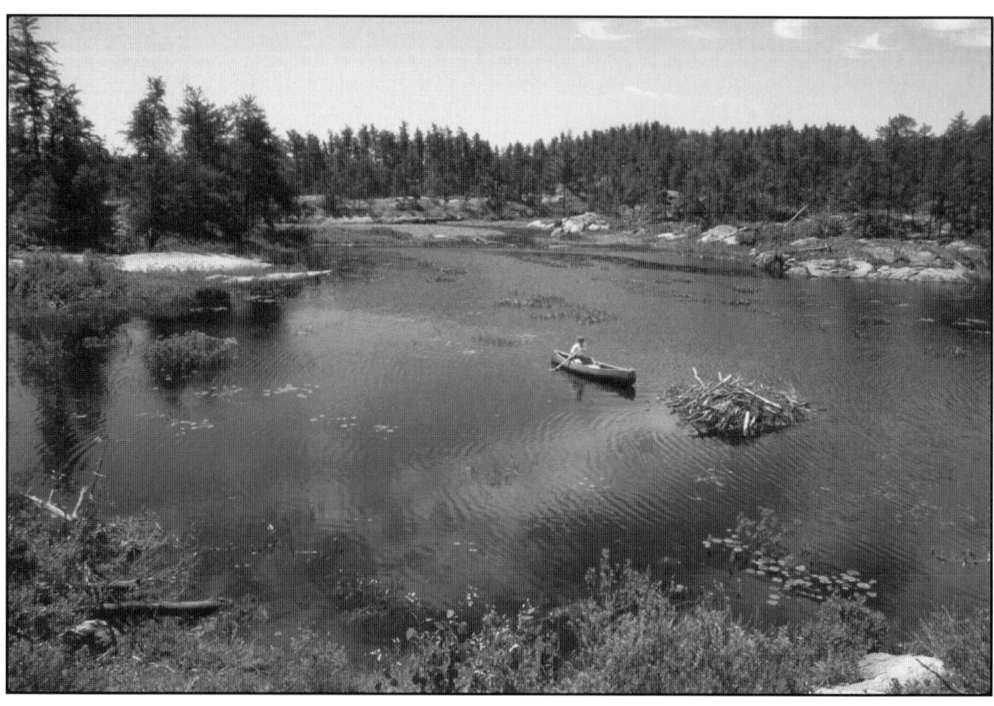

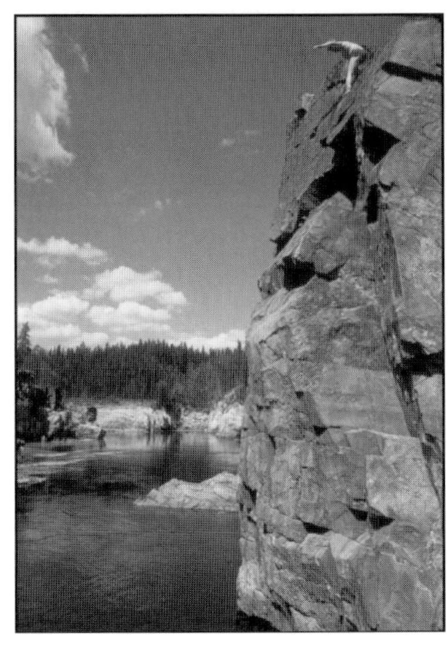

Sometimes a photographer needs more guts to make action shots than the subject does to perform the stunt. I had climbed Conjuring House Rock in the Thunderhouse Falls complex of the Missinaibi River in order to remove a blue nylon strap some inconsiderate visitor had left on top after climbing up and apparently using a rope to get back down. The conspicuous colour of the strap caused severe visual pollution, defacing the solemn Rock to such a degree that I had no choice but to take it off. So up I climbed.

But, lacking a long enough rope, I could not get down again and was stuck on top. I therefore decided to jump into the Missinaibi waters, some 15 metres below, really no big deal because, from the top, the water appeared to be deep enough and clear of rocks.

My wife, Ria, who had to document all this, of course, positioned herself upstream on the large boulders exposed by the low water level of the river, and decided to make three photos, one each of before, during and after the jump. There would be no opportunity to make more than one shot during the jump itself, because she used a pre-focussed manual camera without a motor drive.

All went according to plan. The well-prepared but very apprehensive photographer kept her nerve and did a fine job, her three shots convincingly telling a little story with beginning, middle and end. The middle shot of the sequence is, of course, the main one, and Ria caught me beautifully in mid-jump, clearly visible against the white cloud in the sky. In stressful situations

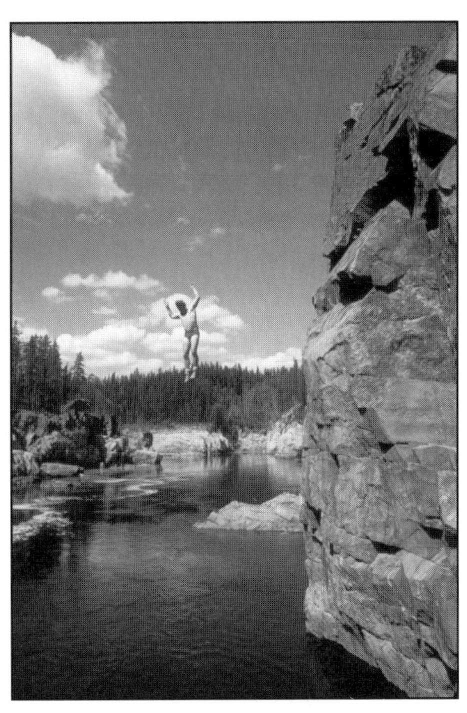

like this it is imperative that the photographer keep her or his cool and not be distracted from the important task at hand. This was, obviously, a clear case of "get the shots first, then deal with your racing heart later."

In retrospect, I would advise against doing a jump like this; it is just too risky for a two-person team without backup. I should have tried to remove the obnoxious nylon strap some other way.

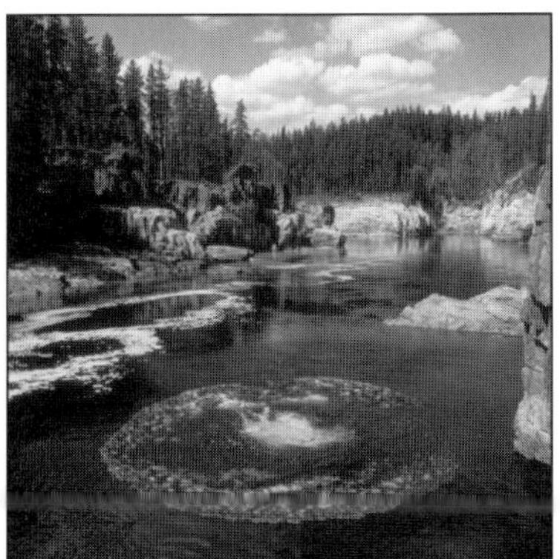

Little or No Current—Recreational Paddling

For many people, taking a solo canoe into the outdoors is a favourite aspect of recreational paddling. To be away on your own for days on end can give tremendous satisfaction and, especially for a photographer, this can be a fruitful time of creativity and soul-searching. With nobody around to hurry you on, you can take your time to experiment and play with various ideas.

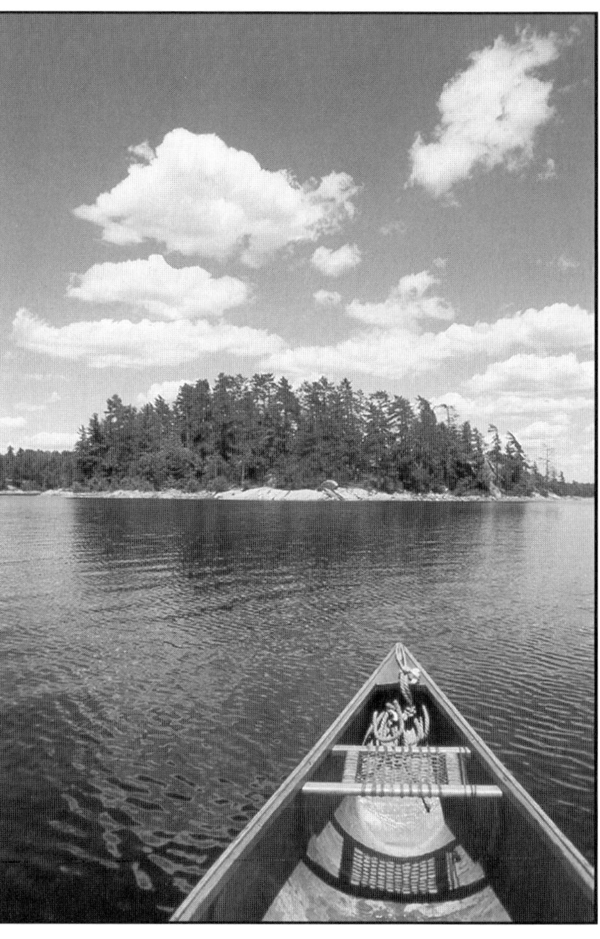

You could, for instance, concentrate on making photos while sitting in your canoe and enjoying the aesthetically pleasing activity of paddling alone on a quiet lake; photos like this one, that can be used on the cover of your trip report or even a book you may want to publish. The vertical format leaves lots of room at the top for the title and, on the left side and just below the middle of the picture, words and short sentences can be printed about contents and author.

The picture was made with a 24-120 mm zoom lens, making easy framing of the composition possible from the back of the canoe. There is a pleasant balance between the various elements in the photo: canoe, rippling water surface, island and sky with clouds. The triangular part of the canoe in the foreground, pointing away from the viewer, provides an interesting visual contrast with the natural shape of the island, also creating a strong feeling of depth. In many cases, putting the horizon in the middle makes for a rather static image, but here it works because the clouds in the large expanse of the sky balance the canoe at the bottom.

The part of the canoe visible in the picture is kept clean of distracting objects such as paddles and life jackets. The hard noon light creates an interesting shadow on the bottom, emphasizing the rounded shape of the canoe.

It is a good idea to try this kind of photography again at the end (or beginning) of the day when the coloured light from the low sun produces very different images. You could also experiment with different compositions such as horizontals. Take your time; you are paddling solo in a world all your own, enjoying a private relationship with nature.

Little or No Current—Recreational Paddling

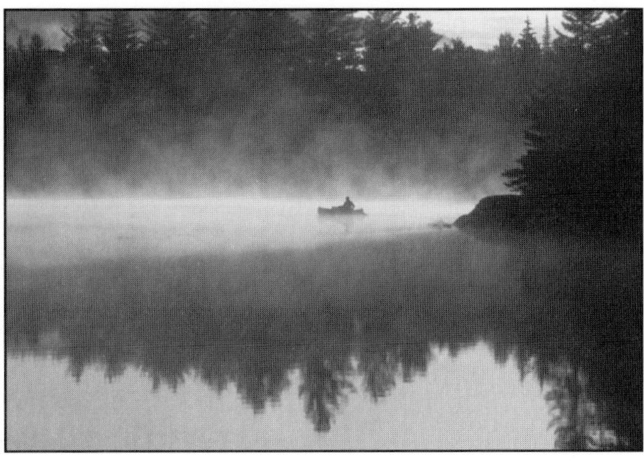

Without a doubt it will be to your great advantage to carefully analyze not only your own pictures, but also those made by other people, such as the ones published in books, magazines and catalogues. Of course, your fellow paddlers too can provide a large numbers of snapshots ready for examination, leading you to a better understanding of what paddling photography is all about.

This photo, for instance, was made by a talented but relatively inexperienced (in paddling photography) amateur photographer, Harry Litz, on Lower Spectacle Lake in Algonquin Park. He recorded the lone paddler early in the morning when the fog was slowly rising from the water, producing a well-observed sharp photograph.

However, this can be made into a much better, even excellent one by simply removing the areas of light sky at the top, thereby eliminating some small but very distracting details. The canoe, floating in the horizontal band of fog enveloping the boat in a delicate veil of minuscule water droplets, makes for a strong centre of interest. The upsidedown reflections of the trees on the unblemished surface of the water give the mood-filled picture something mysterious. (Notice that the top of the tree reflection at the bottom is *not* cut off by the border!) It is fascinating to see how much a photograph can be improved by some simple cropping.

The picture works quite well in black-and-white as presented here; to be expected as the original slide has very little colour in it.

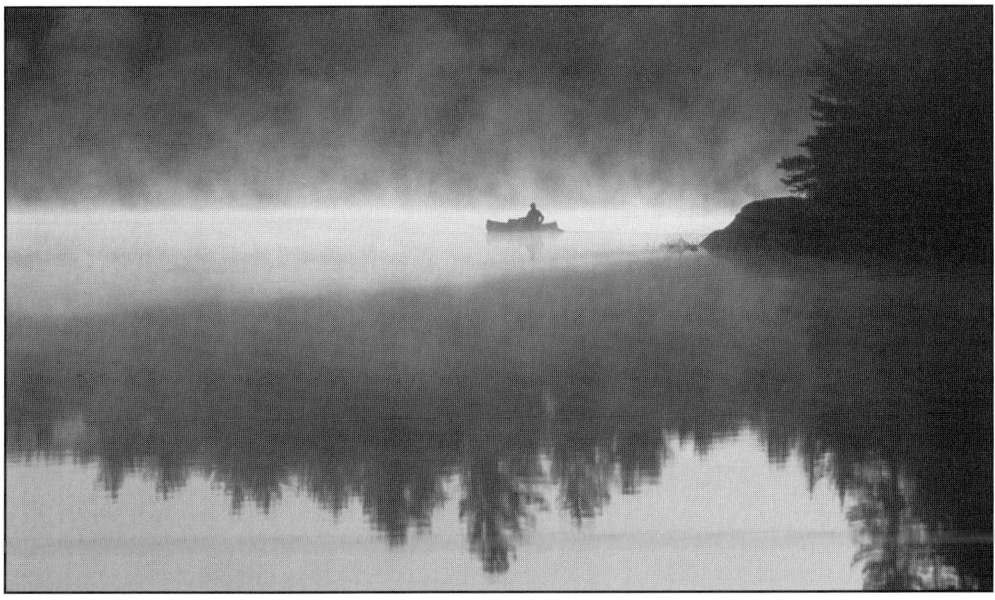

Little or No Current—Recreational Paddling

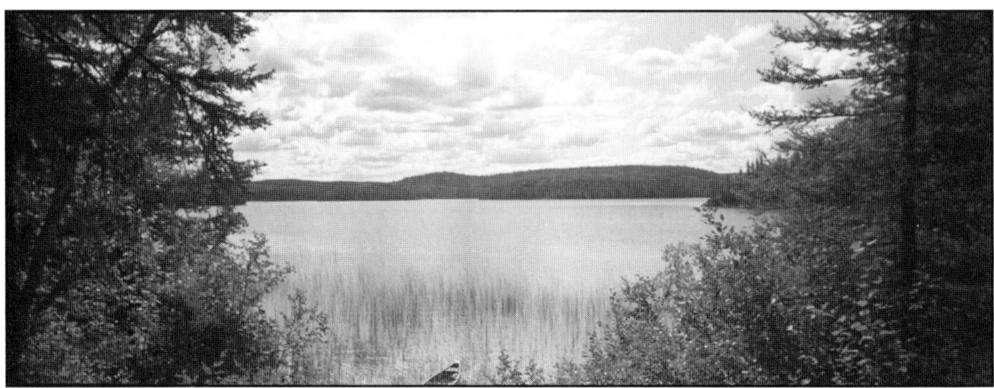

It is the human eye that sees the picture and the person that makes it, not the camera; it is just a tool used to record what you observe.

To illustrate the (relative) unimportance of equipment in photography, these two pictures are presented here. They were each made with the help of an inexpensive, single-use, weather-resistant throw-away camera loaded with ISO 400 print film. If you do not want to make big enlargements, these simple point-and-shoots, although limited in what they can do for you, are still able to produce quite acceptable results. Explore their possibilities and note their limitations, such as some lack of contrast and sharpness.

Both shots were made in a panoramic picture format, which means that the horizontal dimension is much larger than in the case of photos made with a non-panoramic 'normal' camera. If you select the right subjects, such as trees and narrow waterfalls, panoramic cameras can also be used to make vertical pictures.

A problem, however, when using many of these simple cameras is their rather awkward viewfinder. Since looking through the viewfinder without losing parts of the image at the edges of the picture frame takes some getting used to, it is easy to cut off something important. That happened with both photos on this page: in the top one the canoe at the lower edge is cut through the middle; the bottom photo has a very narrow sky with the horizon much too close to the top border of the frame.

In spite of their shortcomings, these little cameras can be most convenient in special situations; for instance, when you absolutely need a rain-resistant or even waterproof camera (some models come that way), or if you have forgotten your regular camera. Make sure the cameras are recycled when you have them processed at the photo store.

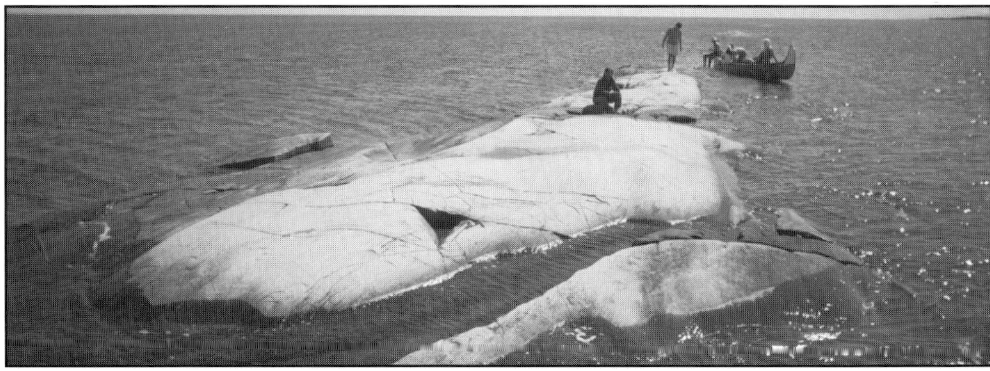

Little or No Current—Recreational Paddling

This is by far the worst picture in the book. However, it is here for the very good reason that it can demonstrate how you can learn from your own mistakes by carefully, even ruthlessly, studying and analyzing your pictures, trying to find out what makes some of them work and others not.

The two dark blotches in the middle and top-left of the picture are caused by blackflies sitting on the front element of the lens of a single lens reflex camera. Blackflies are so tiny that, when looking through the viewfinder, it is easy to miss them when they are on the lens. So watch for them and check the camera when these little monsters are around.

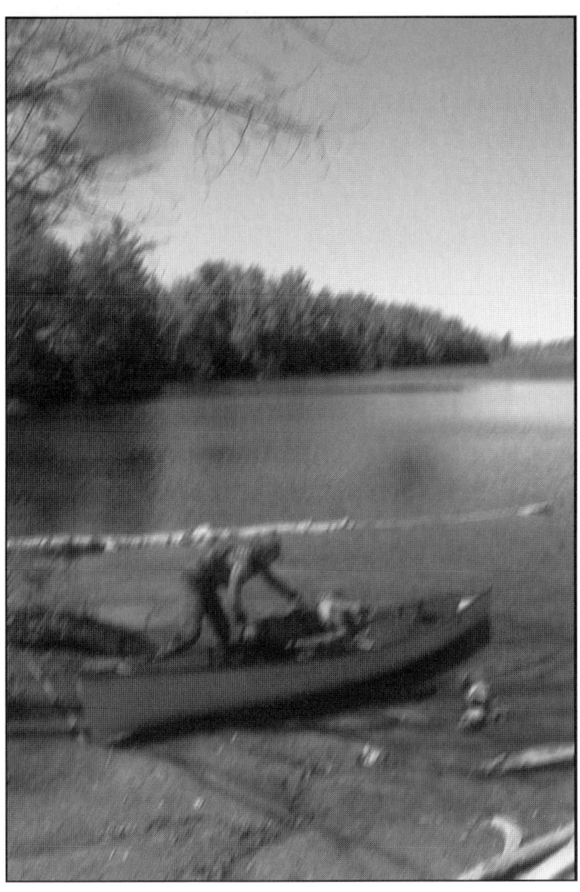

The severe lack of sharpness of the picture is also caused by a bug, probably a mosquito. At the instant I pushed the button to make this shot, I felt a sharp pain on my hand, a sting by some unknown assailant. Involuntarily I jerked my hand away, shaking the camera and producing this disastrously fuzzy picture. (By the way, fuzziness can also result from a dirty lens front element contaminated by any combination of particles, grease, water droplets and finger prints. Clean the lens regularly when you are working in a hazardous environment.)

Besides these two major flaws, there are other shortcomings in the picture worth mentioning. The pieces of wood in the foreground are distracting and could have been avoided by moving the camera forward a bit. The conspicuous light-coloured tree trunk in the water just above the paddler takes away the viewer's attention. It might have less impact if a higher viewpoint had been selected and/or if the camera had been moved to the left. The composition is uninspired and boring; maybe a horizontal picture would have been better. The sunlight is coming from top-left and leaves much of the person and the canoe in the shadow. The bland sky is cloudless. All in al, not a great picture; truly one that should not have been made in the first place.

Obviously, dissecting a disastrous picture like this one can be very instructive after the initial disappointment. Be honest and clear; that is the only way to go. However, do not hesitate to pat yourself on the back if your photograph is exceptional. If you deserve it, let praise be yours!

Little or No Current—Recreational Paddling

This rather eerie-looking picture of a canoe floating in the clouds is the result of a deliberate effort to create an image that was something out of the ordinary, one with a dream-like feeling to it. After observing the clouds reflected in the glassy water surface of Lac Dumoine, I had selected a location where I could make interesting photos using various elements already present in the scene, and also add some new ones. I took some time to identify what attracted me in the picture, then started playing with the various components of the composition.

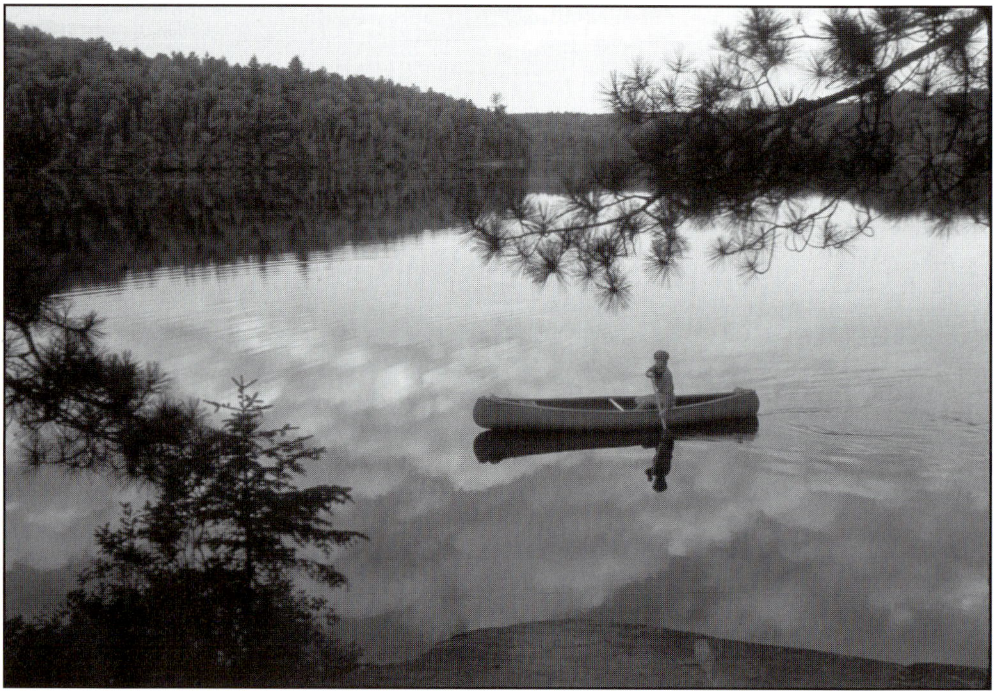

The reflections of the clouds determine the atmosphere of the image, although the canoe with its sharp reflection is the obvious centre of interest. The canoe has been placed deliberately in a preferred rule-of-thirds position. It is moving into the picture from the right, giving an appealing sense of direction to the photograph.

The picture can be improved by cropping the flat rocks at the bottom. Determining the correct exposure of this image brought some complications because, in order to get the right exposure for the canoe and the light-coloured clouds reflected in the water, the overhanging branches as well as the branches and the small tree on the left became underexposed, making them almost into silhouettes.

Because the camera was mounted on a tripod, it was easy to experiment with various compositions by looking through the viewfinder and selecting what to record. For instance, when the human presence is removed by taking out the canoe with the paddler, a different kind of image is found (see page 157). And by concentrating on a small section in the centre of that picture, again another image is created, a vertical one (see page 118). These are only a few of the experiments I made with that scene.

Trying to find such pictures within a picture is a fascinating exercise to heighten your photographic awareness and a wonderful way to improve your talent for *seeing*.

Little or No Current—Recreational Paddling

According to a dictionary definition, an abstract image "achieves its effect by grouping shapes and colours in satisfying patterns rather than by the recognizable representation of physical reality." Nature abounds with abstract images. If you are a perceptive paddler, you can discover many of them on the ever-changing face of water, offering marvellous opportunities to sharpen your sense of seeing shapes, lines and patterns.

The picture above consists of a small reflection of the sun, resting on the slowly undulating bow waves of a canoe and gently moving with them. The diagonal lines create a feeling of energy, and the bright spot located in a pleasing rule-of-thirds position immediately attracts the eye. The simple purity of design and lines and the interaction between water surface and light make this a visually stimulating image of great beauty. As a photographer you feel privileged to be allowed to see and record it.

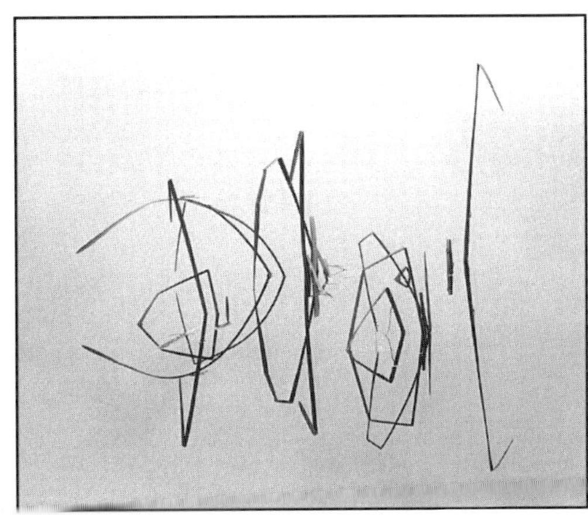

The bottom picture looks like a collection of random lines suspended in space, but it actually consists of several reeds and their reflections, standing in seamless water. There is neither horizon nor sense of depth or scale. The composition of this abstract image is very simple, its pure lines are positioned in the middle of the frame. Train your eye to see those captivating abstract designs in nature; they are too often missed by the casual observer.

Both photos were made with a good-quality digital camera

In canoe country, silhouettes are everywhere. Look for objects that are themselves not illuminated and are placed in front of a light background, thus making them appear as dark shadows without grey details, i.e. without a continuous range of tones from light to dark. Good silhouettes have a distinct pen-and-ink quality that emphasizes pattern and texture, often creating unusual and dramatic pictures of stark simplicity. These can bring an intriguing graphic touch to your photo collection.

The highly textured branches and leaves of the trees in this peaceful photograph form a tight frame around the centrally placed canoe, the centre of interest. The sun reflecting off the water makes the canoe stand out strongly against the silvery water surface. There is a powerful feeling of depth in the picture, with the trees on both sides acting as a window through which we look out at the sun-drenched lake with the island in the distance and the opposite shore even farther away.

The original slide, from which this black-and-white image is made, has very little colour in it. Adding colour to silhouettes, however, can create superb images. Silhouettes made at sunrises and sunsets often exhibit a wonderful contrast between the black silhouette and the vividly coloured background. See the photos in the section Colour.

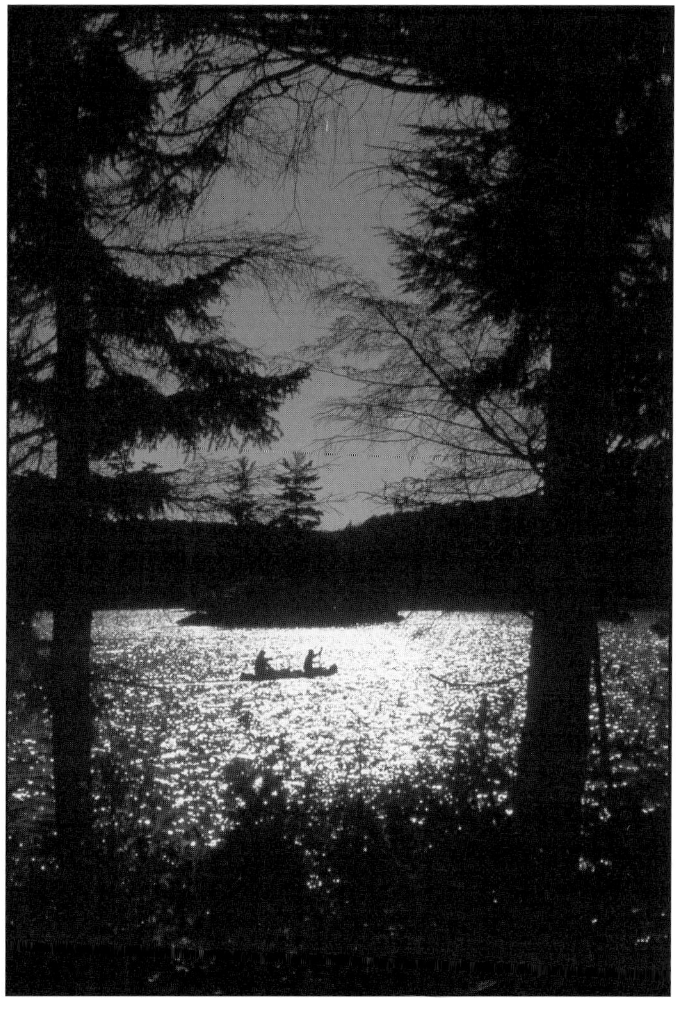

Little or No Current—Recreational Paddling

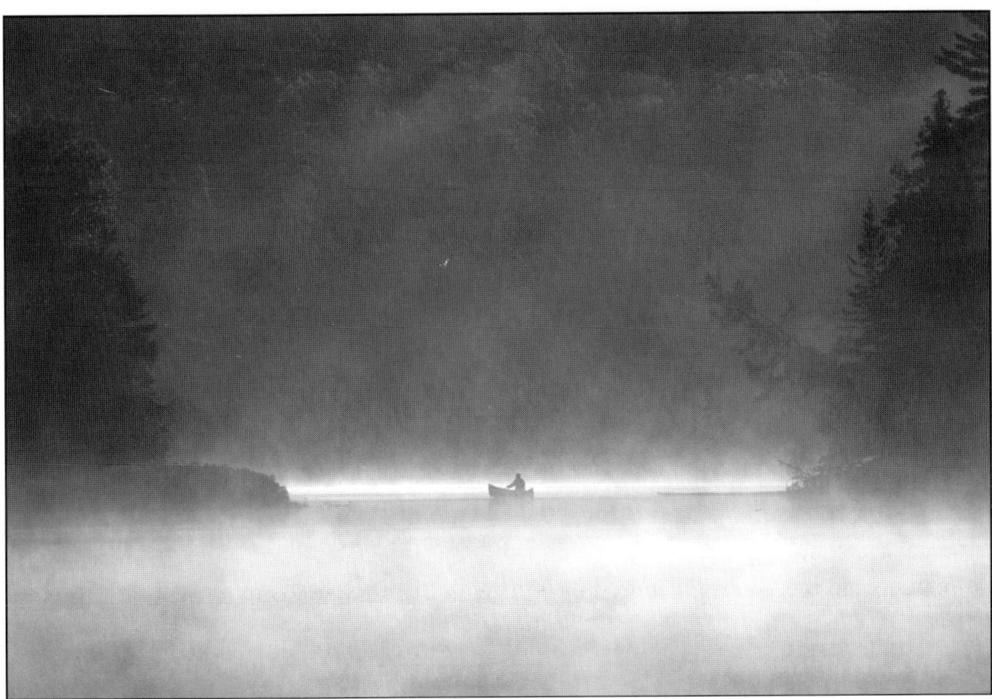

As a dedicated photographer you should always have your camera within easy reach, otherwise you risk missing some of the best shots you might unexpectedly encounter. I should have followed this advice when, early one morning before leaving our last campsite of the trip, I paid a final visit to Crescent Lake in the southern end of Lake Superior Provincial Park.

The lake was covered by a shimmering veil of wispy fog, slowly rising in the crisp air and filling the scene with a mesmerizing golden-brown colour. While I stood there on the beach, absorbing the beauty of the place, a canoe slowly came into the picture, changing the scene from a merely pretty one into something that would drive all perceptive outdoors photographers crazy.

I started running the few hundred metres to our tent site to pick up my camera. But then remembered to deliberately slow down to a walk, because I knew that if I was breathing hard while shooting, my hands would tremble too much to make sharp shots with a hand-held telephoto lens. After picking up the camera and the 300 mm lens, I forced myself to walk slowly to the beach. The canoe had now reached the middle of the lake and appeared to be suspended in the mist between buttresses of trees on both sides, like the wings of a theatre.

Keeping the paddler in the viewfinder just below the middle of the frame, I pushed the button when the scene looked perfect. The fog lasted for only about 20 seconds. I made eight photos, doing all the right things learned over the years: I stood firm and stable with my legs slightly spread, elbows tucked against my sides, holding my breath when I slowly pushed the button, doing everything I could to give the camera all possible support to be able to shoot at 1/60th of a second on ISO 100 slide film.

I got the shots I wanted, thanks to knowledge and self-control. Now I always take my camera with me when saying goodbye to a lake.

Little or No Current—Recreational Paddling

This solitary, beautifully backlit figure sitting on a rock, is performing 'mind photography,' probably the most instructive activity you can do in all picture taking. It means *thinking* about photography, creating images in your head and experimenting with their composition, arranging and rearranging visual elements that are floating in your mind or that you see in front of your eyes. Playing with them, touching them, feeling them with your sense of vision and making them your very own fantasies.

You can even try to solve technical photographic problems in your head: what film to use if your mind picture were a real one; the required lens opening and exposure time; to use a tripod or not; to record it as a vertical or a horizontal. Consider the many technical decisions you have to make when actually using a camera.

The big difference is, you are *not* using a camera and you are *not* registering these pictures on film. You store them in your brain, your memory, thus building a private collection of imagined visual gems you can recall and work on at any moment if you so desire. You can do this wherever you are; while walking, paddling, cooking, doing nothing in particular, before falling asleep even, when remembering the beauty you observed that day and building your own pictures with it.

Once you have worked out the creative and technical problems in your head, you may actually go and produce real photos with your camera, based on the mind pictures you had previously composed. Make practising this kind of virtual photography an integral part of your visual education; it is the least expensive way to go and very entertaining. The more you do it, the better you will become.

Mind photography will not only produce a unique private collection of cherished imaginary pictures, it will also help you very much in your picture-taking by improving the most important aspect of your photographic activities, your ability to *see*.

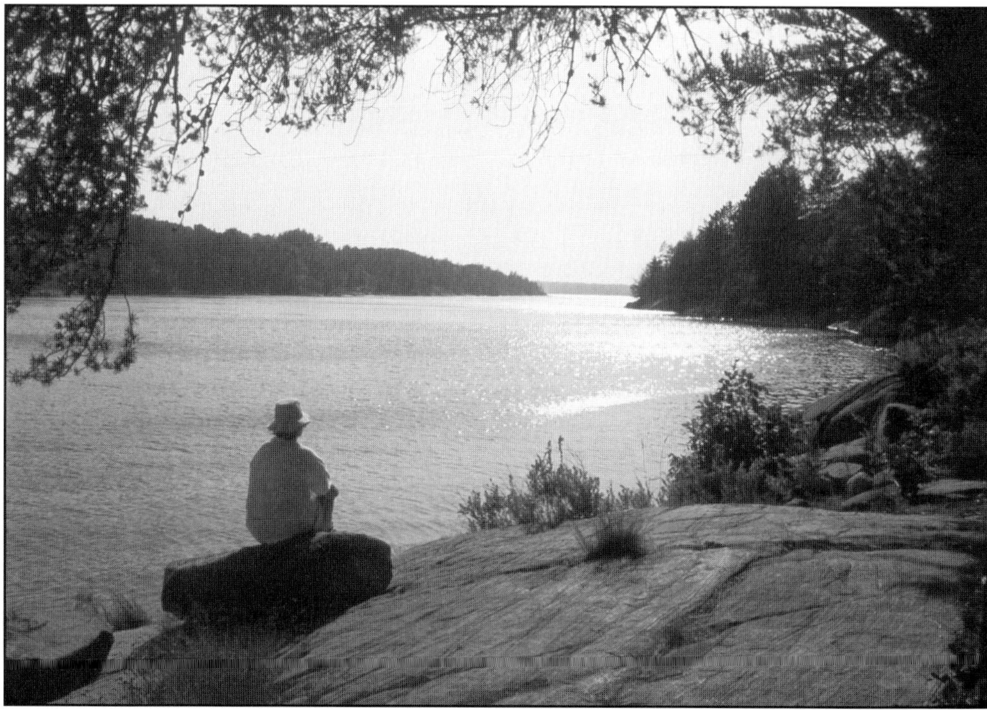

Little or No Current—Recreational Paddling

MARATHON RACING

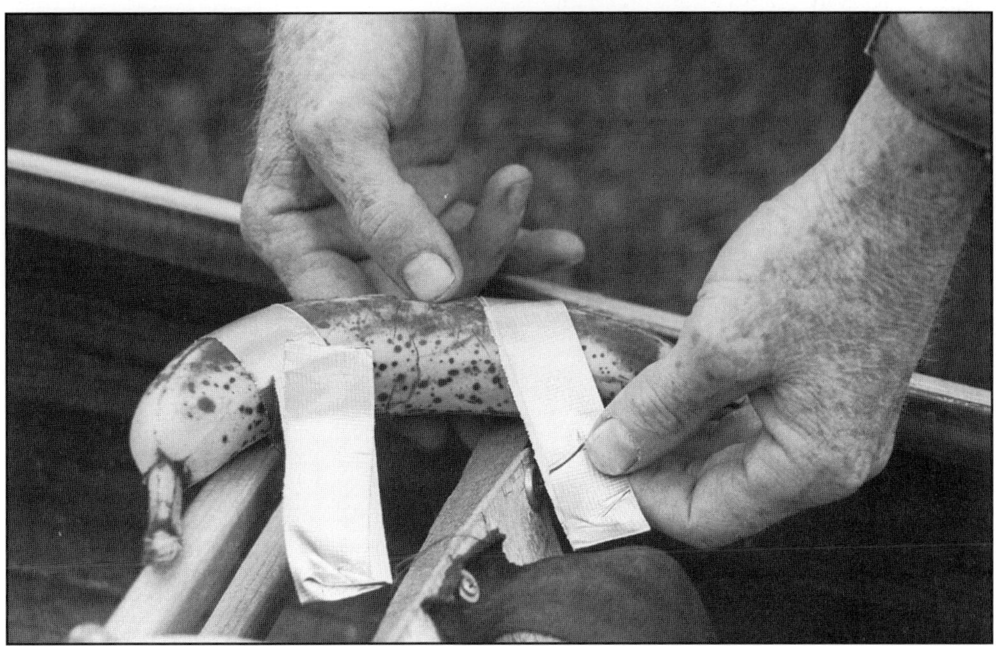

Marathon canoe racing requires the ability to paddle hard for hours over long distances on flatwater—interrupted only by a few running portages—in often distinctive boats powered by light-weight bent-shaft paddles. For the photographer, this continuous action, while creating special problems, also creates possibilities. The canoeists themselves are obviously not in a position to handle a camera because they are far too busy. However, spectators can easily find many opportunities to make unique photos of this exciting sport, the best possibilities being at the start and finish of a race, when the boats are close to the shore or a bridge and when the portages are underway.

It is quite appropriate to open this section with a close-up picture of a pair of hands securing a banana to a thwart by means of duct tape. In the course of a marathon canoe race, the hardworking paddlers expend so much energy that they want something quick and easy to eat when the need arises. And what is more convenient—and photogenic to the photographer!—than a large ripe banana, waiting to be devoured?

There are many such delightful pre-race photographs to be made amidst the hustle and bustle of preparation time. Have your camera ready while hunting for some fine shots to illustrate the activities of the day: such as this man carefully polishing his beloved craft. Here the telling of the story of a marathon canoe race begins.

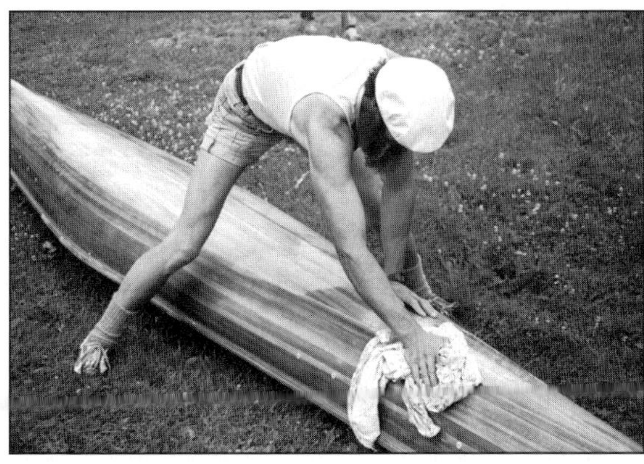

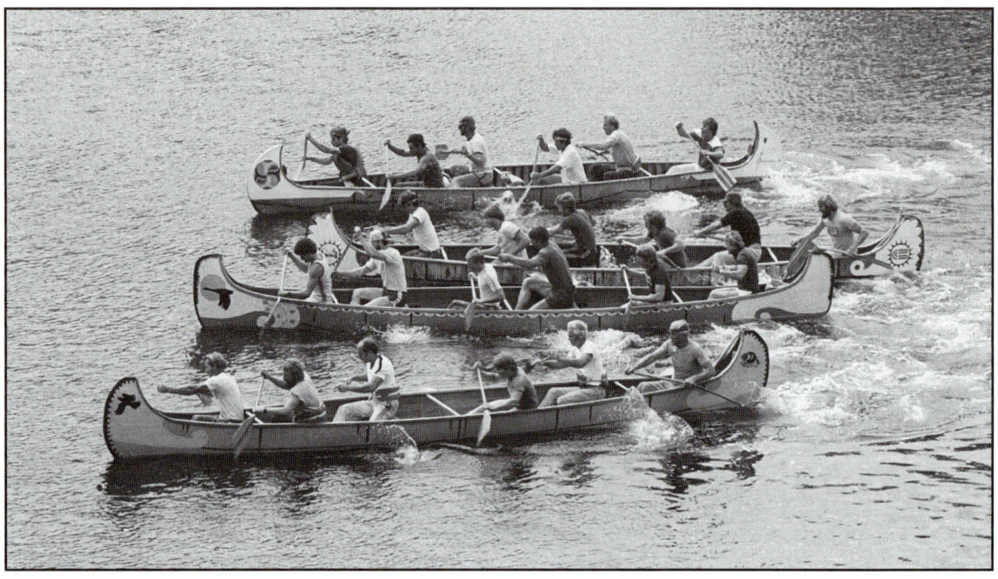

The start of the race is the only time you will be able to record all participants and their boats in one image, so be prepared and select your position carefully. These 7.5-metre-long North canoes were shot from a little hill beside the course; they were still close enough together to form a pack. The few moments it takes to get the starting boats really going are filled with frantic actions. Paddles flash back and forth furiously, as the racers try their utmost to accelerate as fast they can and to gain an important advantage in the first few hundred metres, while the spectators on the shore are enthusiastically yelling their encouragements. Try to make a series of photos, from just before the time the starter's gun goes off to when the canoes are at full speed. This will give you the possibility of selecting the best one(s) from your collection for your story.

The specialized C2 marathon canoes in the bottom photo are the real speed devils of this kind of canoe racing. They can go as fast as 12 km/h. So, make your shot(s) quickly, or the boats will be out of range. This is a rather unspectacular photograph, but it provides a good record of the start. The white canoe in the background is a visual distraction and could be removed by retouching later on, if desired.

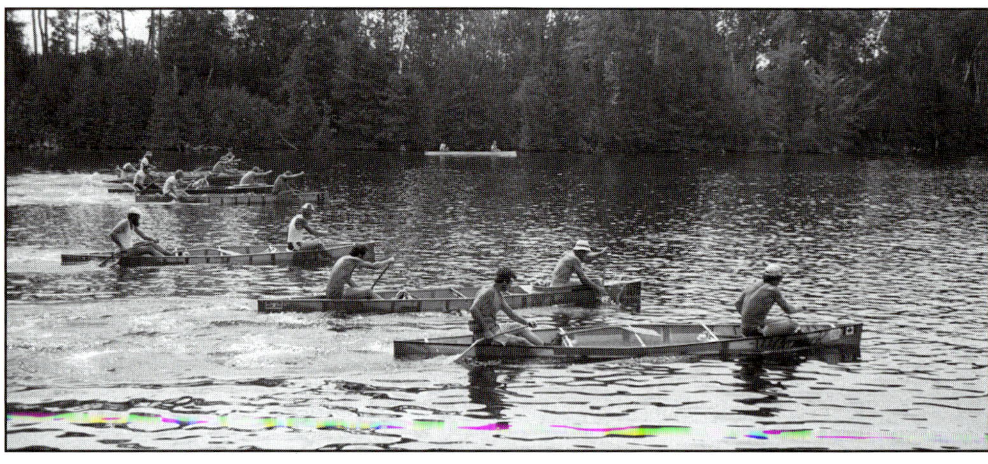

Little or No Current—Marathon Racing

Before the start of the race, carefully scout the course for good locations from which to shoot. Bridges are among the best places; from them you can shoot almost straight down. Once the race is underway, you will have the opportunity to photograph some of the individual boats as they pass underneath. This is also a great opportunity for making vertical photos, something you should always try to do in order to break the monotony of repeatedly using horizontals in your albums or presentations.

This particular shot would make a fine enlargement for the six paddlers to proudly hang on their walls, reminding them of that terrific day they won the trophy! It shows the staggered seating of the men, their bent-shaft paddles just out of the water at the end of the stroke and their faces concentrated on giving this big heavy North canoe the power it needs to move through the water as fast as possible.

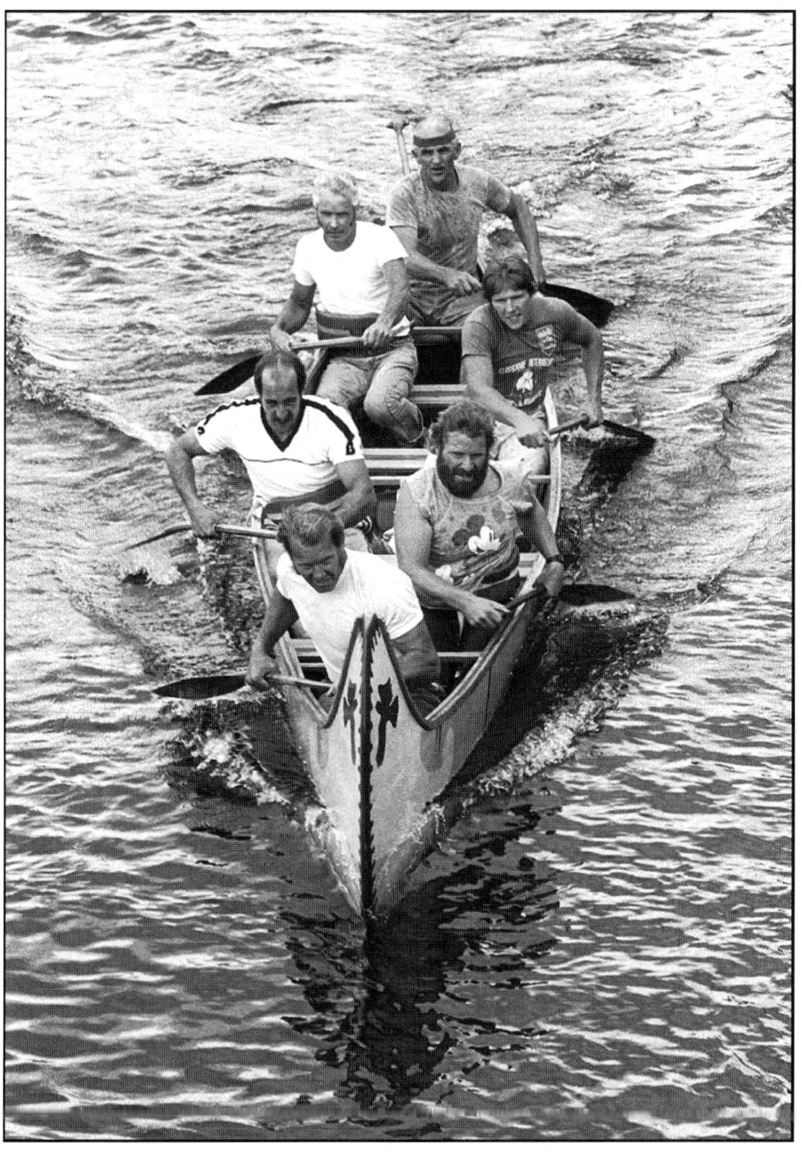

Little or No Current—Marathon Racing

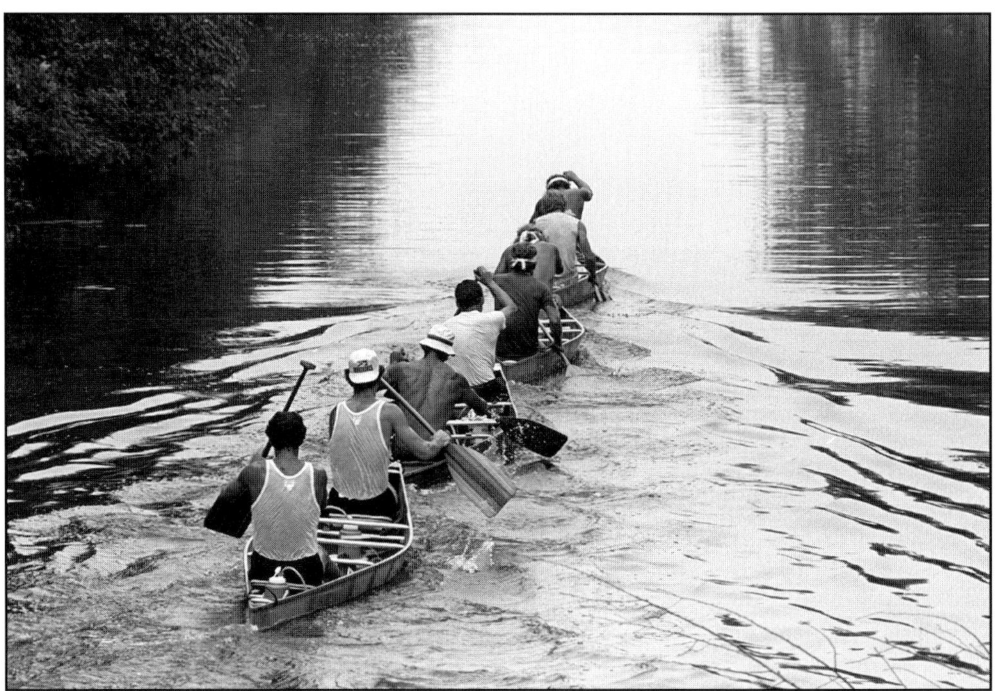

These four boats were shot from a pre-selected position on a low bridge just as they had passed it. The photo clearly shows the characteristic marathon paddling technique where the boats line up behind each other to take advantage of the wake created by the one in front. The last canoe is caught at the exact moment that both men switch paddling sides, following the crisp command HUT!, a procedure used to keep the boat going straight without deliberate (and energy-absorbing) steering.

This is a clean shot. There are no distracting elements and the canoes form a strong line across the picture, emphasizing the sense of movement away from the viewer. Although many different viewpoints are possible, of course, this image presents a fine demonstration of the look and essence of marathon canoe racing.

Because all action is concentrated in the middle of the picture, it could also have been composed as a vertical shot, but would then have had a different 'feel' to it. By covering about 10% of the picture on the left-hand side with some paper and about 20% on the right-hand side, you will see that the interesting wave pattern in the water is now far less prominent and that the wide channel the boats are travelling in is no longer evident. Photo composition is, of course, a matter of personal taste. If you like the way your photo looks, stick to it; but always leave room for experimentation. There are more ways than one to solve the problem of creating a good picture, and the only way you can determine the best is by composing different views and seeing how you react to them.

This photograph was taken with a manual 35-105 mm zoom lens, making the selection of an attractive horizontal composition relatively easy. Because of the bright weather, the high-speed ISO 400 film and the lack of high-contrast whitewater, the focussing, depth of field and (automatic) exposure did not pose real problems.

Little or No Current—Marathon Racing

Often you can make a photograph that satisfies you to some extent at first viewing, but you still feel it can be improved. Such is the case with this photo of a paddler coming straight at you, while being followed by several other boats. It even seems he is making eye contact. What makes this shot so special is the superb reflection on the

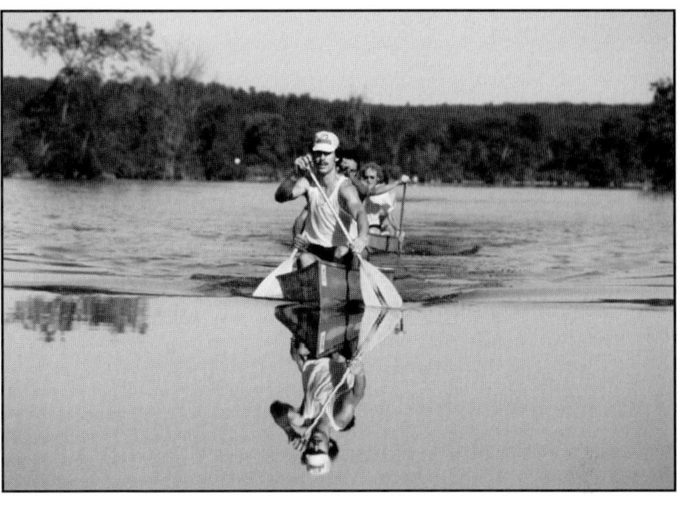

water surface in front of the canoe. But there is too much confusing and unnecessary picture area on both sides of the paddlers. The light sky at the top is a distraction. Also, the horizon is slightly crooked, and there are two irritating white dots, one to the left of the paddler's head and one just to the right of the hand holding the paddle in the background. When the necessary corrections have been made—by cropping, rotating and retouching in either the darkroom or on the computer—the result shows a tremendous

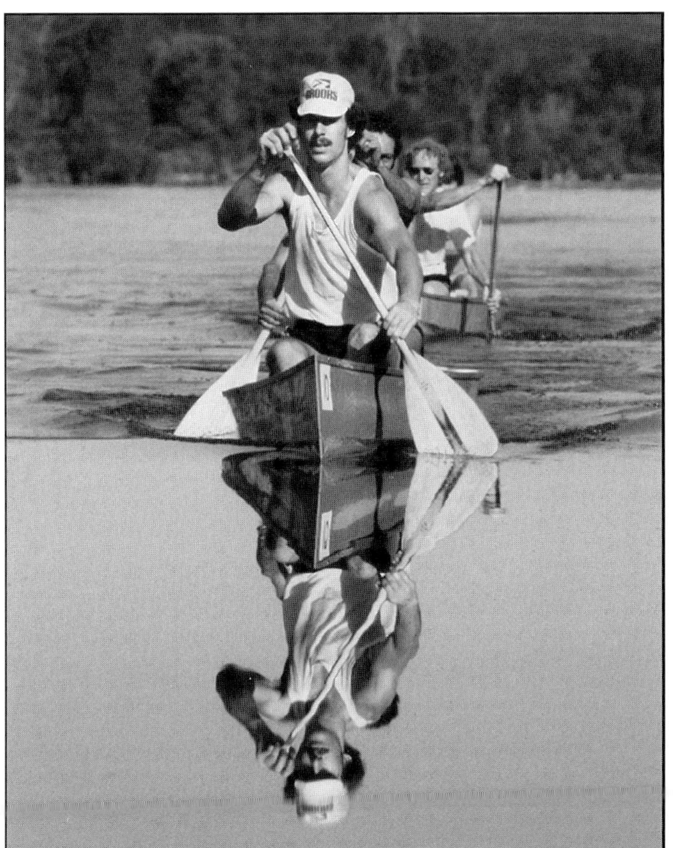

improvement over the original photo. It is now a powerful picture that commands immediate attention. Marathon canoe races will provide remarkable possibilities for making quality photos.

Always cast a critical eye over your photos and try to make their composition and content stronger, preferably at the time you are looking through the viewfinder and actually making the shot. But you can also experiment later with cropping or retouching the photograph itself. You will love the results and recognize the importance of paying attention to details.

Little or No Current—Marathon Racing

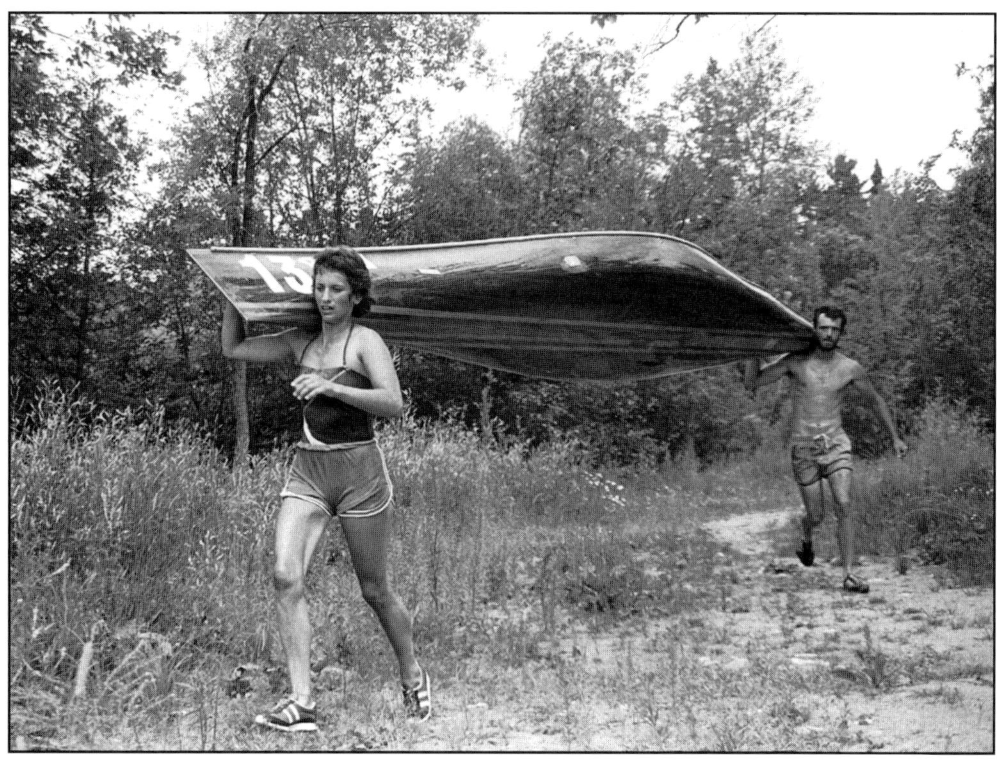

In a race, it is frequently necessary to transport the canoe and everything in it—paddles, life jackets, food, drink—and, of course, yourself and your partner, as quickly as possible between two bodies of water, often over rough ground. The success of your race depends to a large extent upon your capability to use both your legs and your arms efficiently. The art of portaging is, therefore, an essential element of marathon canoe racing, something that is often feared, yet always respected by dedicated racers.

For the photographer, the portage is a fine opportunity to take dramatic action pictures that can help tell the story. But you should select your shooting position with care. Try to anticipate the sequence of events about to happen so that you are ready when the moment to capture some fine photos arrives. The above picture would be less interesting if shot from another angle, without both racers' faces being visible.

Keep your eyes open for the unusual: a novel way of doing things, a clever technique of handling the boat. For instance, this solo kayaker carries everything he has with him and still manages to run fast while balancing the unwieldy kayak. He does this by supporting the boat on his shoulder, using a long rope stretched between bow and stern.

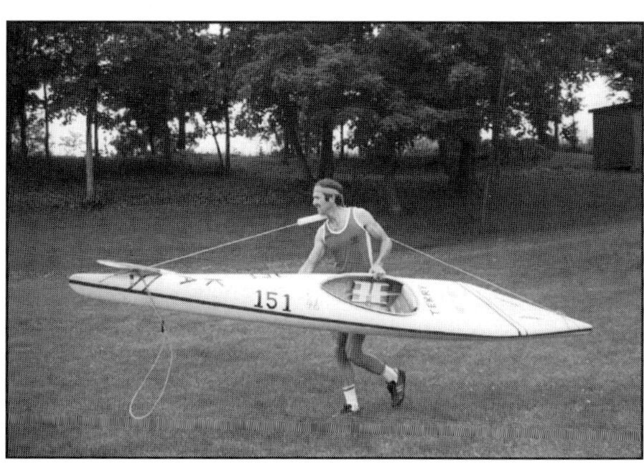

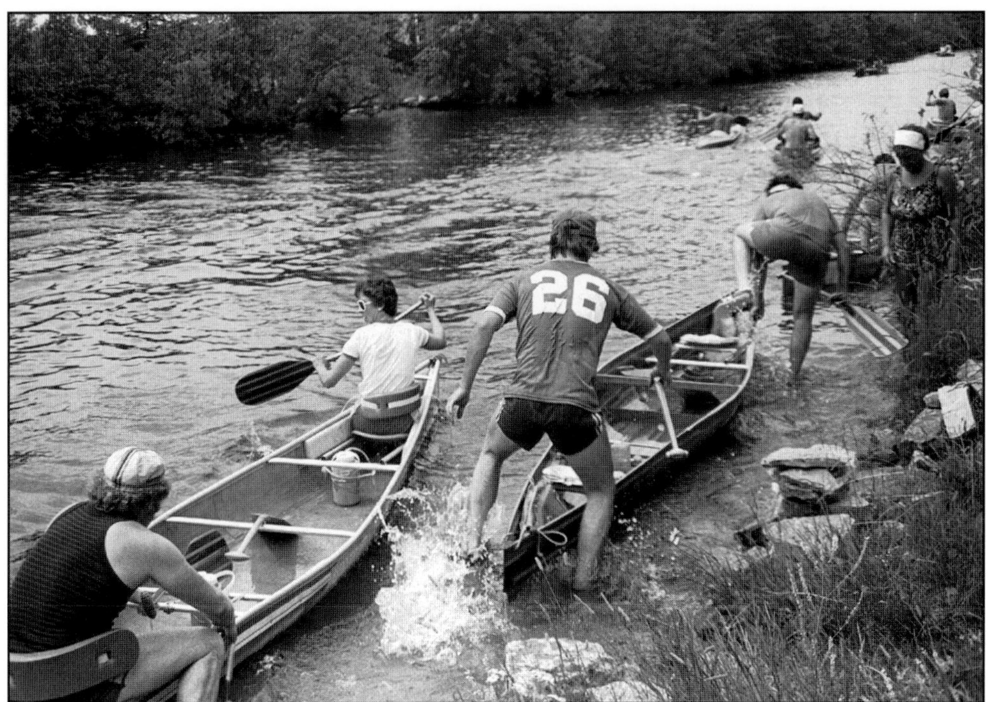

The portage is always followed by a sometimes chaotic put-in. Everybody wants to re-launch their canoe or kayak at about the same time and, because it is all about arriving first, there is a lot of pushing and shoving and yelling (most of the time polite and friendly, but not always). If not very careful, you, the photographer, can be caught in the middle of this fracas and unceremoniously pushed aside by the rushing racers. Understandably so, because who needs another obstacle in this mad dash to get going? Remember, even when you are hunting for precious photographs, the paddlers always have the right of way.

In this photograph, the commotion and urgency at the put-in is well-portrayed, especially because the central character wearing no. 26 is kicking up lots of water in his haste to enter his boat as fast as possible. The picture gives a good overview of the frantic action: from the man in the lower left corner, through the diagonal line filled with boats and people, to the boats already paddling away fast at top right. The woman in the white shirt adds to the strong feeling of urgency, impatiently looking back at her partner in the stern and holding her paddle up, eager to dig it into the water and start the next leg of the race. Everything is shot from the back, giving a strong feeling of movement away from the viewer.

Because marathon canoe races take place over sometimes considerable distances, it is very difficult, if not impossible, for one photographer to make a complete document of the whole race, covering it from start to finish, including portages and other significant events. Even if the portages are accessible by road, getting yourself and all your photographic equipment everywhere on time will be quite a challenge. You might want to recruit friends to help produce a comprehensive document of the race.

Little or No Current—Marathon Racing

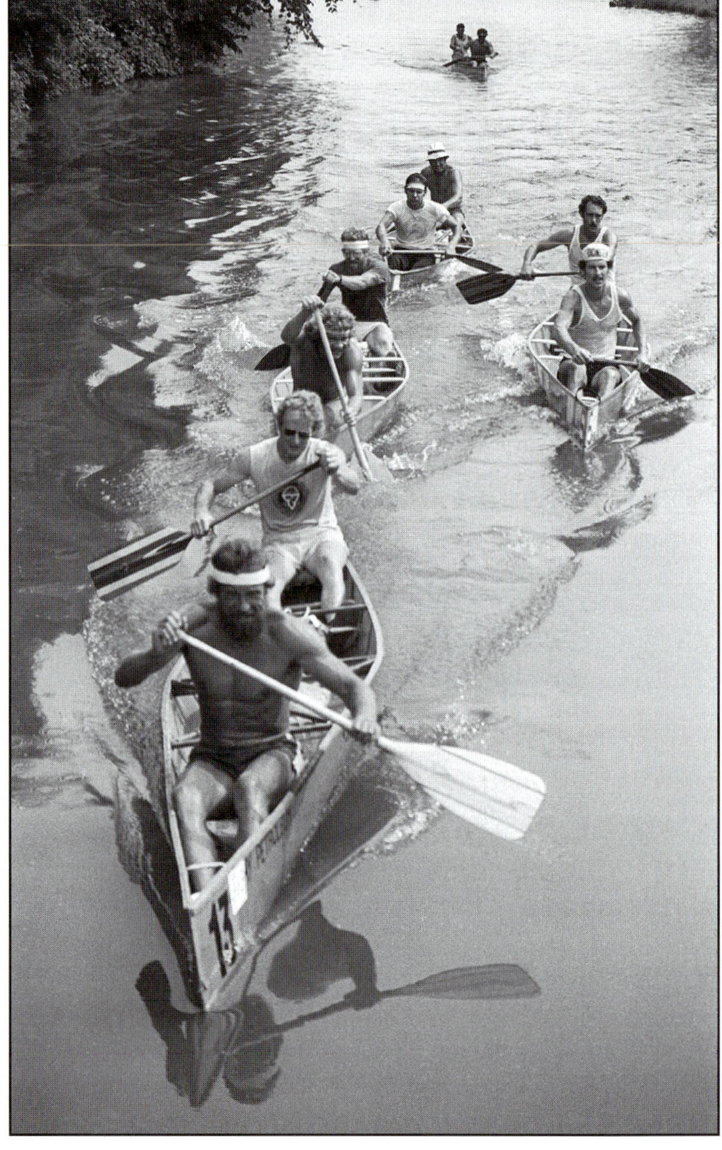

Here we have a fine example of a vertical shot showing the typical marathon canoe racing formation made up of several boats following in each other's wake. This is the same group of paddlers as portrayed earlier, but now there are only three boats, one behind each other. The fourth one has already begun to accelerate, intending to overtake its competitors. Notice how the clean undistorted reflection of the bow paddler in the first canoe creates a pleasing bottom part of the picture. There is also a strong feeling of depth because in going from the first canoe to the one at the top, the boats seem gradually to become smaller.

This picture presents another useful illustration of the importance of cropping. Although the central group of four canoes very much defines the image, the lone canoe at the very top and the little piece of dark shoreline at top-right are quite disturbing and take away from the visual impact of the image. Fortunately, it is very easy to improve this picture tremendously. If you place a sheet of white paper about midway between the white hat of the last paddler of the group and the lone canoe at the top, cutting off the top 10% including the bushes on the left, you will immediately notice a major positive change in the quality of the picture. The four boats now form a single isolated group and you have created a strong image without any distracting elements. All eight paddlers are clearly visible, as are both the distinctive wide mid-section of the classic marathon racing canoe and the wide blades of the bent-shaft paddles used in this demanding endurance sport.

Then, after hours of thoroughly enjoyable hard work, hunger, thirst, aching muscles and possibly even some nasty blisters, the paddlers finally see the finish line appearing in the distance. In some marathons, this may be the least suspenseful part of the race. Because of its length in distance and time, the race can cause the boats to be spread out considerably at the finish line. Often it is hard to find real tension. However, the finish is a very important part of the race and should be properly documented.

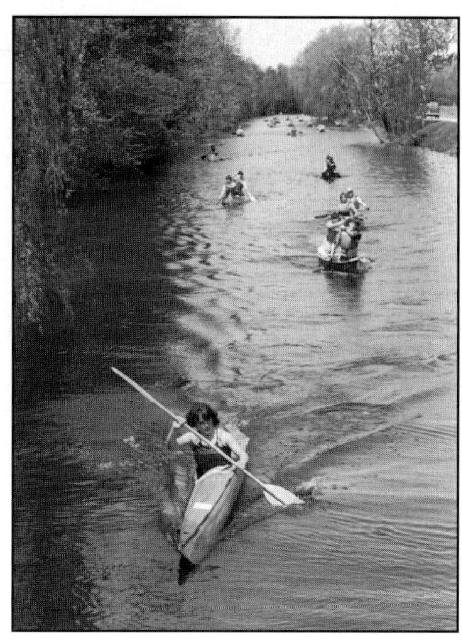

In this vertical shot the boats are still quite close to each other because the race was for junior paddlers over a relatively short distance, with the various classes mixed together. The young woman arriving first in her kayak is sprinting to the finish line, followed by several others. This simple vertical photo gives a nice overview of the final moments.

Even when the finish is lacking in tension, the photographer still has the challenge to make something of it, to record a bit of drama and maybe suspense. The bottom photograph illustrates one way of doing that. It shows the bow of the winning boat just as it crosses the finish line, a ribbon put on top of the water. The paddler is finally allowed to loosen his grip on the paddle and let his boat come to rest on the sandy beach. It is not a picture that may be very popular with the paddler in question, as his face is not visible, but it does clearly illustrate the finish of the race.

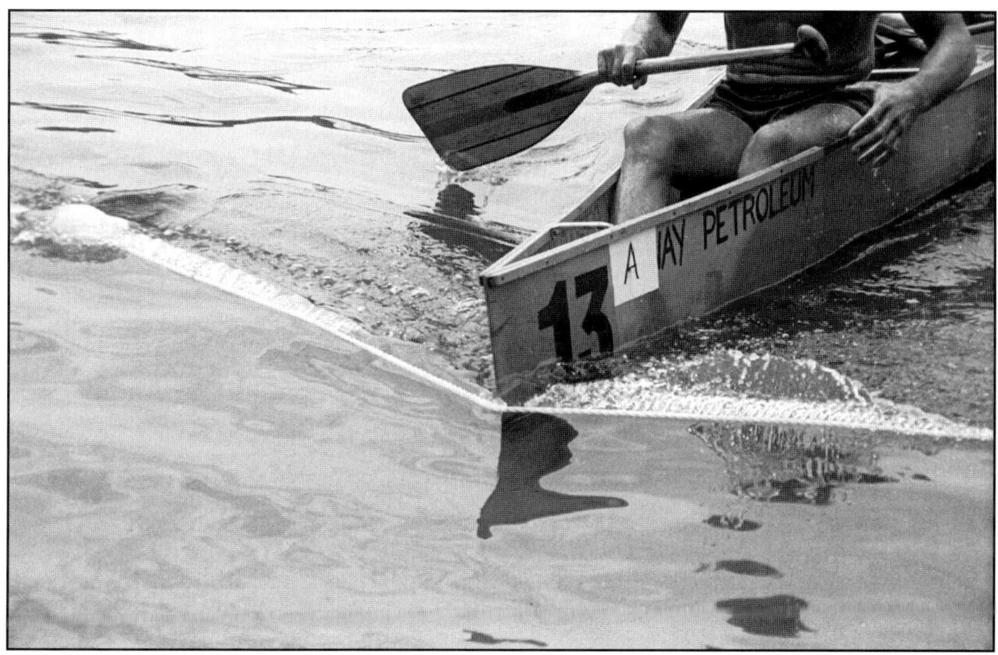

Little or No Current—Marathon Racing

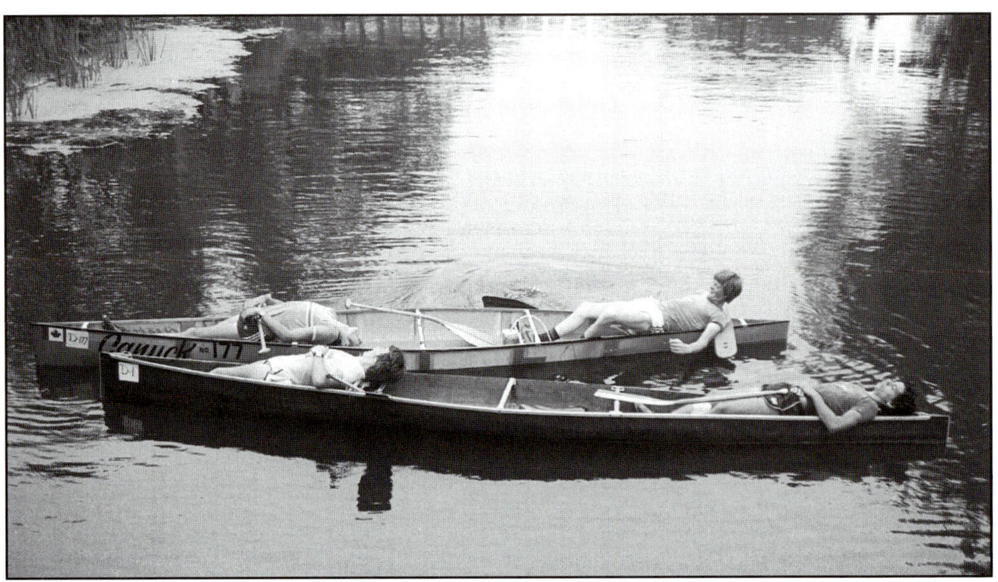

When the race is finally over and the participants collect their belongings, preparing to go home and already thinking about the next race (this sport is addictive!), there is still much to be discovered by the alert photographer. It is wise to prowl the finish area, looking for images that may round off your essay on the race: people are cleaning their boats, maybe finishing off some left-over power food (such as their taped-in bananas shown at the beginning of this section), talking about the race and exchanging stories on what went right or wrong during the long hours on the water and the portages. Many paddlers will be exhausted, some floating blissfully in the water trying to cool off, while others may be stretched out in their canoes, recuperating from the ordeal. These four young people resting in their beautiful racing canoes are typical of what you can find.

And for the final shot of your collection, you might want to photograph the proud winners together with their beloved boat and paddles, the tools of their triumph. To make this shot as clean as possible, I had asked the two men to kneel close to the boat, paddles in hand, and to look directly at the camera. I eliminated the horizon by standing on a low bench with the camera in my hand so that it was high enough to keep all the distracting elements—boats and swimmers in the water, horizon, reflections—out of the picture. To achieve the desired simplicity in your photographs, it is necessary to pay attention to these seemingly minor details. Your photographs will be all the better for it.

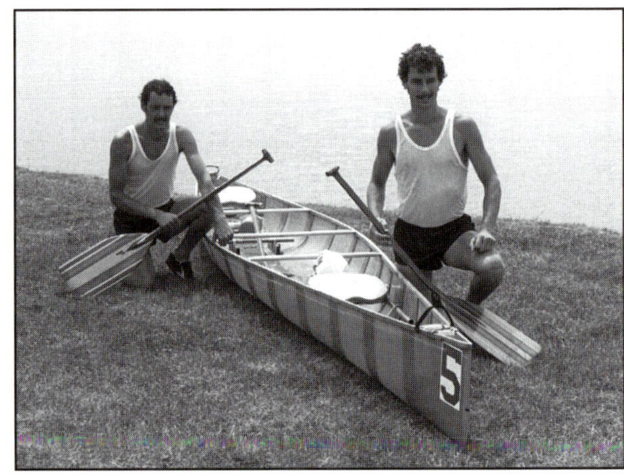

Little or No Current—Marathon Racing

SPRINT RACING

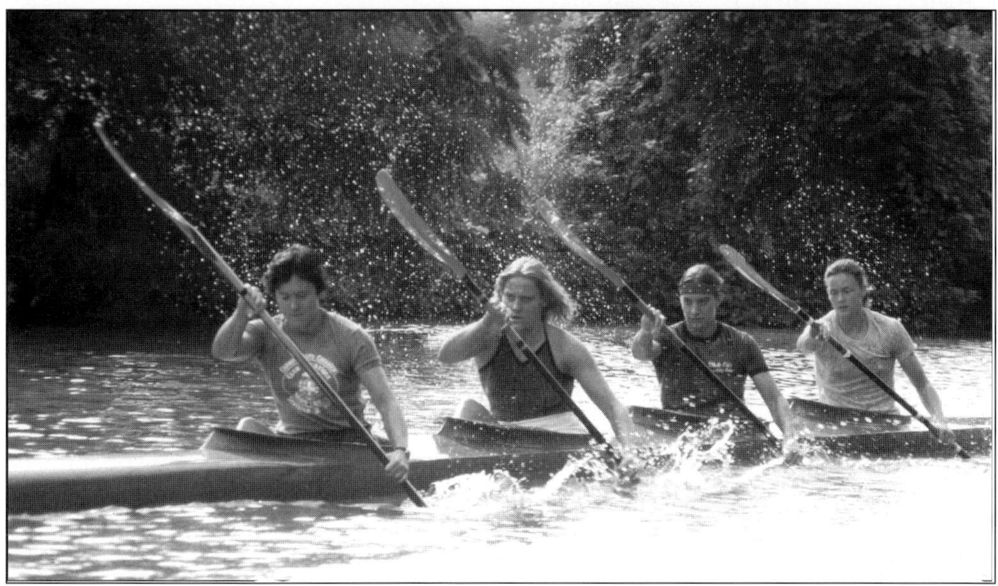

The intense concentration on the faces of these four young women in their long low K4 clearly illustrates the fascination many people feel for this demanding paddling sport that enjoys such a large international following. The rhythmic precision and impeccable teamwork evident in this simple but effective picture are essential elements of canoe and kayak sprint racing.

To photograph the fast movement of arms and paddles is an interesting challenge, requiring the ability to anticipate and record the moment of peak action, that one instant when all elements come together, when one picture tells the whole story of dedicated training, training and more training.

I was sitting on a dock studying the graceful fluid movements of the kayak, which was repeatedly making practice runs on a sheltered stretch of the river. Using a hand-held camera, I could easily follow the approaching boat and select the right moment to click the shutter and catch the desired image. Because I wanted to photograph only the essentials of the scene (the four women and how they handled their paddles) and not include the whole length of the long kayak, I framed the picture carefully, following the subjects through my viewfinder.

The result of all the work—especially by the very patient and obliging paddlers—is quite satisfying. The moment is right, all faces are visible (not covered by arms or paddles), the splashes and drops of the water have been caught by the short exposure time. The four paddles are almost exactly parallel, which not only indicates good paddling technique and style but is also visually interesting. The background is dark enough for the faces to stand out clearly. A bit of a flaw, however, is the light area in the middle of the trees in the background. (In the computer this can be cleaned up by using the cloning tool.) Holding the camera only about 0.7 metre above the ground, I succeeded in keeping the paddlers' heads just above the horizon.

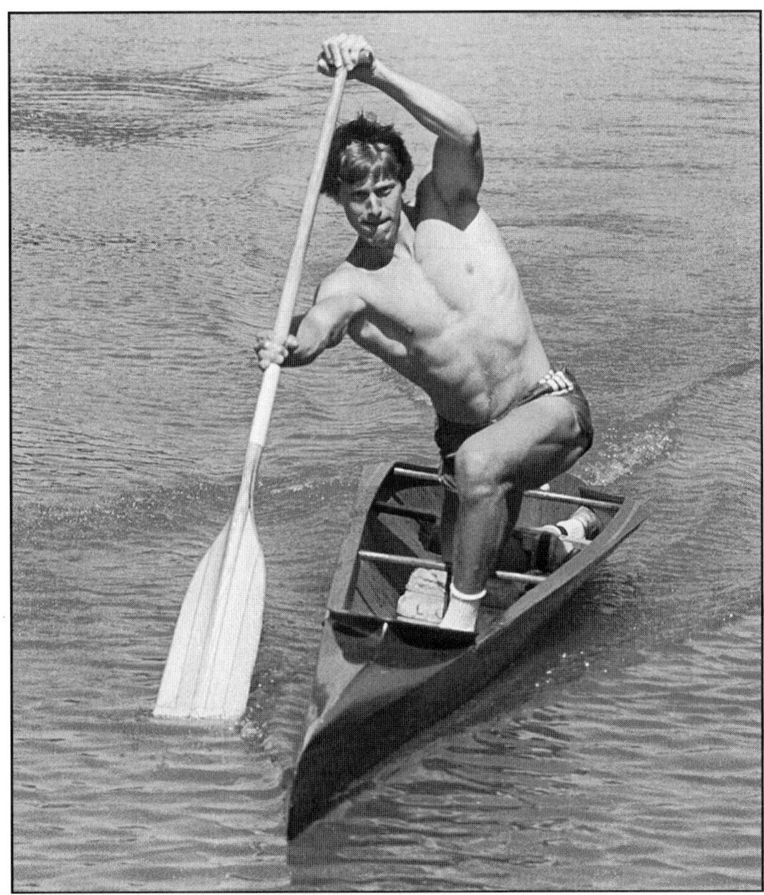

The moment Larry Cain stepped into his exquisite canoe, I knew we would have a winner. When this internationally famous athlete carefully settled on one knee and took the paddle to the water, his superbly sculpted body became one with the low-slung boat, creating a partnership of perfect balance, eager to generate flawless pure speed. Controlling his tremendous physical strength to just the right degree, he propelled the boat forward in a smooth gliding motion, cutting the sharp bow through the water surface with only minimal turbulence trickling down the sides.

Photographing that dynamic unity of man and machine, showing in a single picture everything that makes this whole scene so appealing, would require a careful approach, a well-thought-out arrangement of the various picture elements—such as background, viewing angle, positions of light and shadow, even the condition of the water surface—but above all the selection of the right moment to click the shutter.

I therefore asked Larry to paddle a few times from a considerable distance away, and to head almost straight at me while I was standing on the shore. From my slightly elevated position I could record not only his strong posture at the moment the paddle touched the water, but also provide a glimpse of the inside of the boat. We eventually succeeded in making a fine picture without any distracting elements in the background or around the boat. This shot works perfectly well in black and white because in such a clean yet dynamic composition, colour is not essential.

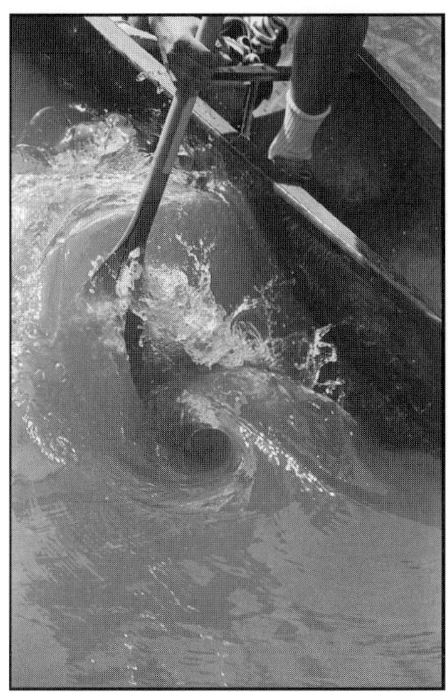

During the several runs Larry made, I had observed the enormous strength he put into his strokes, especially when he used his paddle to accelerate the canoe from stand-still to forward motion in a single explosion of power. This concentrated energy generated a beautiful fascinating swirl in the water behind the moving blade, the water twisting and turning in a tight eddy, with some splashes forming a small crown above it.

While standing on the dock close to the boat, I managed to photograph the scene just as I had observed it, using a short exposure time of 1/500th of a second. Because the image contained too much distracting information at the top and bottom, some cropping was needed to create the final picture of the swirl.

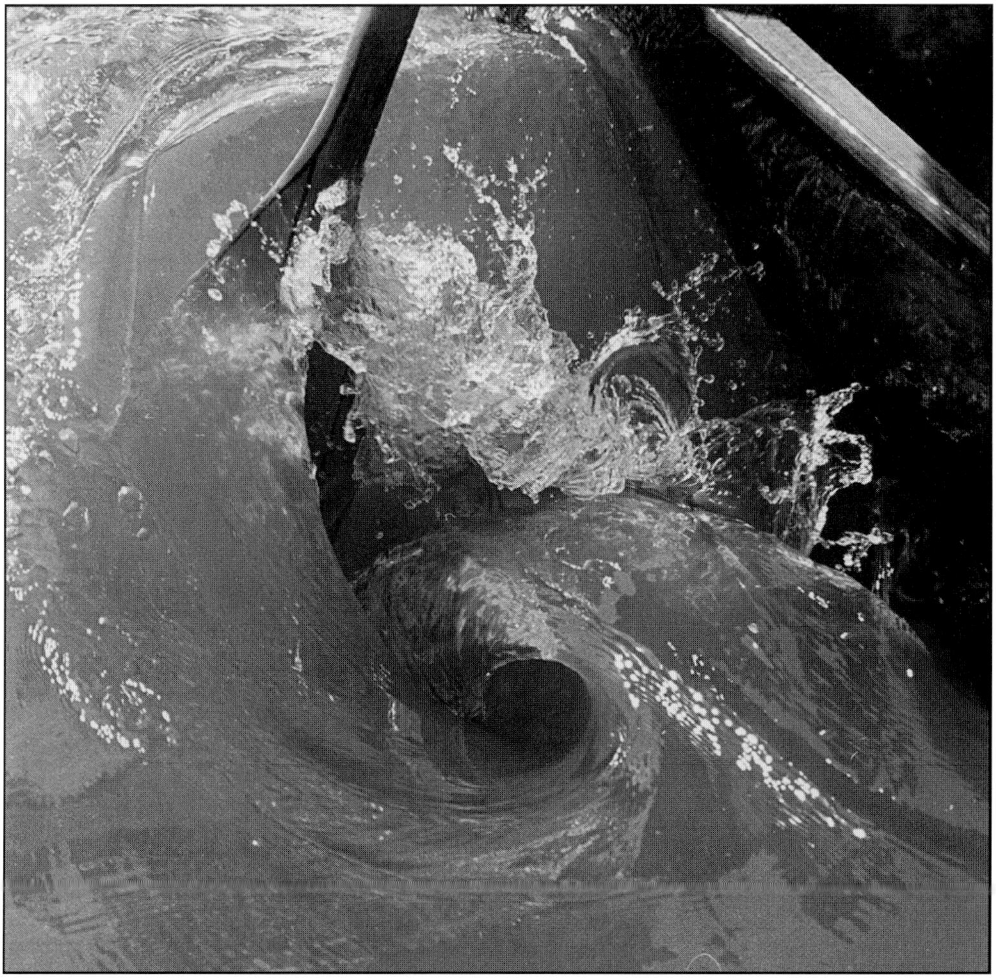

Little or No Current—Sprint Racing

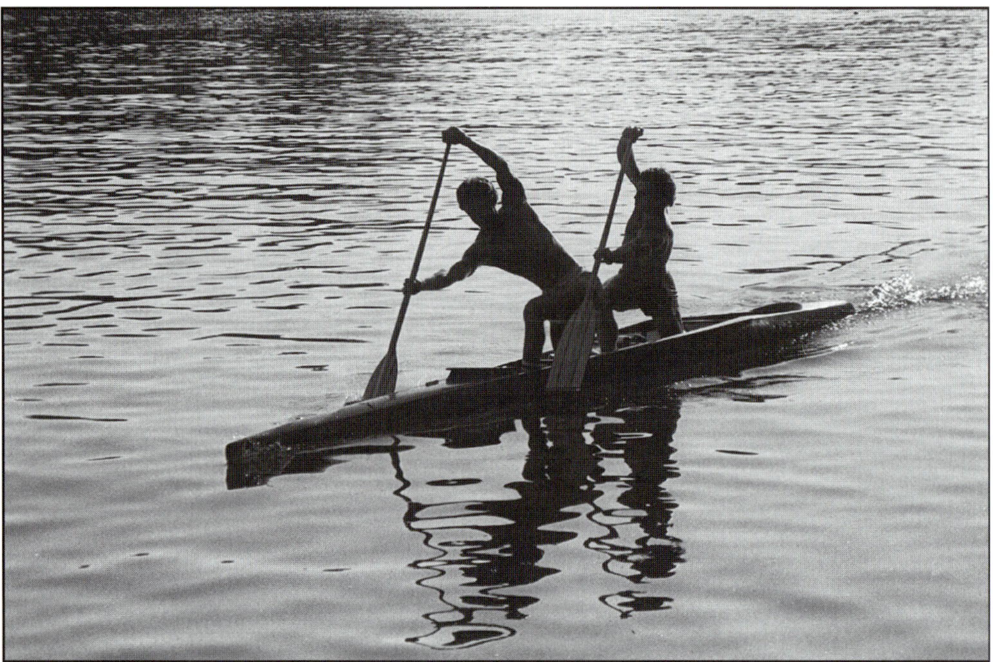

Although this picture of two men in a C2 has some similarities to the one of the C1 on page 56, there are several obvious differences. The previous one is a straightforward but powerful depiction of a champion paddler demonstrating his style and technique. But the photo above is a simple effort to create a more artistic impression of a sprint-racing canoe, showing the anonymous paddlers in silhouette and with their dark reflections playing on the shimmering water surface. The upper part of the background shows a pleasing rippling of the water, giving the picture a feeling of depth. It is of relatively little importance that the two paddles are not quite symmetric relative to the boat, as would be required if this were a shot showing technique and not an impression of a sprint canoe. Again, there are no distracting elements and all the attention of the viewer is focussed on the canoe and the two paddlers.

Looking at the canoe from a different angle, coming almost straight at the viewer, the image becomes more dynamic. While the shore in the background is quite dark, the sunlight coming from the side clearly outlines the bodies of the two men, resulting in a picture with much appealing symmetry. However, both faces are partially covered by the paddle shafts, somewhat spoiling an otherwise fine shot. It does makes sense to try to avoid this type of interference.

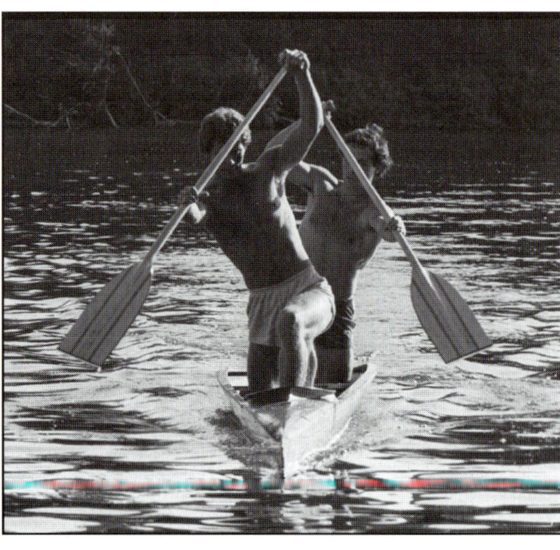

Little or No Current—Sprint Racing

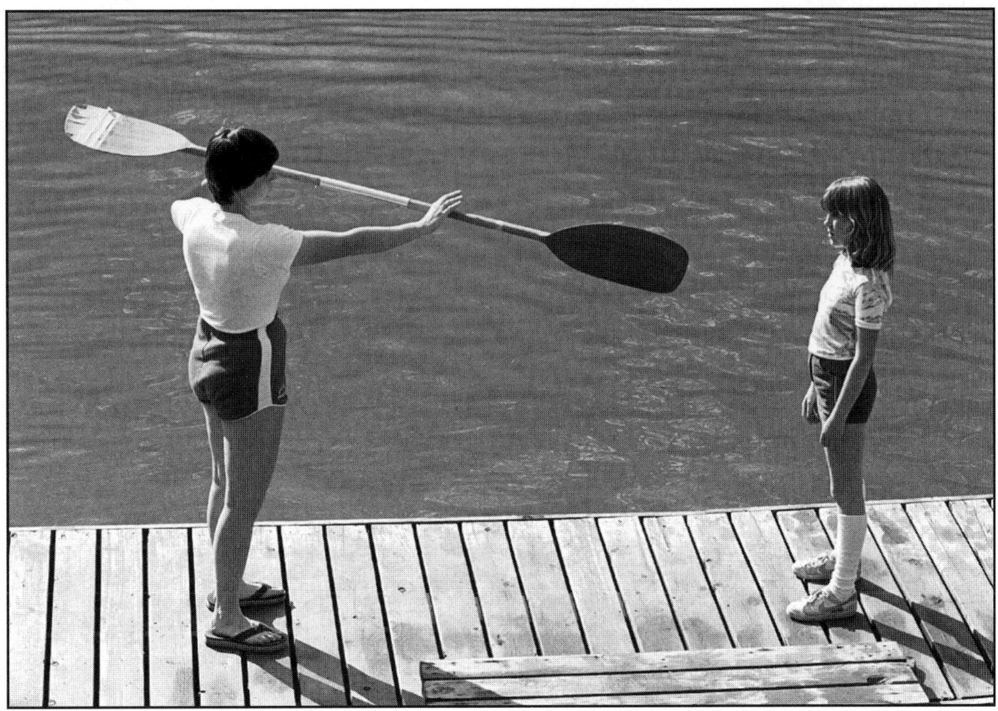

The basis of all successful sprint racing is a well-organized and well-executed training program, especially for the young members of the clubs. If you want to document with your camera what sprint racing is all about, it is important not to neglect the training sessions, on land as well as on water. Training photos may be easier to make than the ones you shoot at actual races, as in many cases you can get quite close to the paddlers. You can also ask them to do something special for the photo.

Opportunities for fine training photographs abound: an adult showing a young girl the correct way to hold her kayak paddle; a young boy strengthening his muscles and improving his technique in order to become another great paddler; a war canoe filled with ferociously paddling bodies; a master paddler getting in his kilometres; and more. You can find appealing scenes by just walking casually on the club grounds, observing the goings-on around you and paying special attention to the young people. Have your camera ready for a quick, perfectly timed shot of an interesting subject. Such photos are as valuable as the action shots made during the races, and they will be treasured by you and the other paddlers for many years to come.

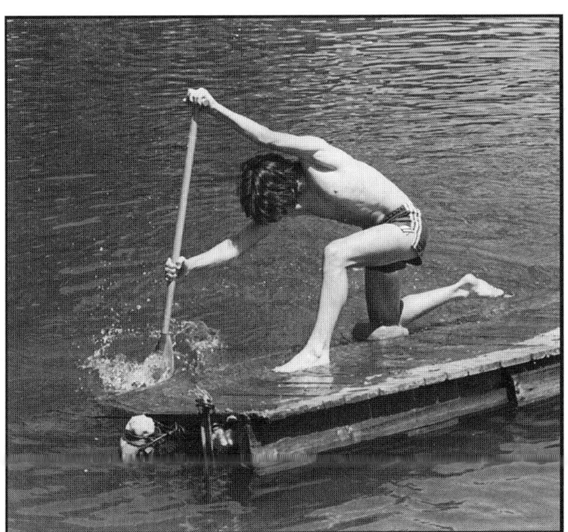

Little or No Current—Sprint Racing

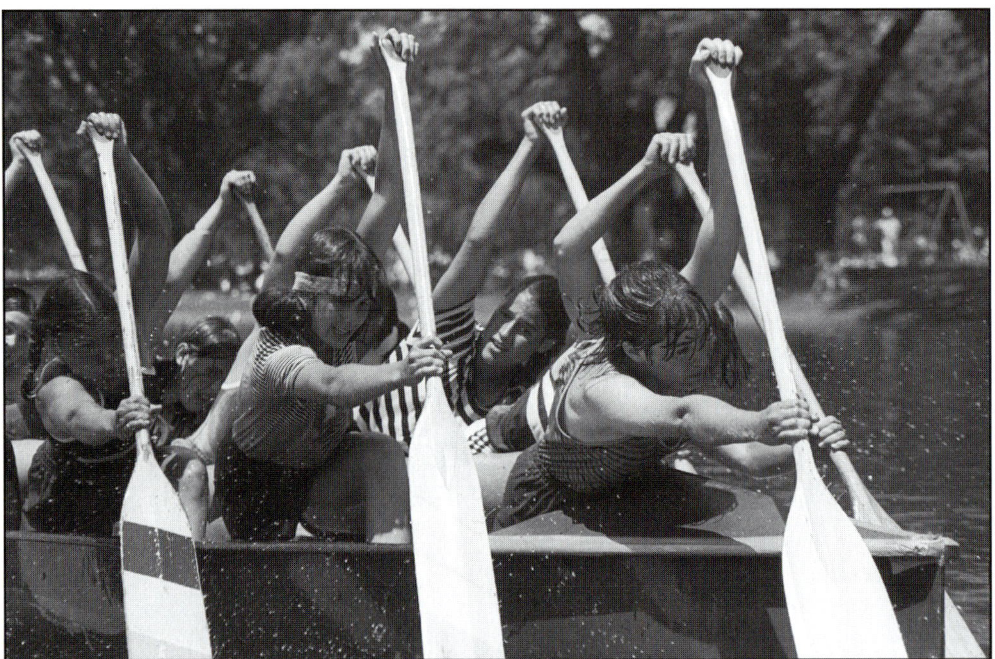

In canoe sprint competition, the 11-metre-long war canoe is often the last and most popular item on the program. The tightly-knit group of 14 paddlers and one steersperson in the stern, working in perfect unison as a well-oiled hard-pumping racing machine, often creates an impressive picture of co-ordinated action that can drive the spectators to wild cheers of enthusiasm.

It is not easy to take effective close-up racing shots from the shore because most of the time the distance is just too great. You would need a good telephoto lens and a tripod, as well as high-speed film, to capture a photograph that convincingly illustrates the essence of sprint canoe and kayak racing: a powerful yet fluid paddling technique propelling the boat forward in a straight line as fast as possible.

To take this photo, I was lucky enough to have access to the trainer's motorboat that, at my request, stayed near the war canoe during several training runs. Sometimes we were so close that the bow wave of the motorboat interfered with the canoe, making it dance up and down even more than usual. I made a number of hand-held shots showing the fierce concentration of the female crew, the sweat pouring off their tense faces, their wet hair, the paddles all held high at the peak of action, the grit and determination, and thus captured a moment of high visual impact.

It is important that all the hands holding the grips of the paddles remain in the picture and are not cut off at the top. The rather dark background is sufficiently out of focus so as not to interfere with the paddlers' arms, which are well separated from the background, thanks also to the early afternoon sunlight illuminating arms and paddles. This shot turned out to be the best one of the about 20 photographs taken at that time. In spite of the difficult shooting conditions caused by the bouncing canoe and motorboat, I succeeded in making a quite successful document of a characteristic moment in a war canoe.

Little or No Current—Sprint Racing

Most of the other photographs were taken from greater distances, showing the whole canoe and all the crew, such as this one. Although this shot is a valuable document, it does not have the visual impact of the previous one taken from a lesser distance. It is more of a record shot of the type that can be used to discuss the paddling technique of the

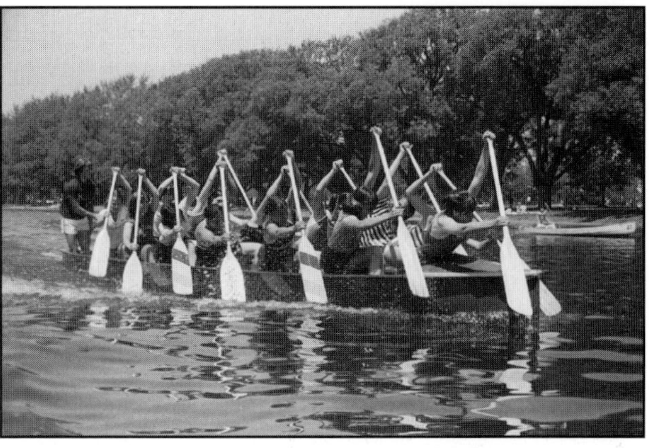

whole crew, including the work of the steersperson. The photograph does show clearly just how large this kind of boat really is and how close to each other the crew members are positioned. The background contains a large expanse of light-coloured sky and the foreground is also visually not very interesting. Had it been possible to make this shot with a glassy smooth water surface instead of a wavy one, the reflection of the crew and the paddles would have made it much more interesting.

Do not stop photographing the scene after the hard work by the paddlers is over. There are still more opportunities to show what takes place in the world of sprint racing, such as these tired paddlers, trying to catch their breath and holding their paddles like little horizontal wings. The canoe seems to be in some danger of swamping because of the disturbance caused by the trainer's motorboat.

Being aware of such 'secondary' moments and photographing them throughout the whole exercise is an important aspect of paddling photography.

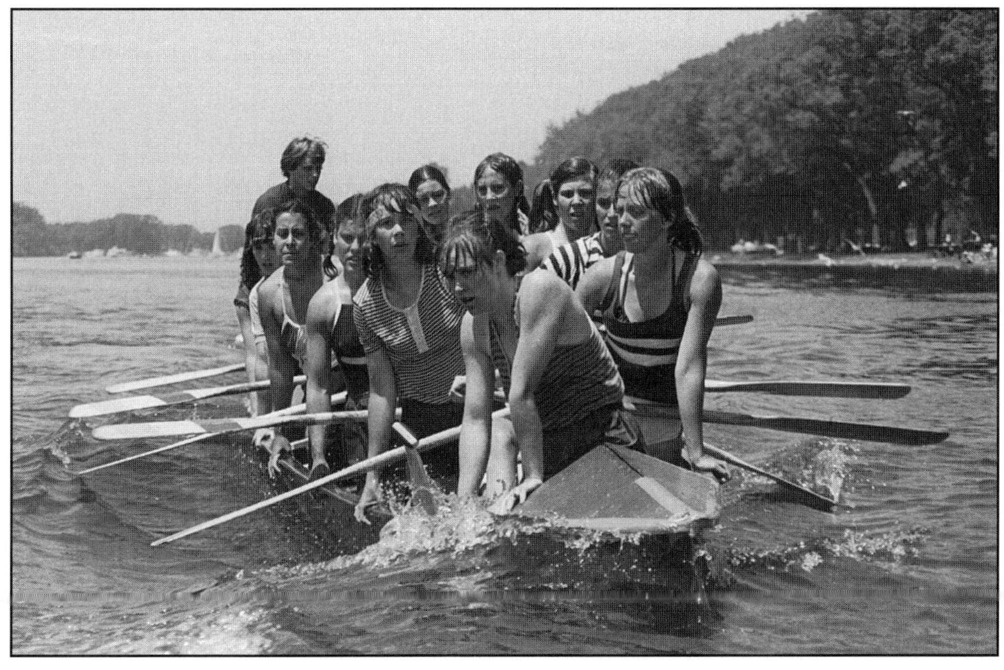

Little or No Current—Sprint Racing

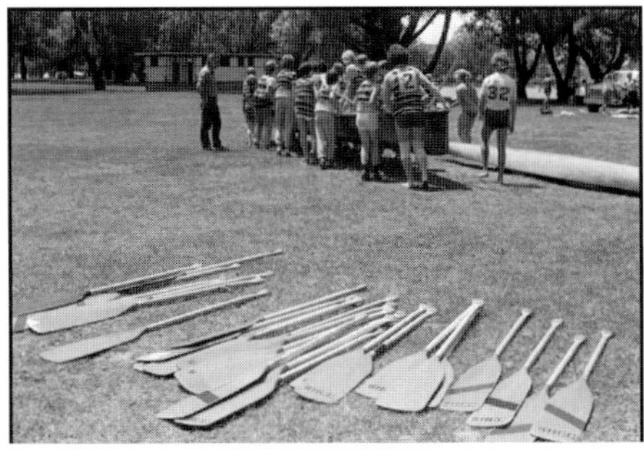

These two photographs offer more examples of the fine pictures that can be discovered by just walking around on the club grounds or in the area where races are held. Keep an eye open for photographic opportunities that are not directly showing sprint racing activities, but illustrate the many picturesque events taking place on the periphery; such as these people, photographed from the back, shown carrying a war canoe across the lawn. That in itself would probably not be sufficiently interesting subject matter, but the addition of the fan-shaped group of paddles in the foreground makes it into a much better composition, creating a nice picture with a subtle appeal.

And then there is that young boy lying on the dock all by himself, staring into the water. Maybe he is fed up with all the training, all that pulling of paddles, all those grown-ups telling him all the time what to do and how to do it and when to do it and where to do it. Or maybe he just loves to touch the water with his hands. Who knows? The important thing for you, the photographer, is to recognize that this is a simple but quite attractive image consisting of just two elements: the large water surface and the dock with the boy occupying an aesthetically pleasing spot in the top-right section of the picture. You can try to analyze the attraction of this or any other photograph as much as you want, but all you really need to work with for now is your gut feeling telling you: I like it! (Or not, of course.) Leave the theories and dissections to others; just enjoy the fascination of photography and learn while you practise seeing and shooting. Once you know more about this wonderful craft (art?), understanding will follow.

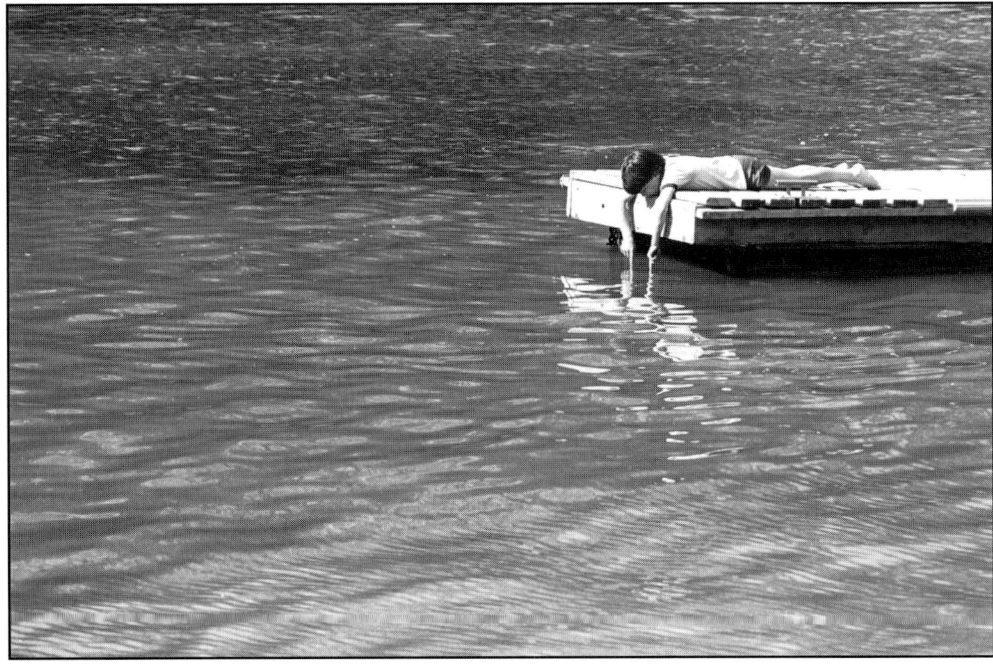

Little or No Current—Sprint Racing

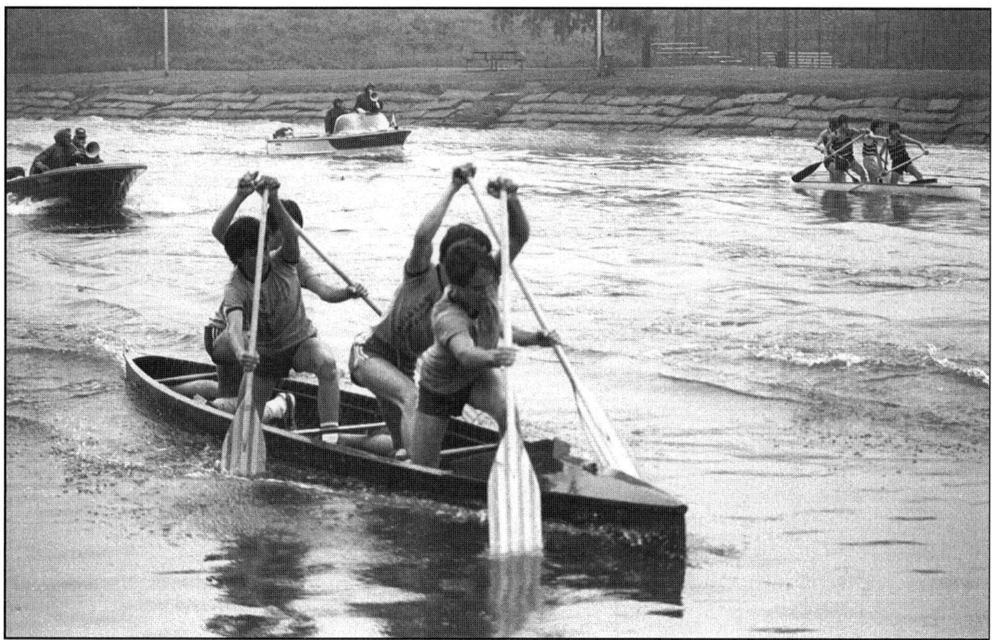

Finally, after al the hard work, the countless hours of training, the many kilometres of exhaustive paddling, there is THE RACE! This, then, is the one big event where all friends and family come to cheer on their favourites, hoping to applaud them in the winners' circle. And what better way to remember all these wonderful happenings than a series of fine photographs? Taking good photos showing the action and intensity of the race is not that easy because you will be located on the shore and the paddlers are far away most of the time. A tele zoom lens supported by a sturdy tripod would, therefore, be a great help. Try to get as close to the action as possible and focus on making shots of the boats nearest the shore. The top photo shows the C4 paddlers concentrating on getting to the finish line first without swamping the tippy craft. Even the officials' motorboats are included, giving the scene an added touch of realism.

In all the excitement, you should also watch for the little things happening around the race. For instance, these two ducks, completely undisturbed by all the human commotion around them, haughtily paddling the other way, showing that this race is farthest from their minds, add a bit of humour. Hunting for such simple images is not only delightful but also important. Teach your eyes and brain to really *see* what is out there in your world.

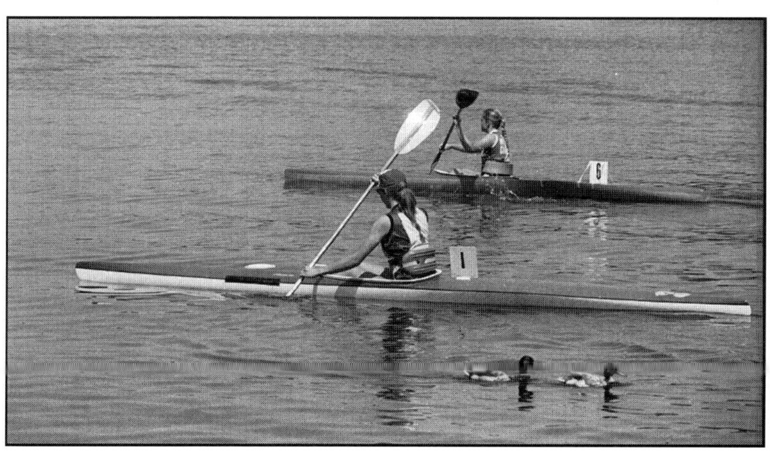

Little or No Current—Sprint Racing

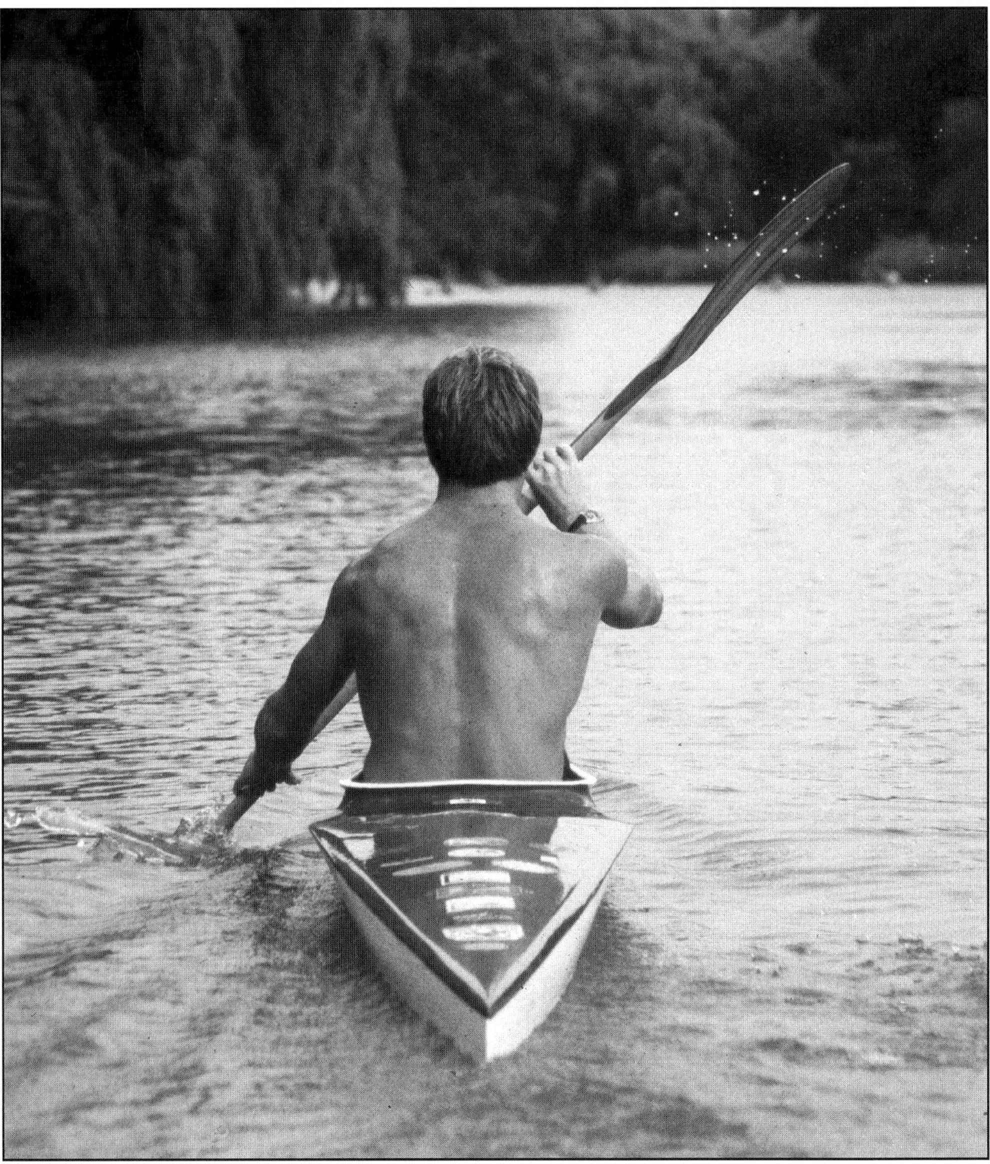

This photo shows a popular sprint racing boat, a K1, from another angle; a different point of view offers interesting visual possibilities. It is a quiet introspective scene, one that does not hint at the excitement of racing. Instead, it shows the paddler in a relaxed mood, very much enjoying the training run he is making. His muscular back and shoulders dominate the picture, providing a clear centre of interest. The shot is also rather rare for a sprint racing photograph because it is a vertical, cropped at the top from a larger picture, one in a series of shots taken from a following motorboat. (Many sprint racing photos tend to be horizontals, because of the horizontal lines of the boats when viewed from the side.) If you present a slide show of your pictures, or are assembling a number of prints to show to friends, this one would make an excellent last image, rounding off your presentation on a relaxed tone.

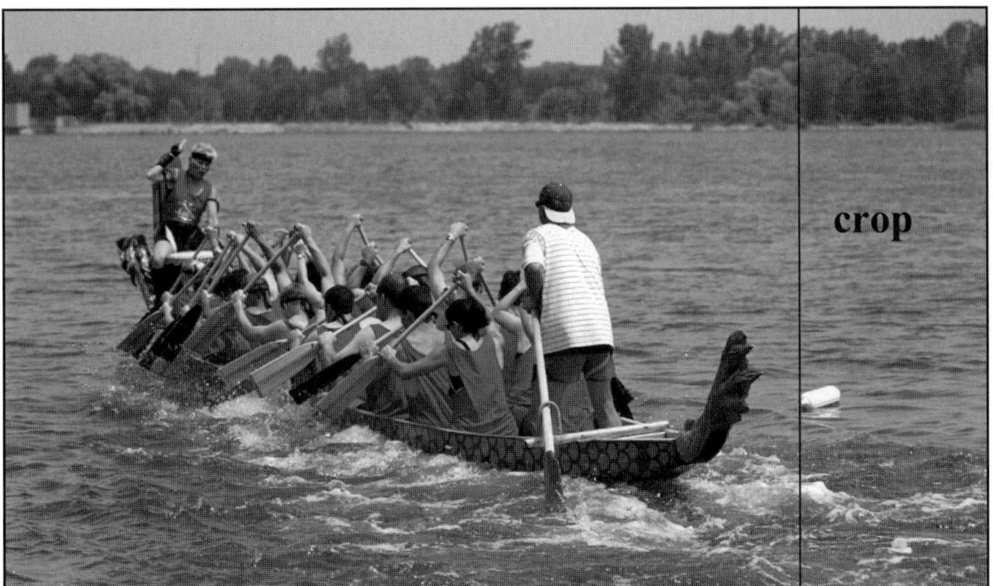

Dragon boat racing is probably the fastest-growing sprint racing paddling sport in the world, with millions of enthusiastic adherents, especially in East Asian countries. It is also the most colourful of the various paddling disciplines, to the delight of both participants and spectators, and particularly photographers. The sleek, long and narrow boats with their often beautifully sculpted and painted dragon-shaped figureheads, the frequently imaginative costumes of the crew, the exotic shapes and vivid hues of the drums, all add up to a true feast for the eye .

The number of people involved in dragon boat races boggles the mind. A typical boat contains 22 people (20 paddlers, one drummer, one steersperson), with several support staff on shore. A race with 50 boats would have more than 1000 people present in the area reserved for the teams! This sea of excited people and colourful boats offers many opportunities for fine pictures.

For the photographer it is convenient to divide the areas where the activities take place into categories: far-from-shore, close-to-shore and on-shore photo opportunities, each with its own possibilities and limitations. If the actual racing takes place some distance from shore, getting sufficiently close to the boats can often be very difficult. The photographer could therefore ask the race organizers to allow access to the safety motorboat that follows the dragon boats from a relatively short distance, thus allowing photographs to be taken of the racers when they fly across the water all the way to the finish.

The above photo was made from such a safety boat; we could not come too close because we did not want to interfere with the furiously racing dragon boats. The composition of the photo can be improved by cropping the lane marker buoy bottle on the right-hand side. Pay attention to the horizon: it should be level.

Closer to shore, when the boats are near or at the dock, there are many more picture opportunities, such as the photo of the dragon head with a boat in the background, shown in the section Colour.

Little or No Current—Sprint Racing

This photo of the drummer with the daringly inventive hat and the club's mascot was also made when her boat was at the dock.

On many of the boats, the race sponsor's names as well as the starting number are often painted on white or light-coloured boards usually attached between the dragon head and the drummer. Try to avoid including this bit of visual nuisance in your pictures. That will not be easy, however, if you shoot the boats from the side.

Numerous interesting photo opportunities are found on shore where so many people are close together, all in a festive mood and enjoying themselves enormously. The crews are awaiting their start or are just back from a race; everybody is in

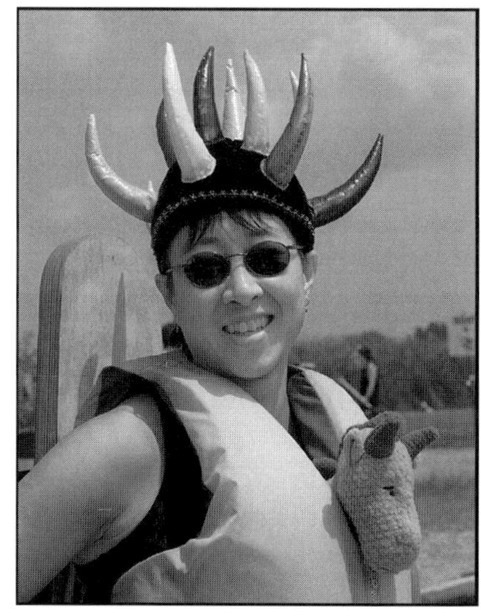

high spirits and there is a boisterous atmosphere of joy and excitement. Some paddlers are stretching their muscles, others are excitedly talking with each other; crews are being hyped up by their coach or are standing close together concentrating on the race to come. The photograph of the high-fiveing team members after a successful race illustrates the passion and enthusiasm of the people involved in dragon boat racing.

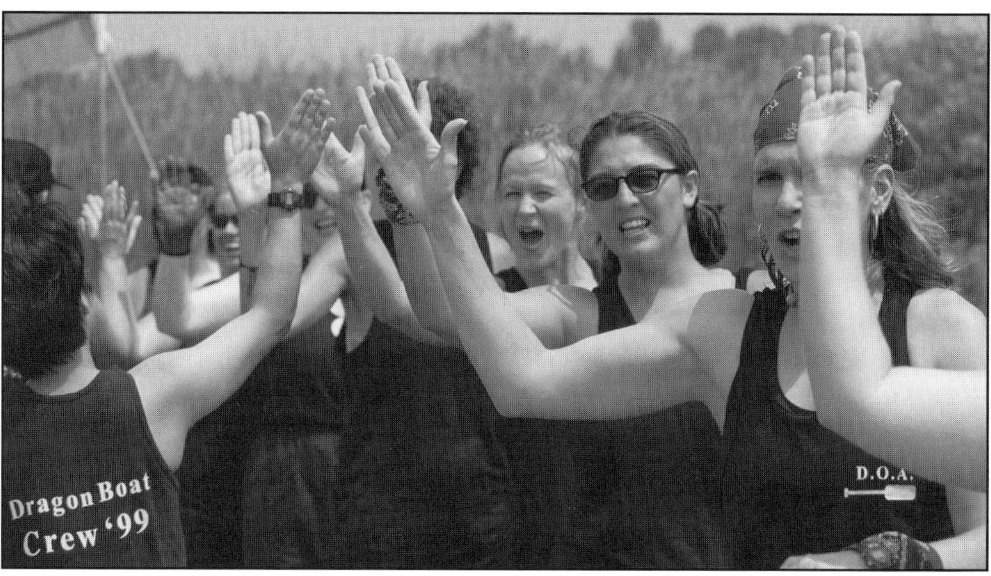

Photographing this kind of rapidly changing action does not require special equipment, almost any kind of camera and lens can be used. However, to be on the safe side, try to shoot with a mid-range tele zoom lens and medium to high-speed film (ISO 200 would do just fine). And to ensure the best possible photos, be at the race site early, get to know the layout of the area and check out the best spots from which to shoot. Introduce yourself to the race organizers and ask their permission for access to the locations you want. Being prepared and politely assertive will help you become a successful photographer.

Little or No Current—Sprint Racing

RECREATIONAL PADDLING

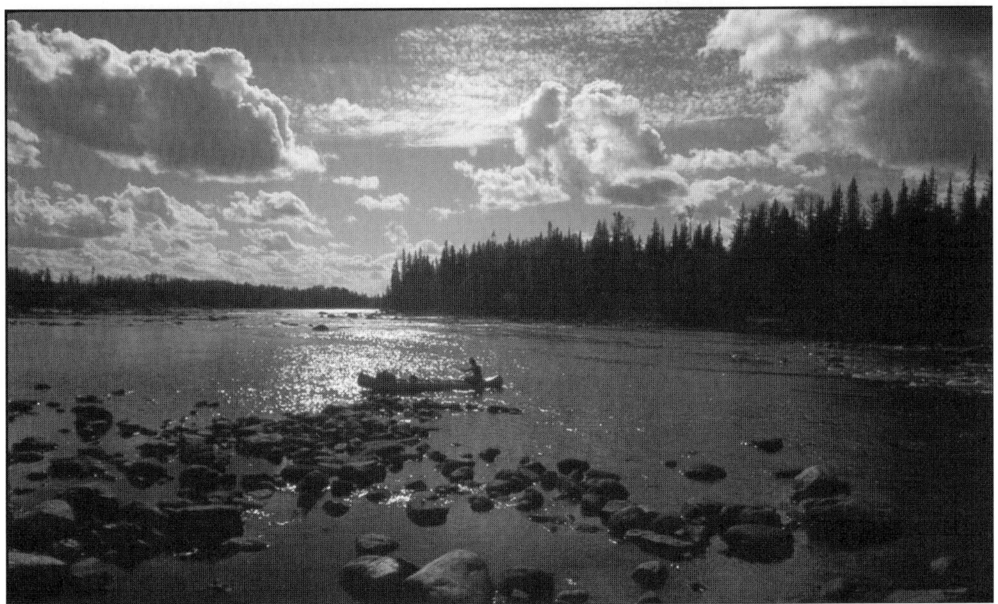

Scenics are among the most important and best-loved photos you can take on your trips in the wilderness. They illustrate the environment through which you are travelling and form the backbone of the story you are weaving.

The paddler in this photograph was a Native friend of ours on his way back upriver to his home town of Mattice, having just spent a few days by himself on his beloved Missinaibi River. This is one of my personal favourites, taken at what I now call the Wrong Channel Rapids. It will always remind me of the quite placid rapid to the right of the picture where I carelessly selected the wrong channel of water flowing between the rocks and managed to place our canoe against a big rock, completely swamping it.

What makes this photo so effective is its mood; the overall feeling of space, vast distances, wildness but also tranquillity, created by the interplay among backlit clouds, rocks, water, silhouetted trees and the solitary canoe. The rocks in the foreground add significantly to the feeling of depth, which is also enhanced by the light reflecting off the surface of the water. If the sky would not have been adorned with such impressive clouds, the photo would have lost much of its appeal.

Note that the sun itself is not in the picture and that there are no disturbing lens flares caused by the sun shining directly into the lens. These flares were avoided by using a hat to cast a shadow on the lens. This is a powerful example of a good centre of interest in a picture; the viewer's attention is inexorably drawn to the canoe and its single occupant.

The photo, which was taken with a 24 mm wide-angle lens on ISO 64 slide film, has been published quite a few times and is included in several private collections. If you have an excellent photo like this one, do not forget to send a print to the person you have photographed; it will surely be much appreciated.

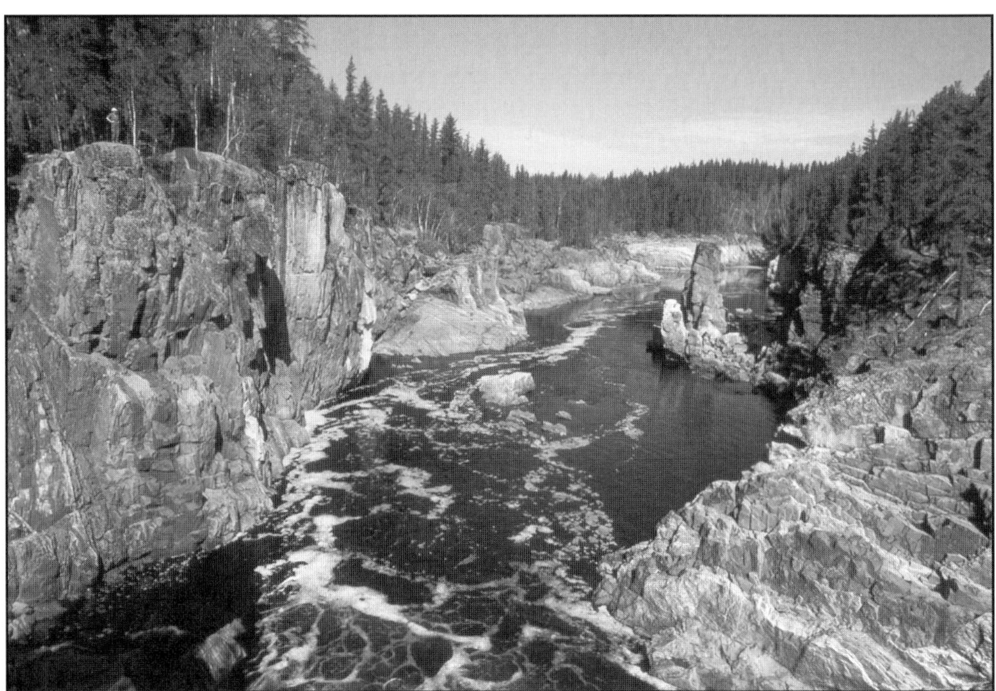

The Thunderhouse Falls complex of the Missinaibi River is a very special place with great religious significance to Native peoples in the North. It is also revered and even feared by many visiting canoeists; its three separate falls are impossible to traverse by canoe and have cost several careless trippers their lives. The free-standing, 15-metre-high Conjuring House Rock dominates the canyon below the last fall.

To make an effective photo of this canyon and its inspiring content, I found the required elevated viewpoint after climbing to a site next to the third fall. This high point of view produces a fine sense of depth and emphasizes the grandeur of the place, with the line of foam on the water surface receding in the distance adding to the feeling of perspective. Notice how the human figure on top of the 21-metre-high vertical wall on the left provides scale to the picture. Although the figure appears small, it stands out well against the dark background between the trees.

Should the opportunity to make aerial photos of the region you will be travelling through arise, you will discover that such a vantage point provides the ideal high viewpoint, presenting you with a great deal of information in one picture. This one, for instance, showing the Dalles Rapids in the Delta region of the French River at relatively high water level, includes in one picture all the significant elements of the rapids: entrance, whitewater, outflow, both shores and the start of the portage trail (notice the two canoes in the lower-left corner).

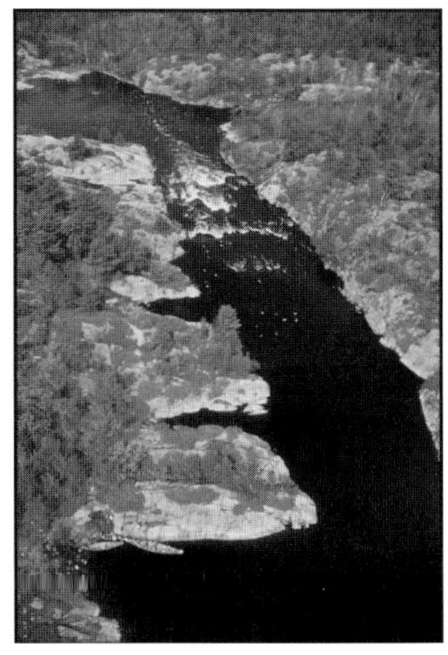

Waterfalls are among the most grandiose spectacles any river has to offer. Finding and observing them can be an exhilarating and rewarding experience for any paddling photographer hunting for their fascinating forms.

In this picture, showing Centre Falls in the North Channel of the Lady Evelyn River, the dominant element is not the waterfall, but the cloud towering over it. This cloud not only makes the photo much more dramatic but also enables it to be made as a vertical one.

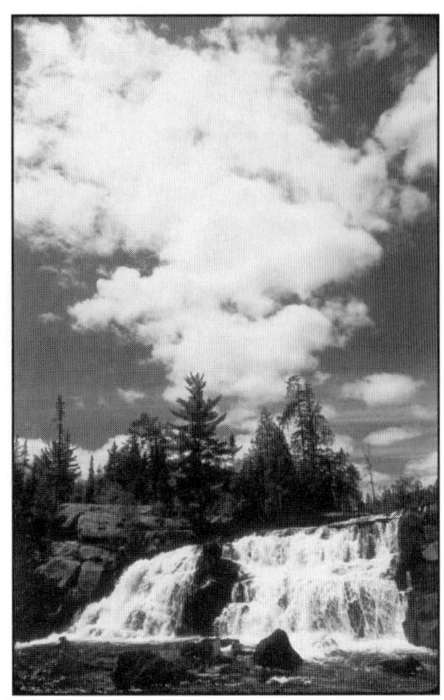

In the large picture, depicting the Paresseux Falls in the Mattawa River, the canoe in the foreground provides a strong feeling of depth and gives a sense of the size of the falls. The canoe's position also leads the eye of the viewer directly to the falls. Without this object in the foreground, the photo would be far less interesting.

Because both shots (as well as the ones on the previous page) were made during mid-morning, the direct sunlight is quite harsh. Less than desirable lighting is often difficult to avoid when one is on a trip without sufficient time to linger and wait for softer late-afternoon light. Still, both photos are good images of demanding subjects. Do the best you can under the circumstances, even if you have to compromise. Another technique for photographing waterfalls is presented in the section Trail.

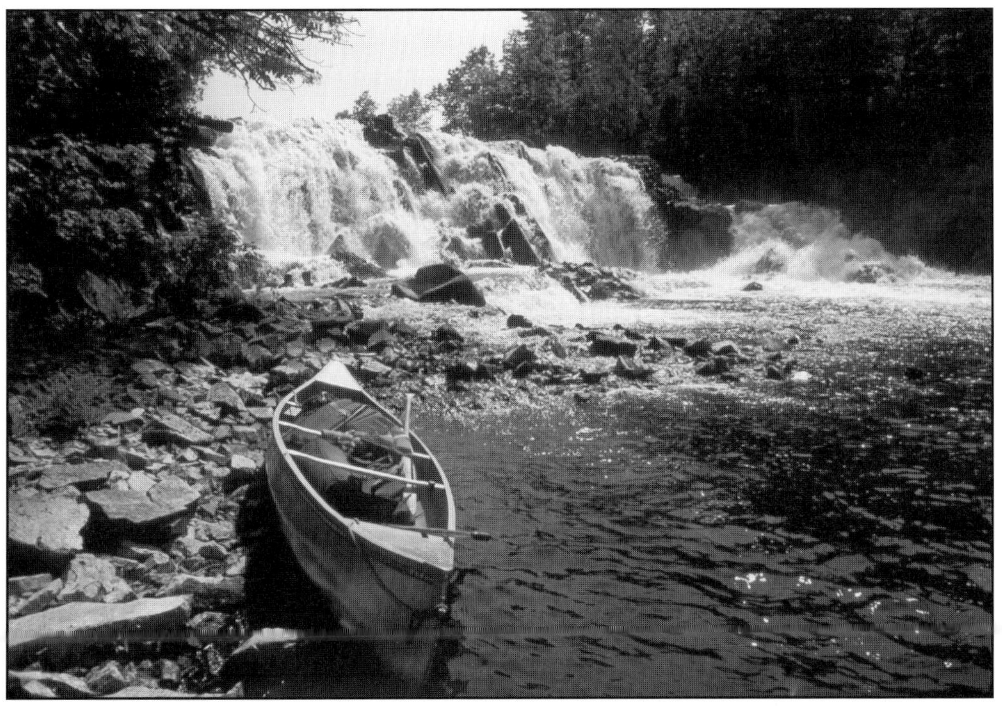

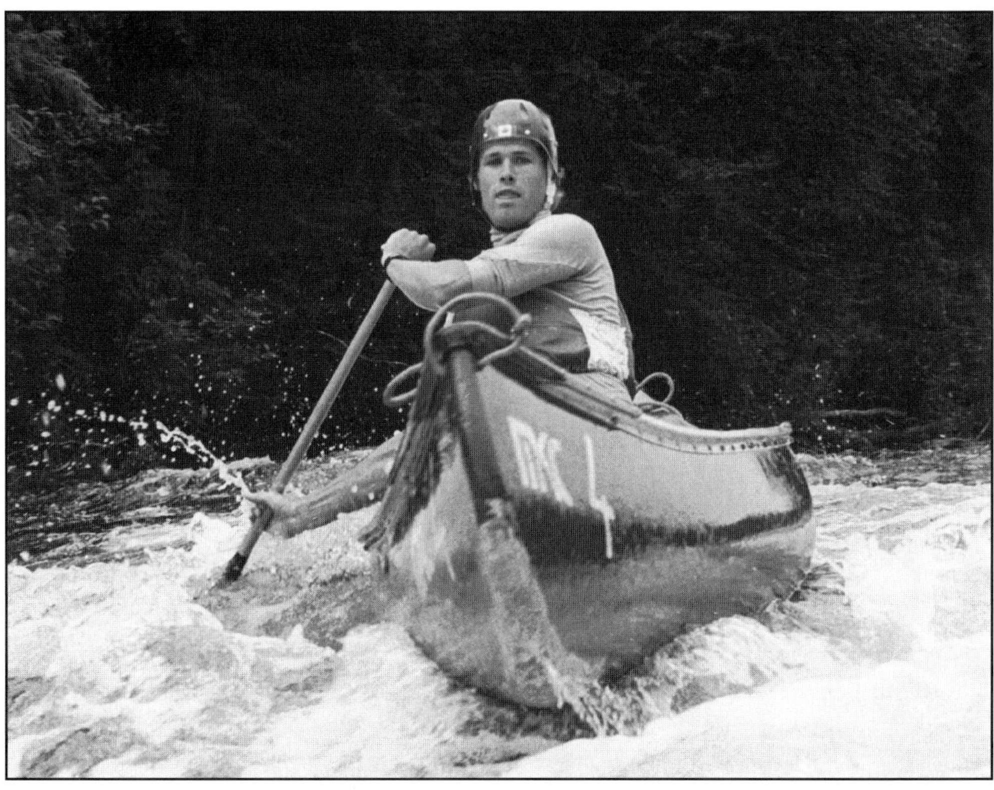

To see a master canoeist flawlessly perform his art is a true joy, warranting a lot of effort and even risk if you want to photograph this compelling accomplishment. The dynamic grace of top-notch canoe handling provides wonderful subjects for paddling photography.

I had asked Dirk Van Wijk, co-owner of the Madawaska Kanu Centre, to paddle past me, as close as he could, as I stood thigh-deep on a submerged rock in the fast whitewater of the Madawaska River. While still on land, I had visualized a situation where I would shoot the canoe at about water level practically head-on as it was coming rapidly toward me. Thus, the photo would possess a powerful feeling of speed and danger, and also of control and elegance. Such positioning was the best way to get the desired image.

Every time we repeated the shot, four times in all (which meant he had to portage his canoe back upriver again and again), Dirk missed me by only a few centimetres. I very much appreciated that he always remained in complete control of his boat; one wrong judgement and he would have collided with me, pushing me into the water and ruining both camera and film. However, that is the risk I took because of wanting to achieve something special. Try this kind of action photography with your own friends. You will be pleasantly surprised how exceptional the results can be.

In this photo, both canoe and paddler stand out well against the dark background. Because of the speed of the action, I could only make one pre-focussed shot each of the four times the canoe was in approximately the right spot. A short exposure time of 1/1000th of a second was used to freeze all movement of paddler, boat and water.

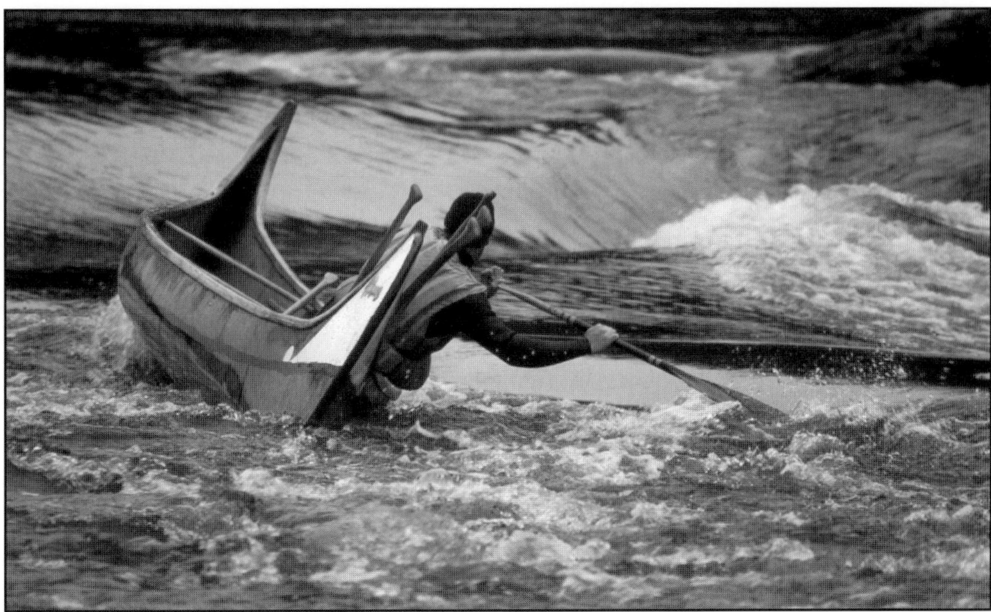

There are those rare precious moments in a photographer's life that, just before clicking the shutter, he or she intuitively knows: "This is it! This is exactly what I have been looking for! The perfect shot! Yessss!"

That is what happened to me when I saw this solo paddler in his large North canoe tackling the fast waters of the Blue Chute in the French River. There he was, hanging way out over the waves in a beautiful high brace, slowly going up the eddy at river right and teasing the craft to catch the water's smooth V-shaped tongue.

I am especially proud of this shot because it was a difficult hand-held one, made on ISO 200 slide film and using automatic exposure from a considerable distance with a 75–300 mm zoom lens set at 300 mm, without the help of a tripod or any other special support. (I took care, though, to tuck in my elbows and hold my breath while I made the shot, trying to be as steady as possible.) It is perfectly framed and quite sharp. There are no distracting elements, all parts of the image have a role to play. This is a truly fine picture of a remarkably beautiful moment in the world of paddling. (By all means, praise yourself when you have done an excellent job!) The photo was used on the cover of my book *French River: Canoeing the River of the Stick-Wavers.*

One of a series I took of this fascinating scene shows the large boat with its sole occupant playing in the rushing waters. I was standing on the shore, following its movements in the viewfinder and clicking the shutter whenever something of particular interest came up. I was also blessed with the somewhat diffuse light from the overcast sky, eliminating unpleasantly hard shadows.

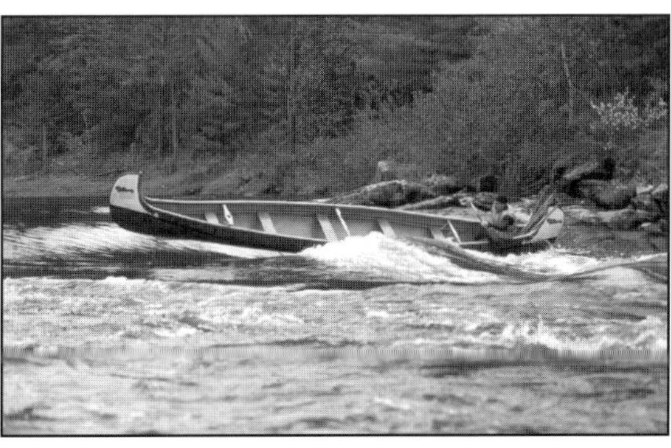

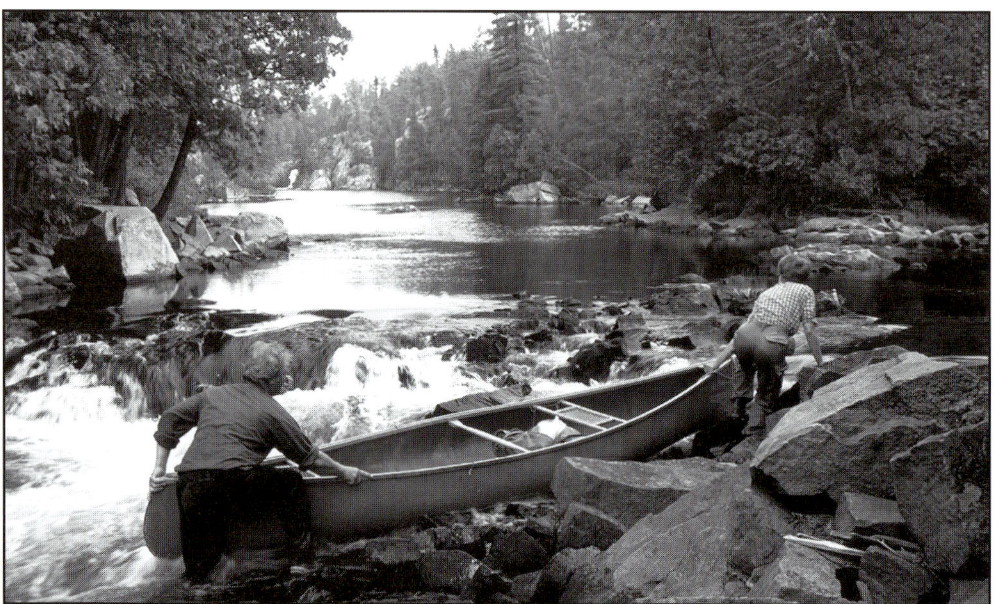

Wading the canoe up a modest drop in the river is very much part of your activities while exploring the intricate waterways of the Canadian Shield. When documenting your trip, it is important to have several photos such as this one, showing people being actively involved. Sometimes you need to deliberately set up such 'working' photos, as you could not have obtained them any other way. This may slow down your travelling pace, but the resulting variety of pictures will tell the story better. Convince the people in your party that they will enjoy the photos later at home and you will surely get their co-operation.

Always, it is more complicated if there are no other people around to make photos of you in action. As happens often out of necessity on our one-canoe-two-people trips, the above photo was made with the help of a tripod, a self-timer, some creative thinking and a fair bit of acting. Because all the action happened so close to the water, I made sure that the tripod legs were secured in place by some large rocks, thus preventing the camera from falling. The rocks lying scattered on the ground between tripod and canoe were quite wet and slippery, hence it was crucial for me to be extra careful and not stumble when moving as fast as possible from the camera to my position at the stern of the canoe, after having triggered the self-timer. Several test runs were required to determine how much time was needed to get from the camera to the canoe.

The photo shows more than only the wading action and the small drop in the river. The shores and the river upstream are also included. In the background are the steep rocks leading to the Fat Man's Portage, a well-known landmark in this part of the South Channel of the Lady Evelyn River in the Temagami area.

Of course, these posed 'working' photographs should look natural, as if somebody else had actually taken the shot of two people struggling to get their canoe over the rocks. Plan your actions well and take your time. With some practice and attention to detail the results can be extremely satisfying.

Because making suitable 'working' photographs is so important when telling your story, here is another example. This time the action took place in the Little Thompson Rapids of the Petawawa River and involved a tripod, two(!) self-timers and a lot of running. This presented a considerably more difficult and dangerous effort than the photo discussed on the previous page.

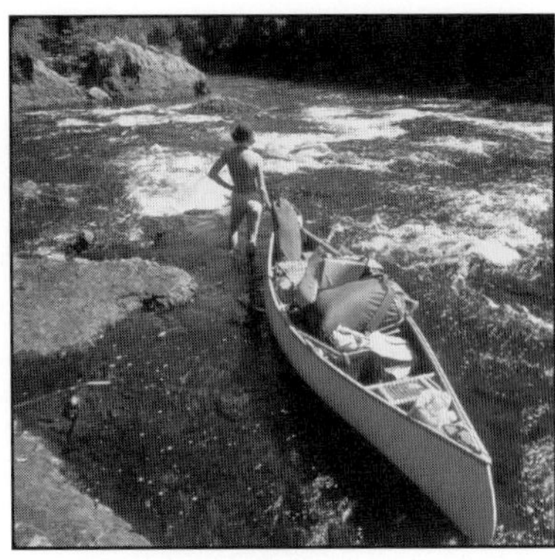

We had decided not to risk paddling down the rapid because the waves looked rather rough and also because we were alone and carried much gear for our three-week trip. Still, I really wanted a record of that part of the river, preferably while we were wading down on river left. I therefore I set up the tripod on a large rock facing the canoe (visible in the top-left corner of the small picture) and put two mechanical self-timers on top of each other on the camera, so that when the first one had run its course, it would trigger the second, giving me about 20 seconds to get from the camera to the boat. Although the total running distance was only maybe 50 metres, the ground between camera and boat was extremely rocky and uneven. I had to move quickly, but with utmost caution so as not to trip on the sharp rocks.

It took three trial runs, all timed by Ria who was standing at the bow of the canoe, to determine that I needed at least 18 seconds to get to the canoe without breaking my neck. This photo shows one of the trial runs, when I was just too slow. The fourth one was successful and shows me standing near the stern, having arrived just in time before the triggering of the camera. I was really tired after all he excitement. But we had the shot!

It may seem to be a lot of work for making simple pictures of everyday events that happen during a canoe trip, but these are among our most cherished photographs. We fondly remember the crazy fun we had making them.

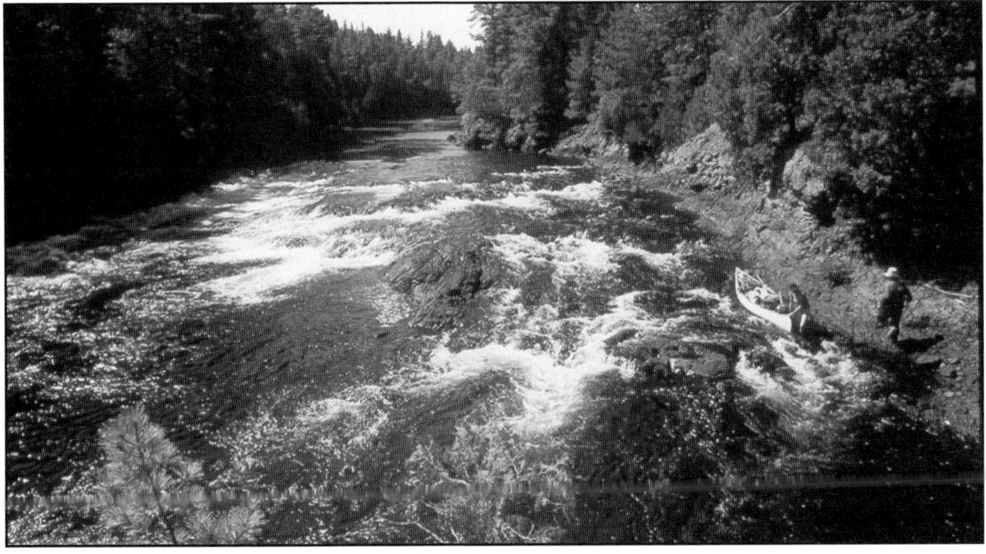

Current—Recreational Paddling

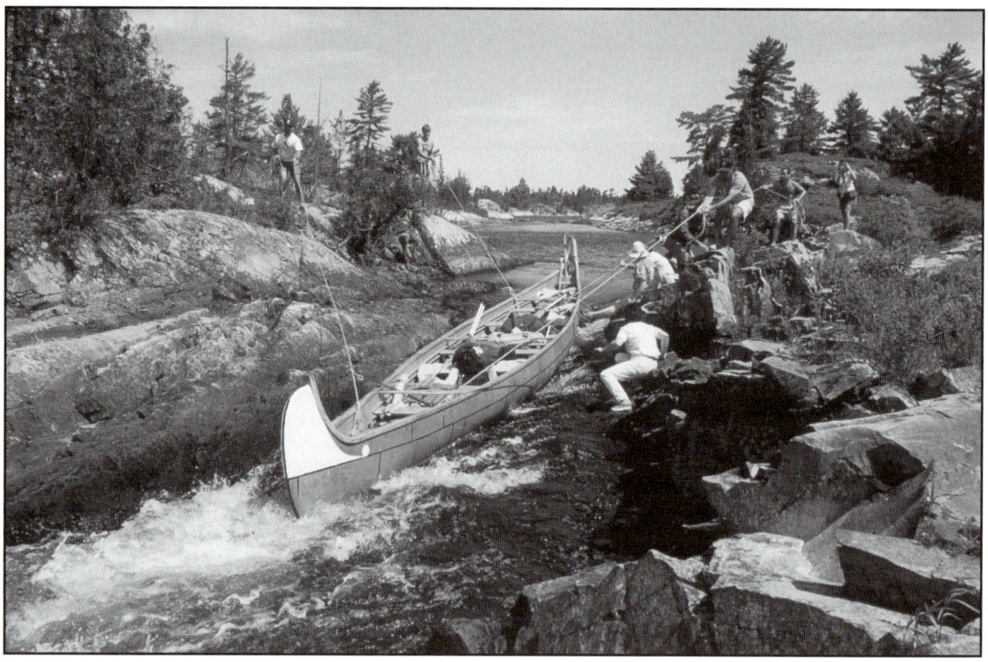

These two pictures were neither set up, nor posed. They are records of spontaneously happening events. In both cases I had made a deal with the trip participants that I would not be required to help with portaging gear or manipulating the boat (except for paddling, of course), but would concentrate on making photographs only. This gave me the freedom to move about as I wished and leave much of the slogging to the others. (Still, I impressed upon them that photography also is hard work.)

The top photo is a remarkable document of a rare event, showing an 11-metre-long Montreal canoe being lined down the Herring Chute in the Western Outlets of the French River. This is an out-of-the-way channel not normally used by these very large canoes. All action is concentrated in the middle of the picture with each team member looking at the boat. There is enough space downriver of the canoe, which occupies a strong diagonal line, to show where it is going. On purpose, I selected a vantage point that allowed inclusion of a considerable amount of surrounding area, thus documenting the whole scene and not just focussing on the action itself.

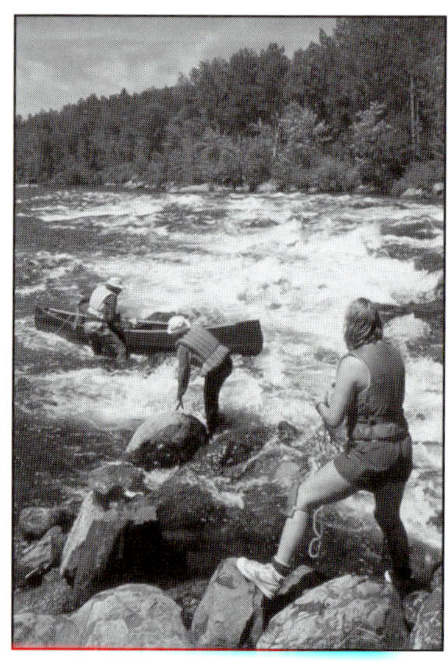

The small picture shows a canoe being lined down a rapids in the Temagami River. Here I was able to make a vertical shot, which ensures variety among the many horizontals naturally occurring in tripping photography, an always welcome diversion in slide shows.

Because we were on the move, both pictures had to be made in the hard mid-morning sunlight. However, they are still quite acceptable, in spite of the rather high contrast between light and dark areas.

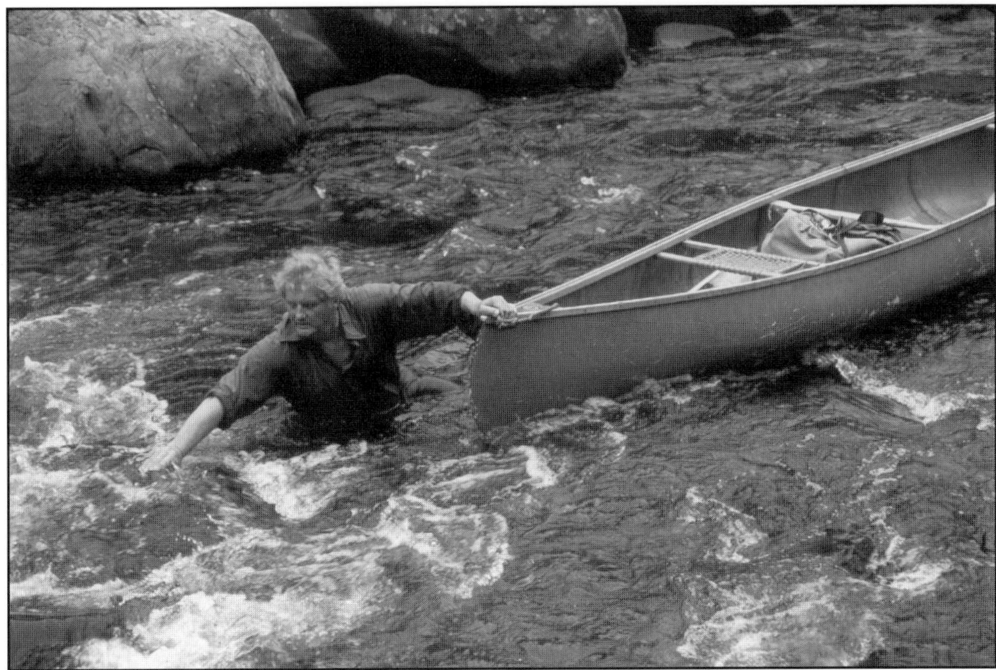

In order to get dramatic true-to-life shots, it is crucial that the photographer keeps her or his cool under difficult circumstances, and not forget that the first priority of the dedicated photographer is 'to get the picture first and try to deal with the consequences later.' This may not always be the most humane path to follow, but it can lead to some unique photos, especially when the events happen unexpectedly.

While wading the canoe up the chest-deep river (lining or portaging was out of the question because of the most unsuitable shore), I reached out to grasp a rock under water, cutting my hand on a sharp edge. Ria, who was photographing the scene, wisely decided to continue shooting once she realized that the cut in my hand was not really serious, in spite of the blood she could see. She knew from experience it would be great to have several pictures showing what had happened in the river.

Maybe such events are not moments of great importance in wilderness canoe tripping, but they are all part of travelling in the wild, of taking risks and encountering unforeseen challenges. You should, therefore, make a habit of having your camera loaded with film and ready to shoot when unexpected happenings occur. Photos like these will greatly enrich the story of your wilderness adventure.

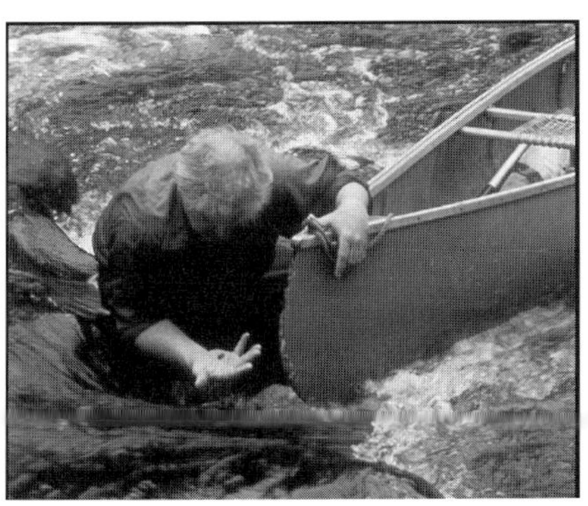

Notice that the small picture has been cropped to show only the important elements. By eliminating the non-essential details around the central scene, the image concentrates the viewer's attention on the act of me looking at my hand. To do this kind of framing when shooting from a fixed position, a zoom lens will be most effective.

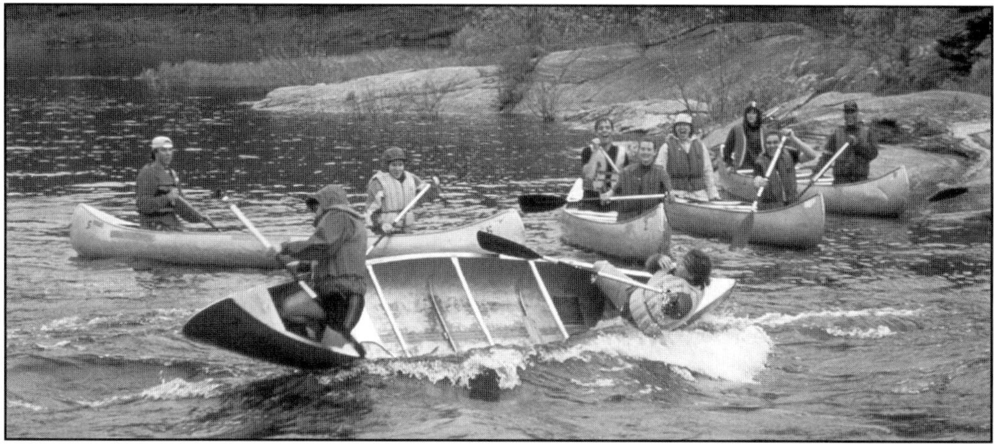

When people paddle, accidents happen. Watching somebody fall out of a canoe can be great fun, as this picture shows. The paddlers in the background are laughing while two of their buddies go swimming. But canoeing accidents may also be potentially dangerous, as depicted by the scene in the bottom picture.

While trying to line the fully loaded canoe down a small drop, the upstream gunnel was caught by the water and pulled under, instantly swamping the canoe. We only lost a paddle, but much of the gear was soaked. Fortunately, the camera was packed in a small home-made waterproof case (visible at the bottom-left corner of the photo) and was not damaged. We could, therefore, make several shots of the unpleasant, even embarrassing situation, while the canoe was still under water. There was no real harm done, except, of course, to my pride. (Be very careful indeed, when trying to line fully loaded canoes; it is a recipe for disaster!)

Always be on the alert for unplanned photo opportunities like these; keep your trigger finger well oiled. And waterproof all your gear.

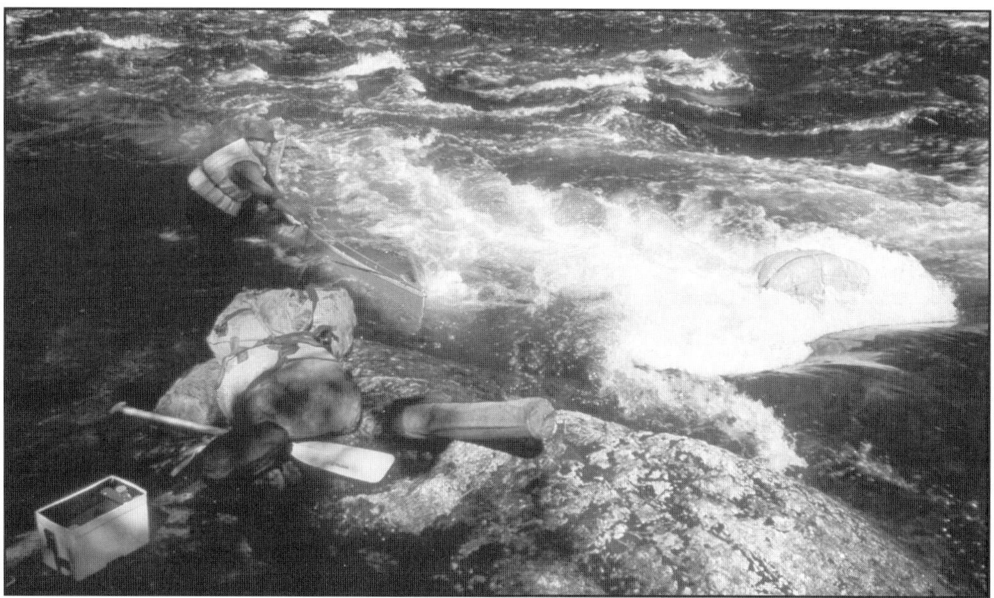

Even if all pieces of your photo equipment are waterproofed, mishaps can happen. Also minor accidents can have unpleasant consequences. While changing the film in my camera, I dropped the cassette on a beach where it was quickly swallowed by an incoming wave. Immediately I retrieved the cassette, but the water had already penetrated inside and soaked the film. By keeping the film wet and having it processed as soon as we got back from the trip, several of the images were saved, although the damage caused by the water can be easily seen in this picture.

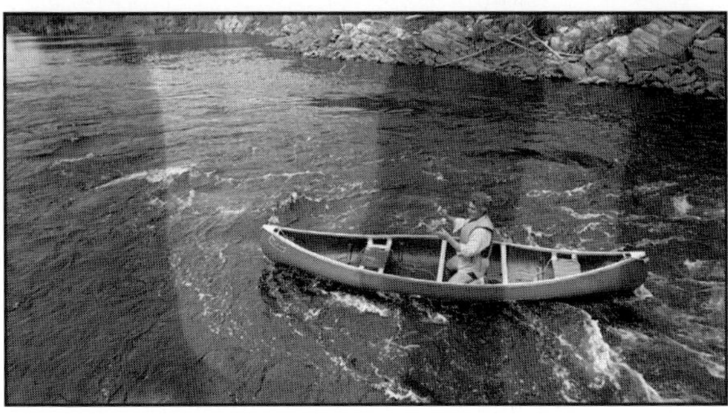

Camera equipment and water are deadly enemies and should be religiously kept from touching each other. However, if something does happen and you are left with a waterlogged camera and wet film, there are ways to save them from total ruin. But success is by no means guaranteed. In the case of a fully electronic camera you will likely loose it, no matter what you do, but you can always try your luck.

First of all: rewind the film, if possible, and then remove *all* batteries right away. Next, immediately take the still wet damaged goods to a repair shop (camera, lens) or processing lab (film). If that is out of the question because you are on a canoe trip days away from help, try the following steps. Keep your fingers crossed.

In case of a primarily mechanical camera or lens, shake the water out of it the best you can, then try to dry it out slowly and very carefully in clean warm air. For instance, the photo on page 171 shows a camera body and a lens held over a butane burner set at low heat. Alternatively, you could place the camera on a flat rock in the sun, but *never* hang it over a smoking wood fire. Be careful not to overheat it. The drying process may take hours, so do not rush.

If it is not possible to dry out the equipment, put the wet camera or lens in a tightly closed plastic bag or other airtight container to *keep* it wet. Deliver this package to the repair shop as soon you can. The more electronic components there are in the camera, the less chance you have of recovery. Also remember, repairing a water-damaged camera can be very expensive. Buying a new one may be a better solution to your problems. If you dropped your camera in salt water, desalinate thoroughly by rinsing in fresh water, before putting the camera in a plastic bag to keep it wet.

There is a somewhat greater chance of success with wet film. Immediately rewind it into the cassette. Place this in the canister to keep the film wet and put the closed waterproof canister in a tightly shut plastic bag. Do not try to dry the film in the camera or the cassette, as you would surely ruin the film for it would only stick together.

These are just the most basic of tips; talk with your camera dealer and repair shop people for more information. Of course, it is much better to take precautions and not dunk the camera in the first place. Probably the wisest thing you can do is to insure your equipment before a trip. Then, at least, you may get your money back.

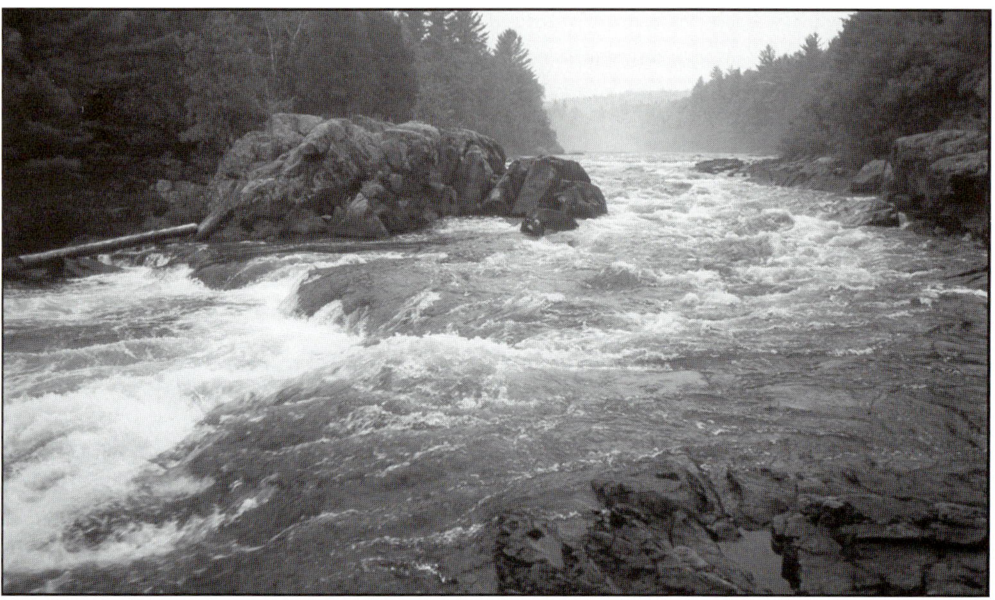

The unorthodox way this solo paddler ran the Petawawa River's Crooked Chute, shown above, was startling but effective. After carefully scouting the rapid from the shore on river right and portaging his gear to the end of the trail, he went down the dangerous chute cautiously, deliberately and always in complete control, sometimes paddling while sitting, sometimes standing up to determine which path to take.

It was a joy to observe him guiding his canoe so expertly down the rough water, over and between the treacherous ledges and rocks hidden below, always searching for the deepest current to take him further. He did not seem bothered by the many lives the dangerous S-shaped Crooked has claimed over the years: lives taken from careless trippers who had neglected to correctly read the river's topography, convinced that this rapid was a piece of cake. Well, it surely is not!

In spite of the unpleasant and very dark fall weather with intermittent drizzle and some wet snow, I succeeded in making a series of shots of the man, using high-speed ISO 400 film. Even then, none of the hand-held shots, all taken from the big rock in the middle of the large photo, is really sharp, but I am still very pleased to have such an interesting series of photos of this extraordinary paddler. It can indeed pay off if you keep your eyes and ears open for anonymous passers-by who may give you some fine moments of real paddling magic.

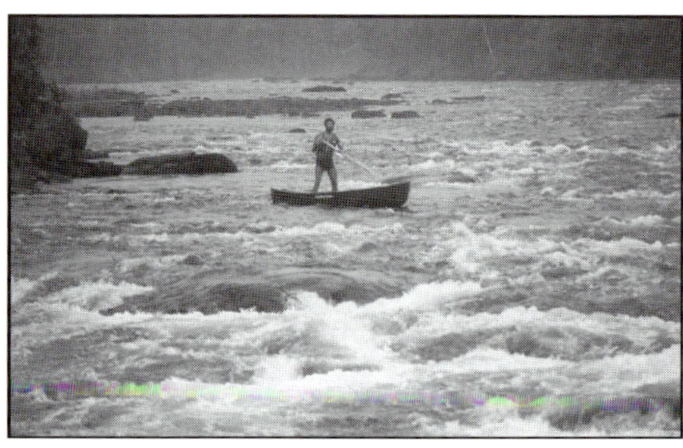 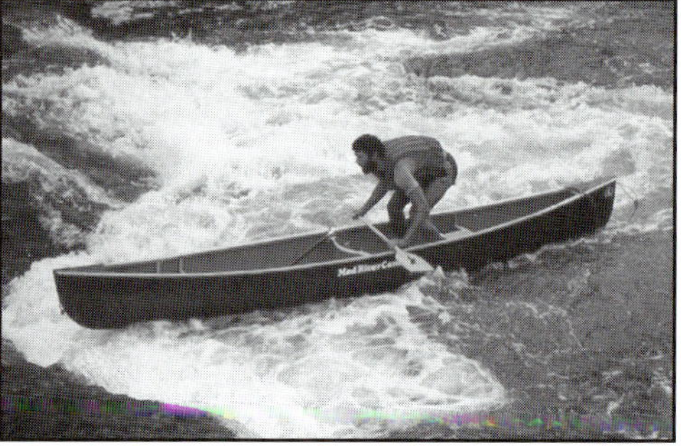

This photograph is another example of the interesting images you can collect, if you keep yourself open for events that may unexpectedly come your way.

We were camped at the Barron River, upstream from Brigham Lake, and busy doing camping chores when I heard the clanking sound aluminum canoes often make when they bang against rocks. Realizing there would probably be an opportunity to take some 'working' photos of trippers outside of my own group (something I am always looking for, because that is also part of what I observe on any trip), I grabbed my camera and ran to the shore. There, I saw four people wading two canoes down the shallow river, pulling and pushing them between the numerous rocks, the front canoe even floating for a short while when there was enough water. The trippers did not pay any attention to me and I did not have the audacity to tell them they could have avoided this long rock garden by doing several portages between a few small lakes to the southeast. (Some people try to avoid portages at almost all cost.)

What struck me immediately in the image I saw was the way the two front men were sitting on, not in, their canoe. But above all, I noticed the powerful, almost horizontal morning sunlight shining directly into their faces, sculpting the bowman into a well-rounded image of light and shadow. I made a frame-filling shot with the two canoes on a strong diagonal line, showing the four people working in the beautiful light. Because the canoes are coming in the direction of the viewer, the picture creates a strong feeling of depth. I tried to keep the rock on the right-hand side out of the picture, but that was not possible without me stepping into the water (something I was not prepared to do so early in the morning). This was the only shot I made then, enough to give me a nice feeling of having communicated with others.

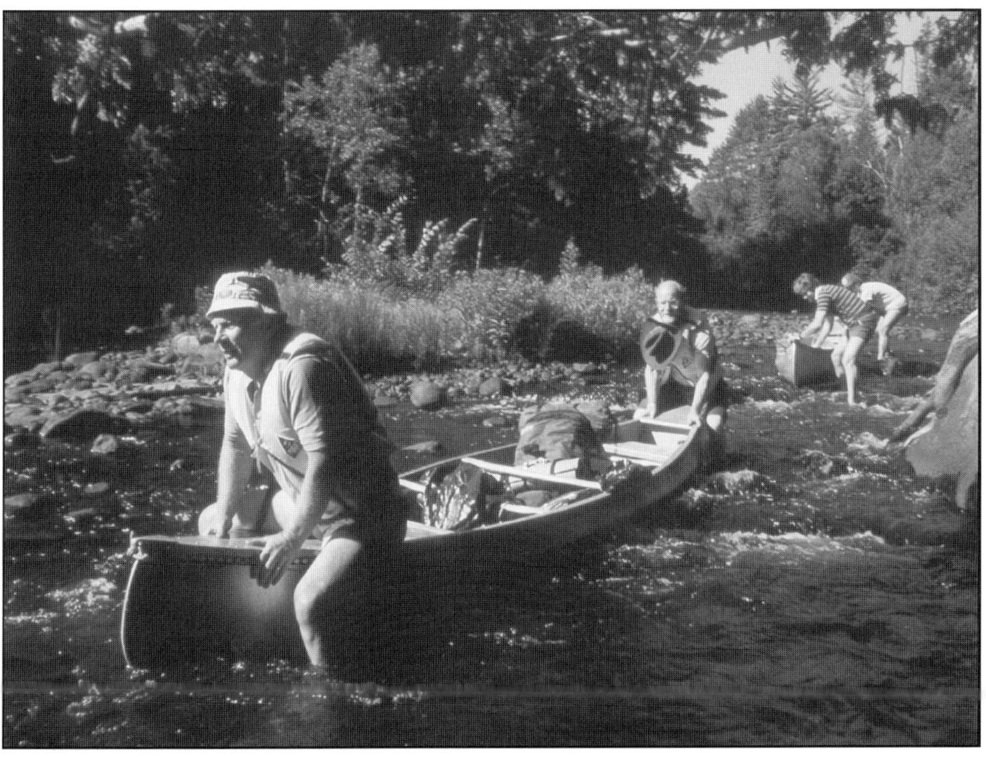

Current—Recreational Paddling

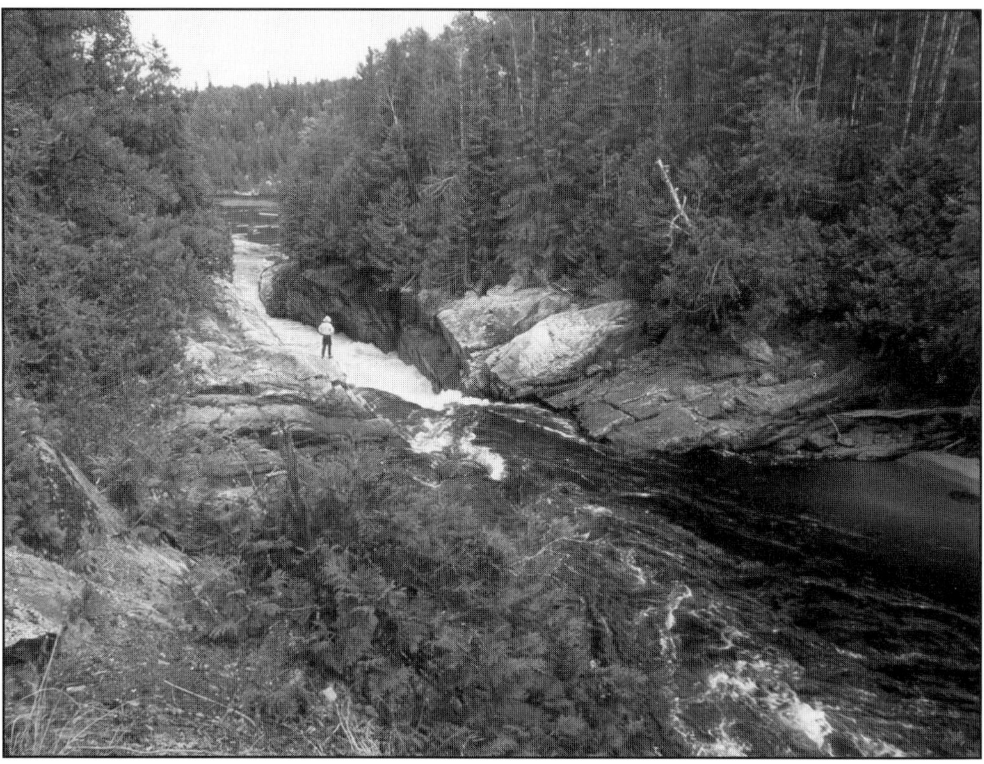

Serendipity, defined as "the faculty of making happy and unexpected discoveries by accident," certainly plays a major role in the quality of this picture, taken at the Split Rock Falls of the Missinaibi River. The tiny figure, looking at the waters rushing through the narrows between the angled rocks, is dressed in dark trousers and a light shirt, which, serendipitously, are in perfect contrast with the background of white-coloured water and dark rocks behind the man, making him easily visible. Had it been the other way around, i.e. light trousers and a dark shirt, he would have blended into the background, possibly disappearing from the picture. Normally, one should try to avoid photographing someone dressed in light clothing against a dark background, because of the large contrast, but in this case it works well.

The figure also provides scale to the picture, making it possible for the viewer to get an idea of the size of everything in this section of the Missinaibi. Split Rock Falls is an intriguing area with all kinds of possibilities for making photographs. Unfortunately, too many trippers portage around the falls without so much as a second look, ignoring the beauty of the place: probably because they are controlled by the dreaded tripper's curse: "Hurry, we're late!" What canoeists should do, if at all possible, is camp here for at least one day and explore the area around the falls, go searching for all kinds of angles from which to view the river and maybe shoot some pleasing pictures. For instance, very few people have ever been on the opposite side of the river, observing the falls from river right. Try it; you will like it.

There is much more to wilderness canoeing than running rapids and pumping adrenaline. For the photographer, there is also the hunt for beautiful images, and the sublime satisfaction of capturing the pictures you want.

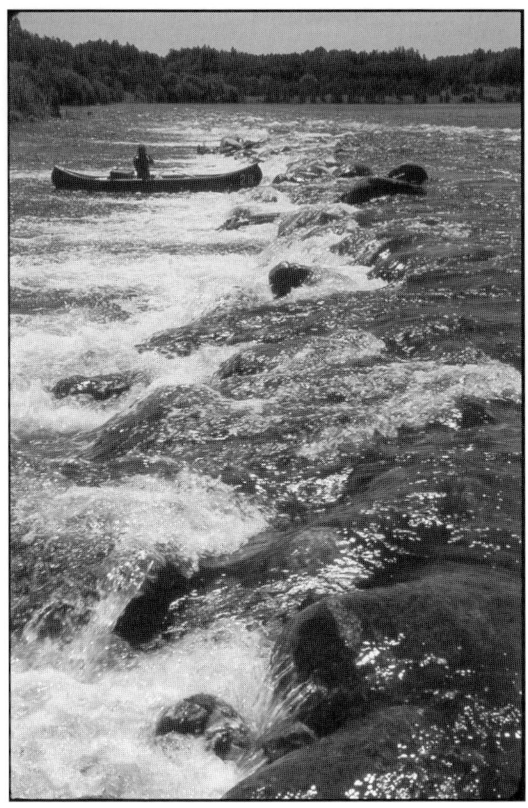

Rivers have many faces, each one different, each one an object of great beauty, each one a living world in itself.

There are few water-related activities in nature as fascinating as seeing a river, born as a trickle, gradually quicken its pace, widen into a stream, play in rapids, tumble over falls and finally empty into a lake or sea. Observing flowing water can be a truly spellbinding experience.

Of all the faces of the river, rapids are among the most spectacular and awe-inspiring, creating wave and current patterns that are manna for the photographer's soul. Interesting ways to make photos that present a fresh perspective on the appearance of rapids include: selecting a dramatic vertical format as shown in these two pictures; pointing the camera down and using a wide-angle lens, if available. This perspective creates a tremendous feeling of depth, accentuated by the placement of the centre of interest, the canoe, near the top.

These pictures, both very effective and visually exciting verticals, show different aspects of whitewater. Notice the hard backlight in the top photo, whereas the bottom one is illuminated by the soft light from an overcast sky, eliminating all shadows.

The ability to see such details clearly and accurately is important for success as a photographer. It will transform images and events into photos with a unique novel look, ones that are distinctive. By learning to understand the visual language of photography, you are on your way to the making of good, maybe even great photographs.

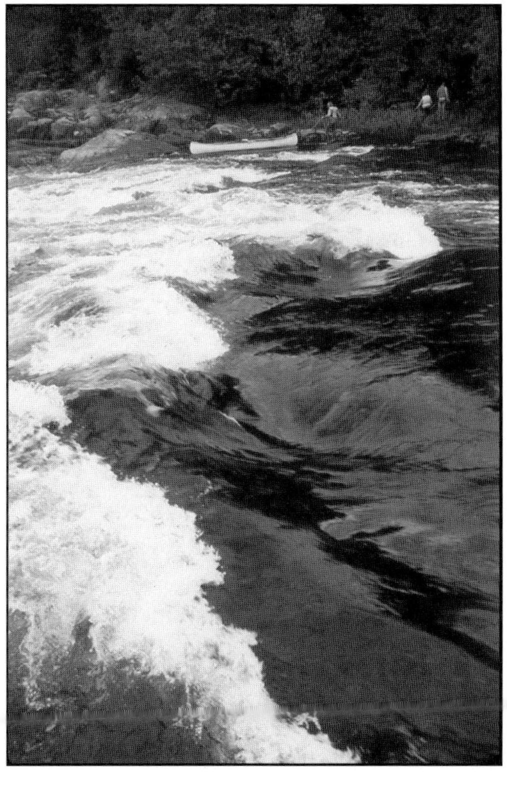

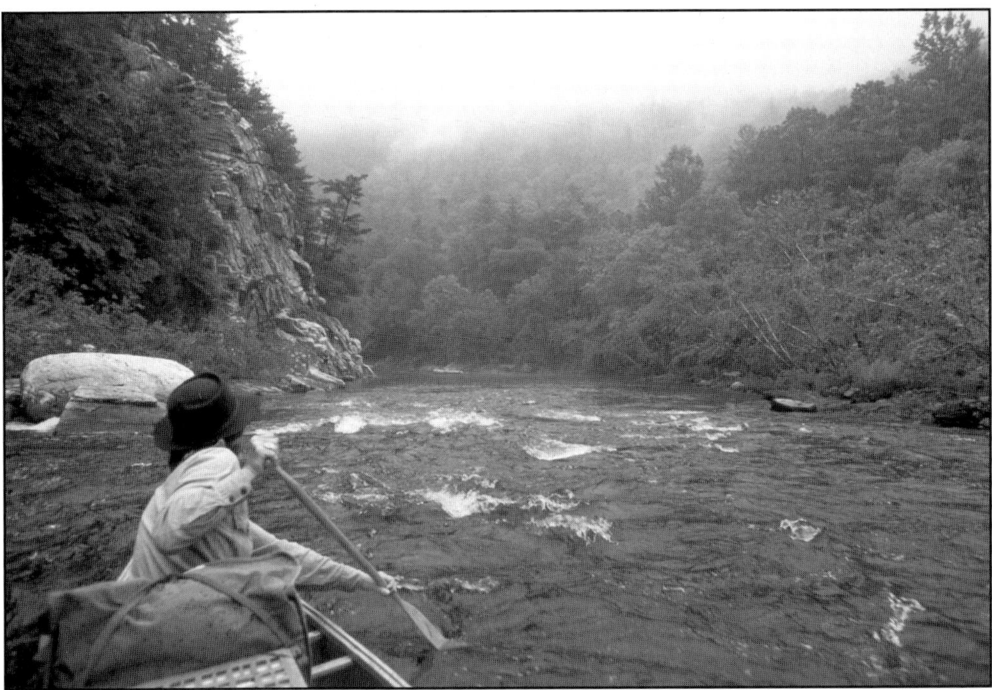

Making photos from inside a canoe while paddling whitewater is tricky, yet very rewarding. It gives the viewer of your picture story some direct access to the experience of being in a canoe going down a wilderness river.

While travelling the Cacapon River in West Virginia, we came upon this narrow section where the water flowed rather quickly, creating some simple waves. Obviously, there were no rocks hidden below the water surface, so we paddled through without scouting from the shore. At the onset of the whitewater, I made this photo while remaining seated in the stern of the canoe. In other situations I have sometimes stood up to get a higher viewpoint, thus showing the bow paddler and the water up front from a different perspective. Of course, that can only be done with a trusting and willing partner, one who is able to keep the canoe steady for the sake of allowing you the photos you wish. Always warn your partner whenever you intend to stand up; it is very easy to loose balance if either of you makes an unexpected movement. (We may not always wear our uncomfortable life jackets in situations like this where the whitewater is not obviously menacing and the risk of mishaps is extremely low.)

A short analysis of this picture is instructive. The bow paddler is placed left of centre while making a cross draw, putting some real canoeing action in the picture. Because of the unobstructed view, the river itself is clearly visible, showing the narrows with the rock wall on the left and the forest on the right. Having the person in the foreground gives the picture a sense of depth, enhanced by the grey fog in the background. Also the whitecaps on the waves receding into the background increase this depth. The overcast sky provides a soft light, giving the photo a rather subdued tone. All in all, this is an effective record shot of quite good photographic quality, depicting a typical tripping scene as viewed from the canoe.

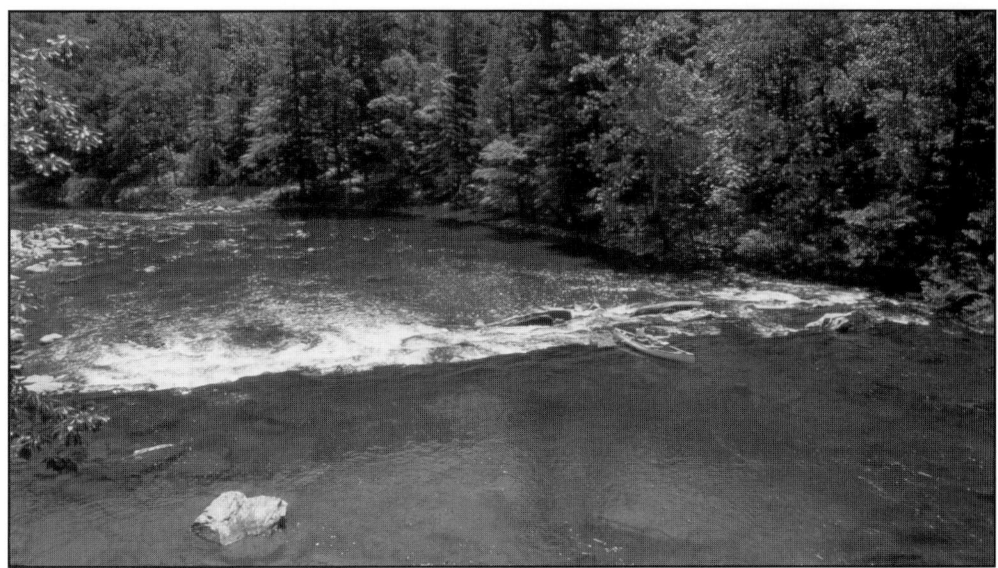

These two photos, also taken at the Cacapon River, illustrate the value of zoom lenses. When we came upon this ledge and tried to find our way through (there was no obvious portage around it), I took the opportunity of making a photographic record of the scene. Well aware of the dangers involved, but with the canoe resting safely (I hoped) against a rock, I got out, scrambled over the mostly submerged ledge to river left and climbed up the steep riverbank.

With my 35-140 mm zoom lens set at a wide 35 mm, I took the first photo of the whole ledge, establishing a proper overview of the situation. Then, from the same spot and zooming out to 140 mm, I shot the second one, showing the boat/ledge relationship in much greater detail.

Making these two different but complementary photos would, of course, also have been possible had I carried two separate lenses of the appropriate focal lengths with me. But the zoom lens made it all much easier and more convenient. The optical quality of many zoom lenses is truly remarkable. They can make life more comfortable for the traveller who does not want to carry around a variety of lenses. Nowadays, most cameras, including the point-and-shoot and digital ones, come equipped with decent-to-excellent zoom lenses.

I realize that, by traversing the wet and slippery rocky ledge, just to take some photographs, I risked my (and my innocent partner's) health and equipment, but my photographic hunting instinct can be very powerful. In the end, we managed to pass the ledge by carefully wading between the rocks on river right.

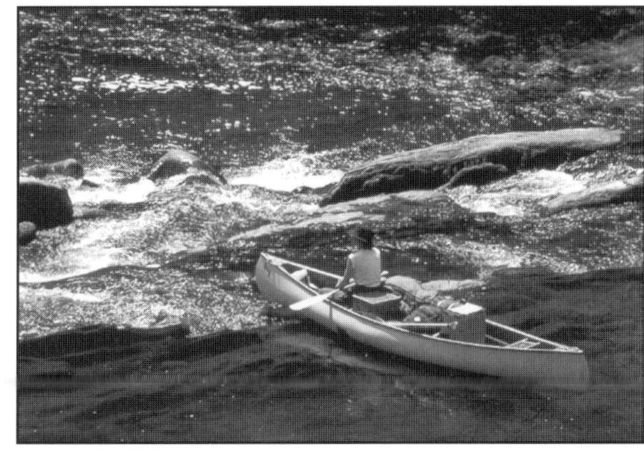

Current—Recreational Paddling

It is an interesting challenge to try and make a picture for a specific purpose, and extremely satisfying if you finally succeed after several attempts. Although a measure of luck and opportunity helps one realize a vision, it is primarily hard work and persistence that are needed. Most importantly, you have to *recognize* the possibilities of a situation before you can set out to take the photograph.

In 1992, when I started thinking about creating this book, it was obvious that a strong attention-grabbing colour picture would be required for the cover; one that would express in a vertical image the power and beauty of paddling, emphasizing its great appeal to all canoeists, kayakers and rafters.

When I saw Glenn Fallis and his crew go down the French River's Blue Chute in a 7.5-metre-long North canoe, I grabbed the opportunity to create just such a cover shot. I knew from observing earlier runs that at a certain point the boat would come almost straight at me, filling the centre of the frame and therefore giving me the required vertical with enough space at top and bottom for the book title and other text. In the photo, the water in the foreground and the rock face in the background are sufficiently undetailed to not seriously interfere with the titling.

When I clicked the shutter of my hand-held camera, equipped with a 75-300 mm zoom lens

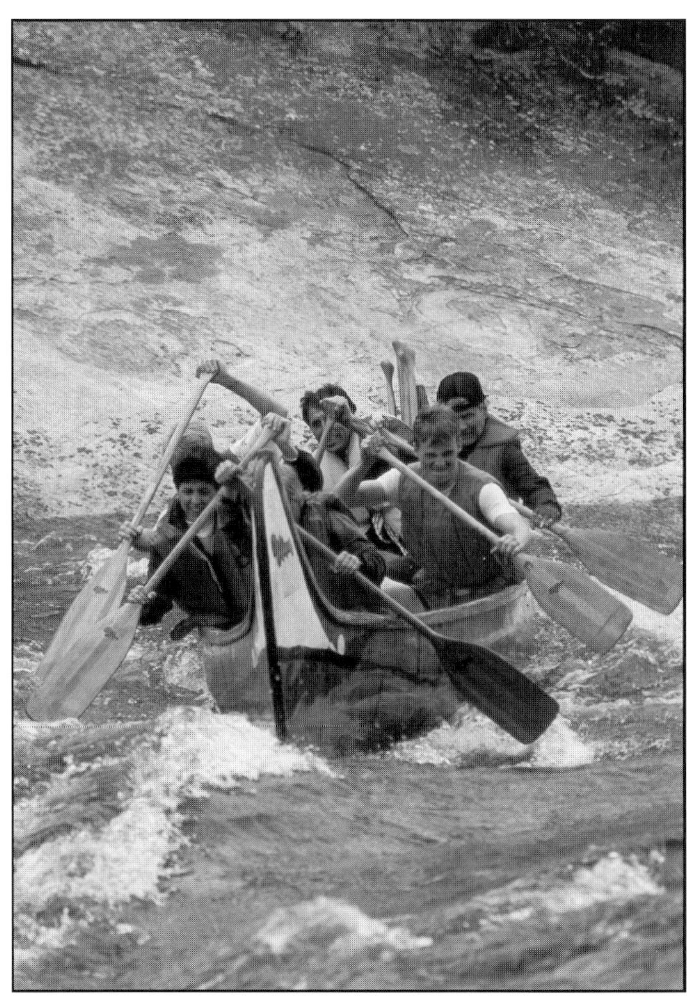

and loaded with ISO 200 slide film, I made sure the paddles were poised just above the water surface, giving the picture tension and a strong sense of speed and power. Only after the film had been processed did I realize that the faces of the paddlers were full of expression, showing the stress of the situation. This was an unexpected but welcome bonus.

The photo indeed turned out the way I had visualized it and now graces the cover of this book. It is interesting to compare the colour and black-and-white renditions of the picture. In this case, colour is clearly more appealing.

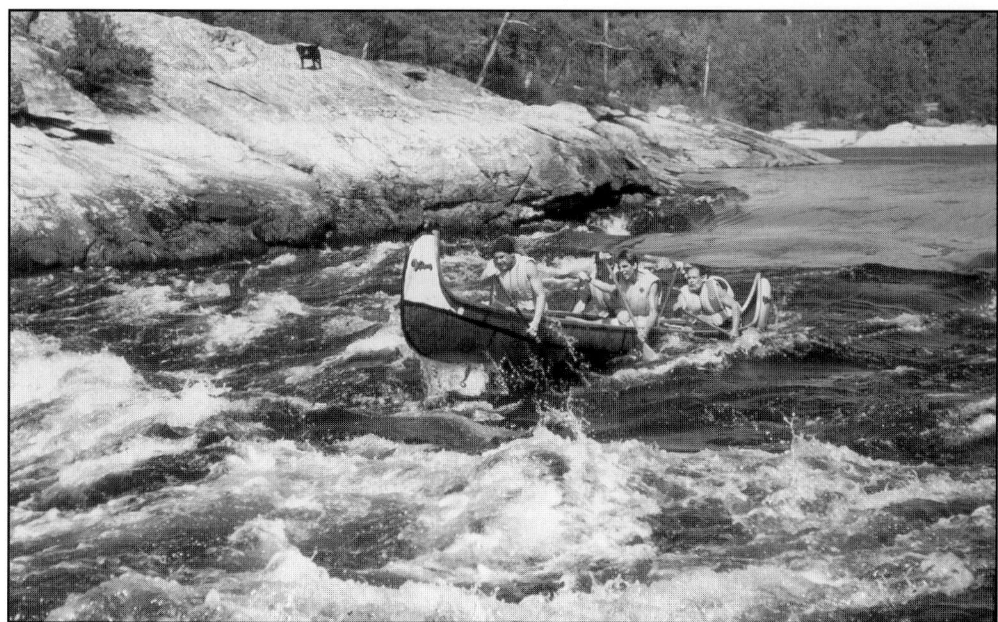

During the fur-trade era, which lasted roughly from the early-17th to the mid-19th century, huge fortunes in trading goods and pelts were transported between the traders' headquarters in the east and the vast interior where the furs originated. In this industry the French River played a central role.

Over the centuries, thousands of heavily laden canoes propelled by tens of thousands of hard-working voyageurs travelled up and down this river. And there are numerous places were the ghosts of these professional paddlers still dwell, heard by those with the imagination to hear them. One of those special places surely is the Blue Chute, which all canoeists had to traverse, either by doing a difficult portage or lining, or by running its challenging waters.

Would those travellers of yesteryear have danced on the waves of the Blue Chute the way this modern canoe does? Would they have deliberately selected the central standing waves for such joyful bouncing up and down as shown here? It is doubtful, because the fur traders were there to make money, not for the thrill of running rapids. Always in a hurry, they did not dare take the risk of damaging their delicate birch-bark craft in the violent waters, just because they wanted to have some fun.

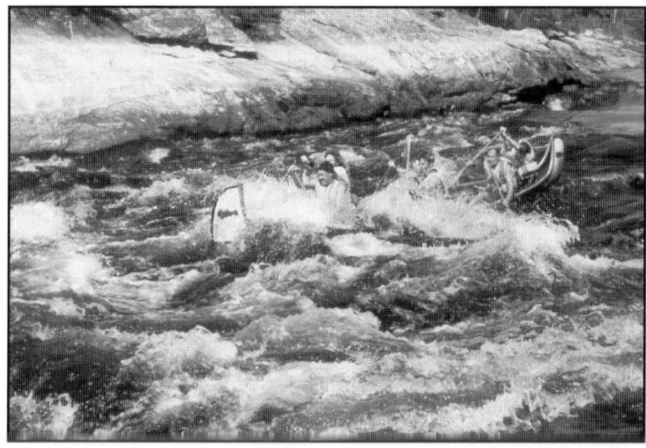

Remember the voyageurs when you paddle these waters. Listen, and hear them sing.

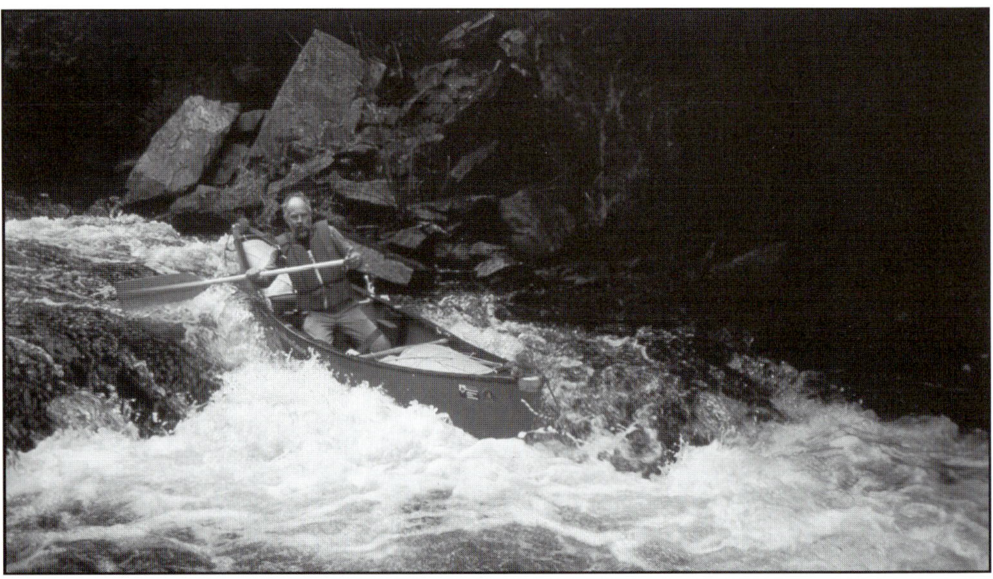

A fine and very productive source of paddling photos can be found in the activities of outdoors clubs that organize canoe and kayak trips to numerous waterways and lakes of all sizes in canoe country.

One of those popular trip destinations is Eels Creek, where many members of the Wilderness Canoe Association and other paddling clubs continue to enjoy the thrill of whitewater on this rather small but very photogenic stream. From a photographer's perspective, Eels Creek offers great opportunities for fine action photography. But as it is quite narrow and often flanked by high trees and rock walls, the creek is also somewhat dark in places, making photography an extra challenge because of the relative lack of light. However, if a sufficiently high film speed is used and some extra care is given to determining correct exposure, the results can be more than acceptable.

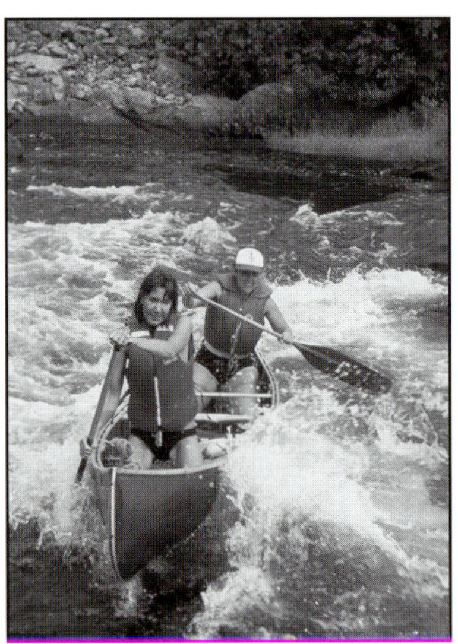

The top photo shows a canoe going down one of the many mild drops in the creek, photographed on ISO 400 slide film with a good quality automatic point-and-shoot camera. Notice the dark rock face in the background, creating an interesting contrast with the much lighter water below in the foreground.

The bottom photo was taken at another WCA outing, at Palmer Rapids in the Madawaska River. Because of the open nature of this place, light was no problem. The photo was taken without special provisions, except that the photographer had to climb onto a rock in the middle of the current in order to obtain the required high angle on this tandem canoe.

Both of these are simple photographs, but fine examples of what can be found at club outings.

Although it makes sense, in many cases, to follow the 'rules' of composition that have been developed over the centuries that visual art has existed, occasionally breaking some or all of those prescriptions can lead to interesting and unexpected results.

This photograph breaks some of those rules. There are no leading lines, no S-curves, no diagonals, all primary lines are horizontals, broken only by the dominant main subject (canoe plus man plus paddle), which is positioned in such a way that the canoeist is paddling out of the picture instead of into it. Granted, there is some adherence to the rule of thirds, where, by placing the main subject in a location about one third of the way from the top or the bottom as well as from both sides of the picture, greater visual interest may be generated.

However, this is a powerful image, with the canoe coming straight at the viewer, imparting a feeling of strength, speed and total control. The paddler's face is clearly visible, and his paddling technique is exemplary. The slight bending of the paddle shaft indicates the power he puts into his stroke. Fortunately, the light coming from the overcast sky is diffuse, so that the whitewater on the left is not too bright. The background is unobtrusive, not taking any attention away from the main subject.

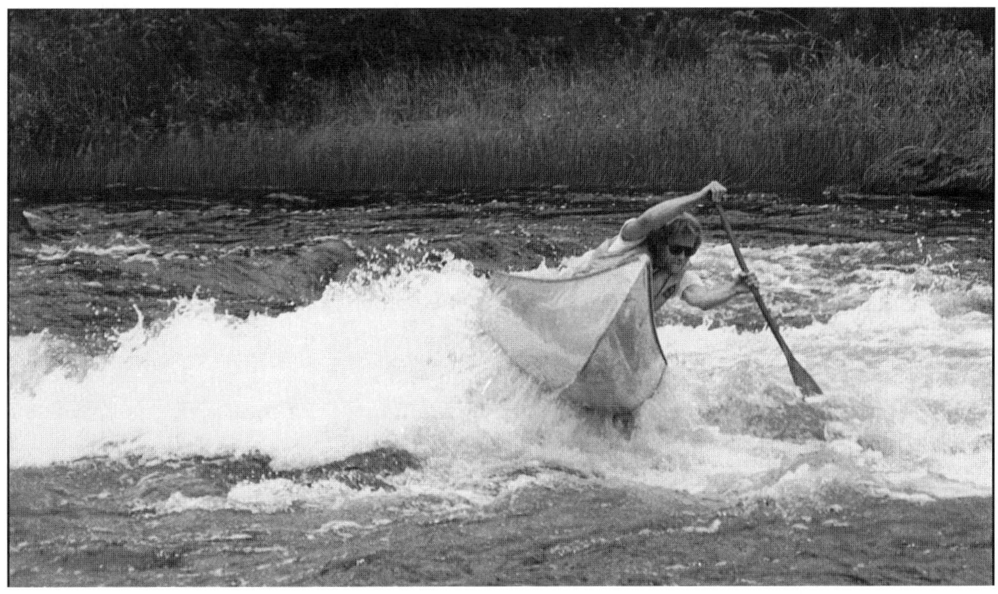

To capture fast-moving pictures like this one, the photographer has to be alert and ready to shoot. This photo is a deceptively simple but very effective recording of a high-intensity action scene shot at the 'decisive moment.' The frothing waves on the left are very important to the impact of the photo. If you were to crop out most of the left and right sections, keeping only the boat and the area immediately around it, much of the impact would disappear and it would become just a mediocre picture.

By analyzing your photographs and, of course, also those made by other people, you strengthen your capability to see, recognize and then record the images around you. Work hard at developing a painter's eye for composition, light and colour, and you will eventually rise above mediocrity. Increasingly, your photographs will become delightful sources of great pride and ones filled with personal expression.

Current—Recreational Paddling

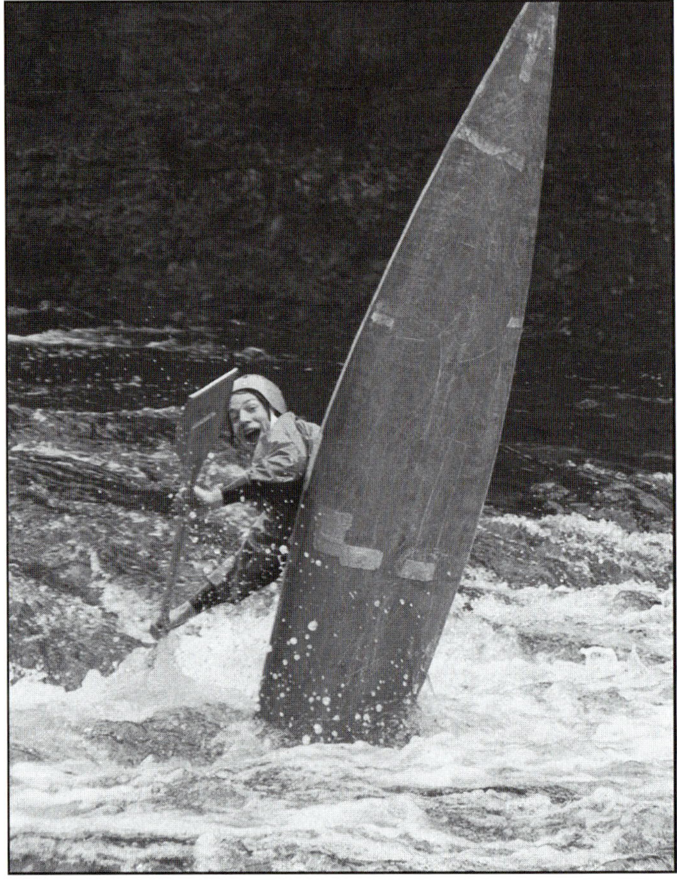

'Extreme' kayaking and canoeing is a form of free-style paddling that appeals to those dare-devils who want to discover how far they can go in their quest for the ulti-mate whitewater thrill. Over the years, a variety of forms and names have been developed for these exuberant expressions of high-energy paddling: rodeo, squirt boating, surfing etc.

This photograph, taken in the Elora Gorge when the Grand River was at low water level, shows an 'ender,' also called 'pop-up,' a basic form of paddle playing out of which various forms of extreme paddling have been developed. I was able to get close to the scene by walking on some exposed riverbed rocks. The obvious joy of the kayaker playing in the waves was contagious; everybody in the group around me had big grins on their faces. A whimsical touch is brought into the picture by the patches of duct tape on the scratched bottom of the craft, indicating a much-used and obviously well-loved kayak.

These water-ballet manoeuvres are performed in the 'hole' created by the recircu-lating water behind a shallow submerged obstacle. As was the case with the action photo on the previous page, this shot was also made at the decisive moment of peak action. By looking directly at the camera and expressing his open-mouthed joy, the paddler clearly demonstrates his superb control of the kayak and the intense fun he is having.

This picture is one of a series I took at that location using a motor drive and black-and-white high-speed film. It is cropped from a horizontal photo that was at least twice as wide as the one presented here. By thus eliminating the distracting surroundings, the picture has become much more interesting and direct in its appeal. In spite of the rig-orous cropping, what is left of the original photo is still reasonably sharp.

A minor shortcoming is the fact that the stern tip of the kayak is missing from the top of the photo, a result of having to shoot very quickly when recording the moment. Because of such fast action, it is easy to be sloppy when framing the photos, so pay close attention to what you observe in the viewfinder.

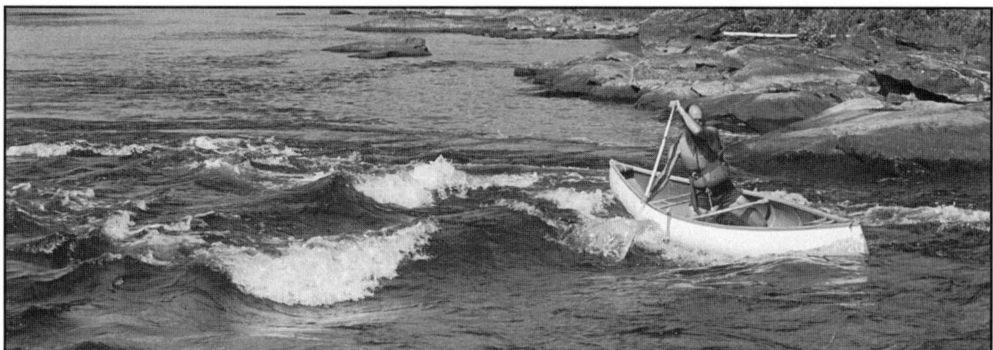

When I discovered this man manoeuvring his canoe so skilfully in the outflow waves of the Madawaska River's Palmer Rapids, I started making several shots of his playful antics, hoping that something spectacular would come up to give me a 'key' image for a series. And yes, possibly because he saw me photographing him, he turned his boat around and jumped out in my direction, making it look convincingly like a real upset.

To say the least, I was most grateful for this voluntary creative act of sacrifice, because I succeeded in getting it all on film. Everything was captured perfectly; I had caught the whole canoe and jumping man at the peak of action, the midday sun illuminated the man and the inside of the boat beautifully and the background did not have any disturbing elements in it. A fine shot, thanks to the courageous paddler.

Eventually, I used six of these photos to accompany a song I had written based on this event. *Ferrying Song* is the story of "a man with a very long beard, who wanted to ferry across, a violent wilderness river, to show it that he was the boss, just to show it that he was the boss." But sadly the canoe tipped over and both the man and his white-water beard drowned because the beard could not swim. A tragic story indeed!

Try to create special photographs that can be used later in unexpected ways. Develop your imagination and creativity. A whole world of fascinating images is available out there in canoe country, waiting to be photographed by you.

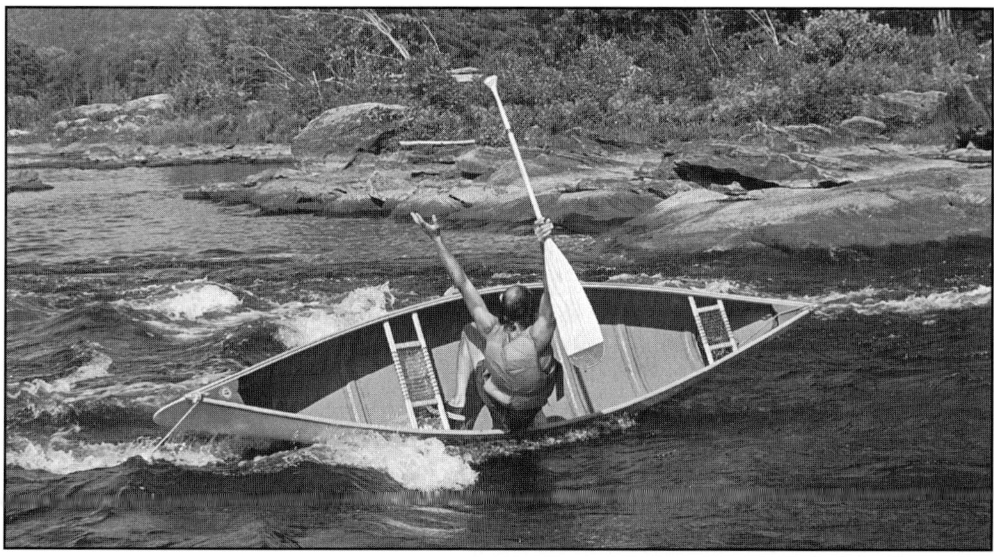

Current—Recreational Paddling

How better to end this section on whitewater recreational paddling than by showing the latest fashion in knee protection?

This teenager was walking around the shore with both her knees wrapped in rough blocks of foam plastic. She had just come out of a canoe after having run some wild rapids and the soaked foam was still dripping with water. Because I am always on the lookout for humorous images, I asked permission to photograph her ingenious contraption. It would, of course, have been possible to make the shot from a distance using a telephoto lens, without her being aware of my presence. However, I prefer to be courteous and get full co-operation from the people I photograph; the whole shooting process will then be much more pleasant for everybody involved. It is encouraging to see how people open up when you approach them with a smile and enthusiasm.

Although the giggling teen was being teased mercilessly by her friends and had trouble standing still, I managed to get close enough to photograph just her legs and the knee pads against an out-of-focus background of water and reeds, eliminating all unnecessary elements. I could only make two photos, of which this one is the best, before the young lady took off and collapsed on the grass, surrounded by the group of her laughing and yelling buddies.

This is nothing more than a very simple unsophisticated picture, a well-observed record shot that only aims to show something amusing in the world of paddling. Such photographs, little slices of paddling life, are like spices sprinkled over the soup of your story—used with discretion, they make the taste so much more delicious.

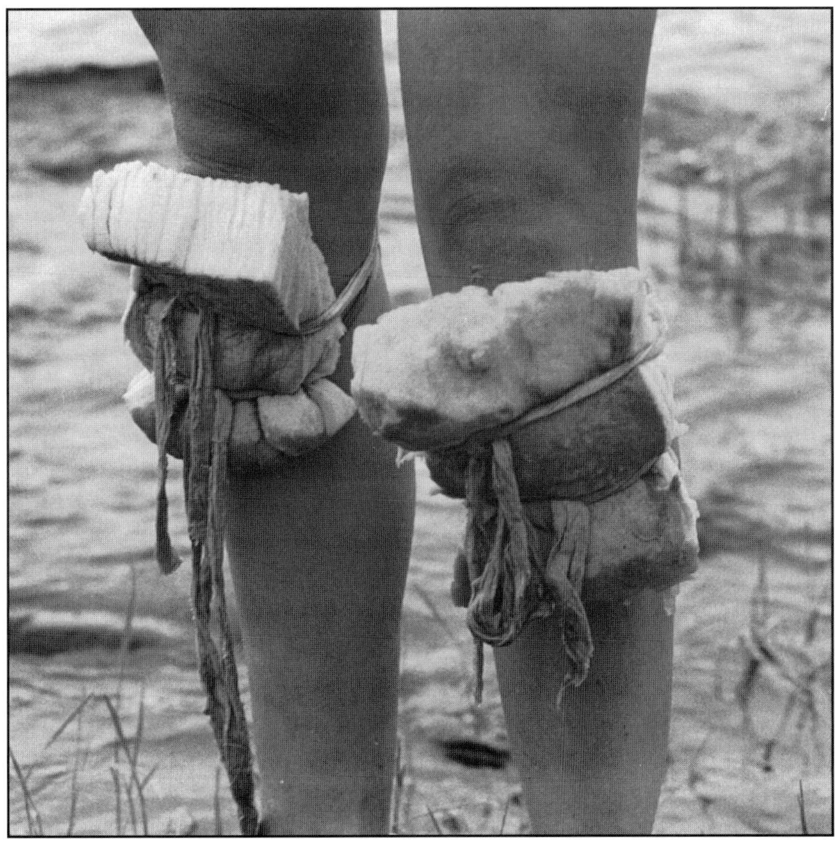

Current—Recreational Paddling

COMPETITION

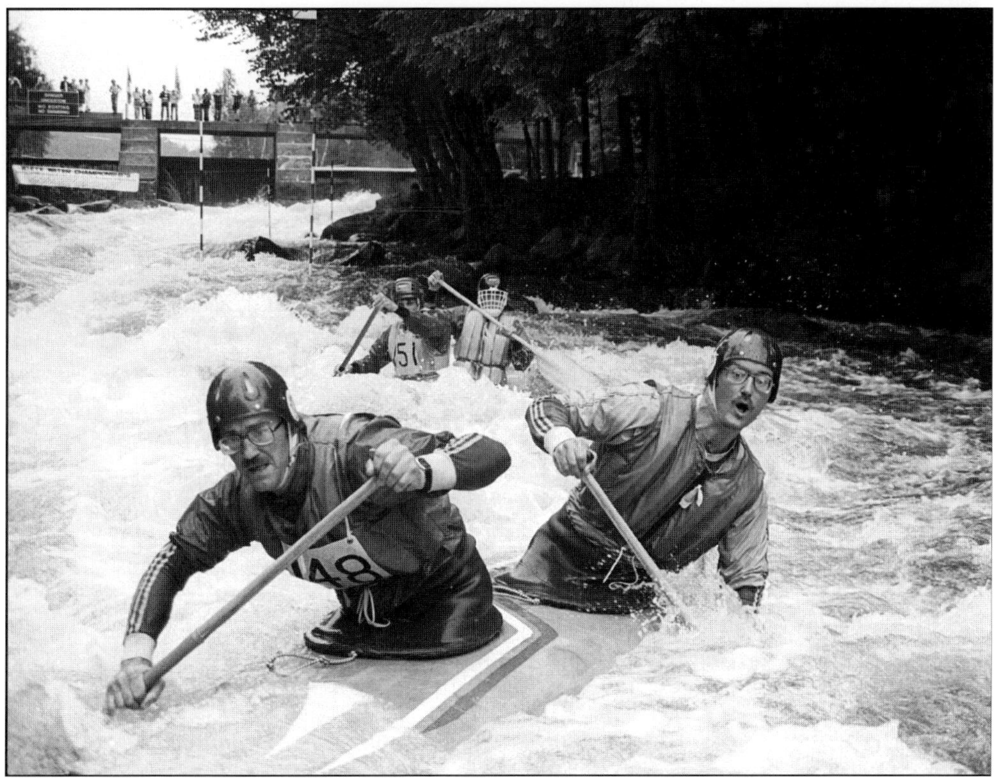

Whitewater slalom competition for kayaks and canoes provides a true test of your ability to react swiftly to fast-moving action. On the racecourse, the colourful boats are engulfed in boiling waves that throw them around in a mad dance of controlled mayhem, creating countless stirring images that will attract the attention of spectators and excite dedicated paddlers.

In order to avoid distracting clutter in the photograph, you have to move as close as possible to the subject and/or use a telephoto lens (in which case you should use some kind of support, such as a tripod, monopod or maybe a friend's shoulder). Ask permission to stand near a gate, if possible; that is where much of the action is to be found.

In this photo, all movement takes place in the middle, showing a decked C2 canoe in a team competition, with the second boat clearly visible in the background. What immediately catches the eye is the intense open-mouthed concentration of the stern paddler focussing on the next gate.

In whitewater competition photography you will have to compose the picture, focus the camera and set the exposure correctly just before you push the release button. Improve your chances of getting good results by practising as much as you can. Plan to be at the racecourse early to find the best locations for you to occupy. Check the position of the sun during the race so you can have the light coming over your shoulder, if possible, in order to avoid placing the paddlers' faces in the shadow.

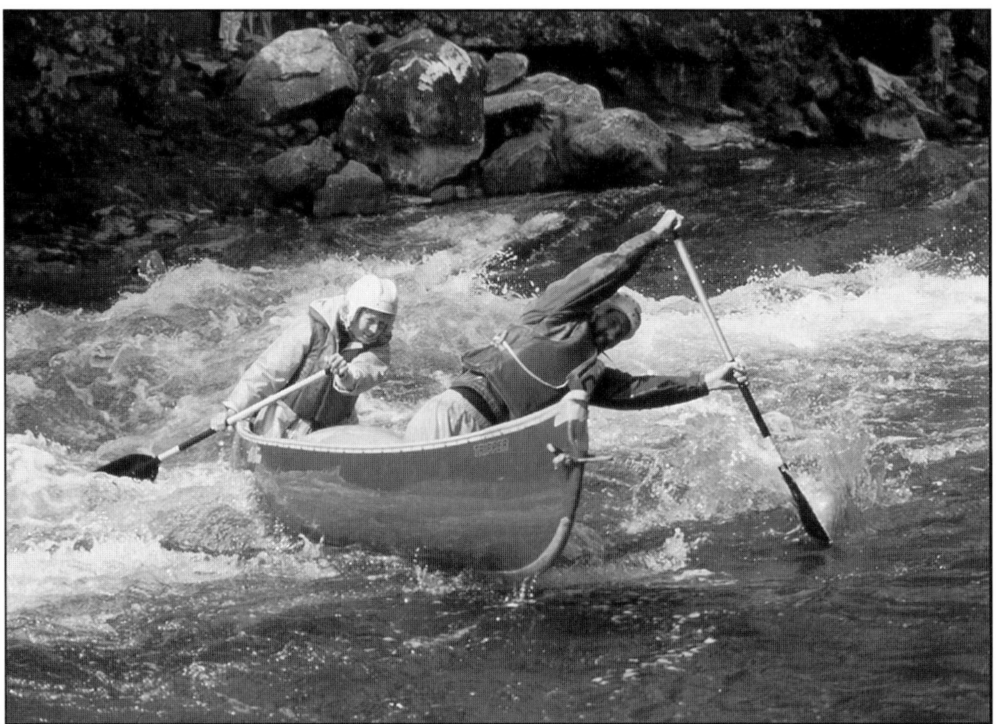

If there is one kind of competition close to the canoe tripper's heart, it is open canoe slalom racing down a turbulent stretch of whitewater filled with rapids and other challenging hazards. Here, the adventurous paddlers can test their mastery of the techniques required to successfully negotiate difficult stretches of rivers in their beloved canoe country. In this picture, the important technique of turning out of the current and getting the boat into the quiet water of an eddy is captured at the right moment. Both competitors as well as their paddles are clearly visible against the white foamy water, and both are exhibiting excellent racing technique.

Note that the background is formed by the rock-filled river shore, photographed at an angle looking somewhat upstream. The line is therefore not horizontal as a true horizon should be, but somewhat slanting down to the left.

In such fast-moving scenes, it is wise to keep the camera glued to your eye, following the canoe through the viewfinder and selecting the right instant of exposure. You should also try to take several shots, because there may be paddles or arms concealing the competitors' faces.

Look for locations where you can get different views and backgrounds, where the action is at a peak, where you can be more creative. Try to find a different angle, a unique perspective. It may even be necessary for you to stand in the water (if allowed by the organizers), so be prepared. And please, be courteous to other photographers, try not to block their view. But do not get pushed around either, be assertive.

Just as it takes years of serious training for whitewater paddlers to become great racers, also photographing competitions requires much time and dedication if you want to attain your very best potential. But even if your commitment is not that intense, you can still have great fun shooting such whitewater action.

Obviously, this kayaker, playing in the turbulent 'hole' behind a small ledge, was not only training to improve his balance and paddle control, but also had a tremendous amount of fun doing it. To be one with your boat is an absolute necessity when participating in whitewater slalom races, and the only way to achieve that is by constantly committing yourself to serious training. Such discipline also greatly improves your chances of success when taking part in the boisterous 'extreme' paddlesport of playboating, also called rodeo, freestyle paddling or aquabatics.

To shoot this photograph (one of dozens taken at the same spot), I sat on a rock on the river shore, using a low tripod to support my 75-300 mm zoom lens, and with an ISO 400 black-and-white film in the camera. It was of paramount importance that the shot be made at exactly the critical moment, while all action was at its peak, showing the flying paddle at maximum height and the outstretched arm and hand ready to grab the paddle (always successfully!), while the paddler was looking up.

This timing requires quick reflexes from the photographer, who needs a keen eye and a sensitive trigger finger to shoot at exactly the right moment. The short but significant delay between the time the finger pushes the button and the time the shutter opens to expose the film begins to play an important role in this kind of split-second action photography. With film-based cameras this time delay may amount to several tenths of a second, and with digital cameras it may even take half a second or more. So you have to learn to anticipate the precise moment to push the button just before the peak of action takes place. This requires much experience. The more you train yourself, the better your photos will become. Keep the camera in front of your eye and learn to anticipate the decisive moment of concentrated action. Eventually, you will surely succeed in making some very powerful pictures.

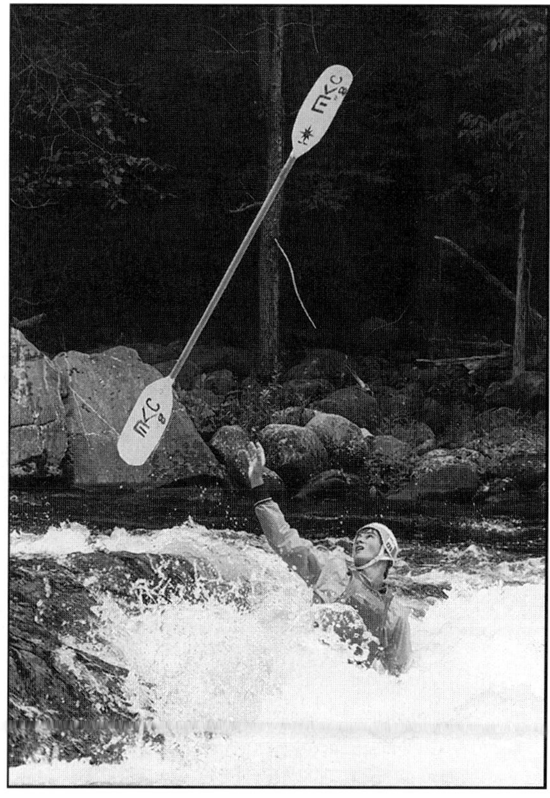

Although I am quite happy with the action and the moment of capture in this picture, I am really bothered by the tree, especially the light-coloured branch behind the paddle (and to a lesser extent also by the small tree on the right). These are disturbing elements that interfere with the cleanliness of the dark background. I should have physically removed at least the (dead) branch before the shoot started, but I failed to see it. Thus, all that can be done to clean up the picture afterwards is to edit out the branch in the computer or darkroom.

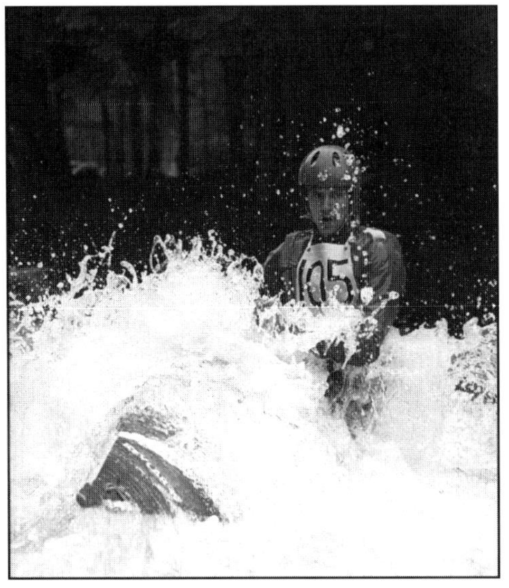

Besides recording their excellent paddling techniques, I wanted above all to photograph the expressions of intense concentration on the faces of these two paddlers I had observed on earlier runs. However, that proved to be easier said than done. Although I am pleased with the composition of both pictures, captured at moments of strong action, the faces are not illuminated well enough to be clearly visible, thus removing some of the appeal. Unfortunately, there is nothing that can be done about the quality and direction of sunlight in situations like this; you have to work with what is available. It therefore makes sense to take as many photos as possible and select the best one(s) later. Above all, choose your shooting location carefully, with the position of the sun in mind.

Because there are only three elements in the pictures—whitewater foreground, paddler in boat and dark background—their uncomplicated graphic quality is quite attractive. These images would make fine enlargements. It is most important that the paddler's right hand in the large picture is not cut off by the border. An only partially visible hand would have ruined the image. Being aware of such seemingly minor details can make or break a picture.

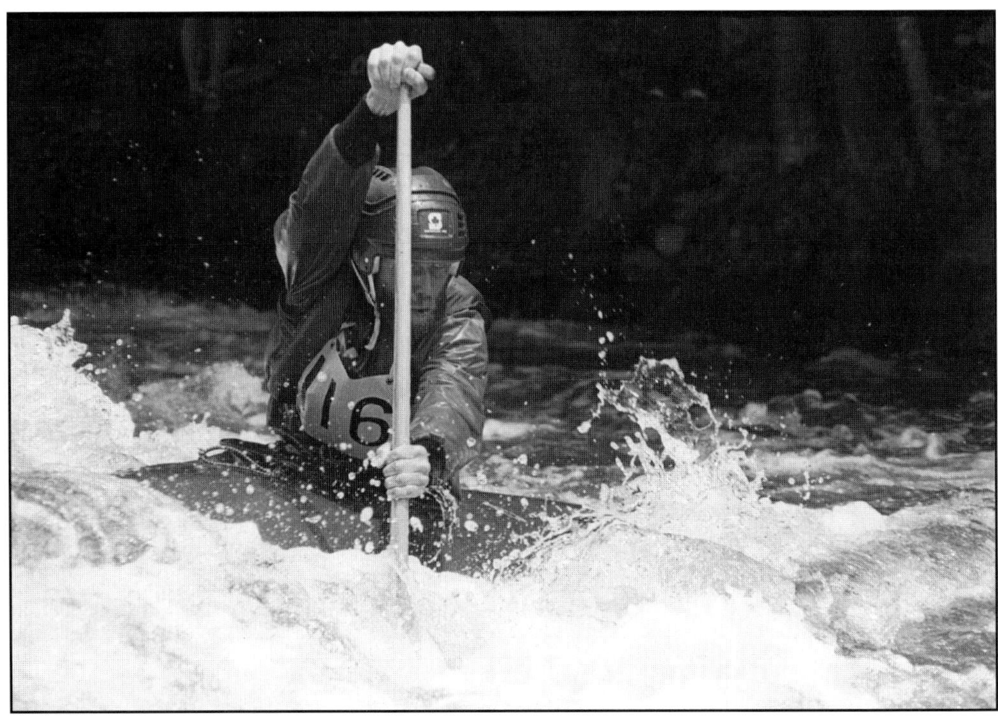

Current—Competition

The story of paddling is, of course, the story of people doing what they like to do best: sitting or kneeling in their watercraft and propelling themselves across the water by their own muscle power.

Whether it is an eight-year-old girl in a kayak doing her best in a slalom competition or an older man in his beautiful self-built wooden open canoe participating in a downriver race, all enjoy the freedom and tremendous feeling of accomplishment that paddling gives them. Paddle sport is a fascinating

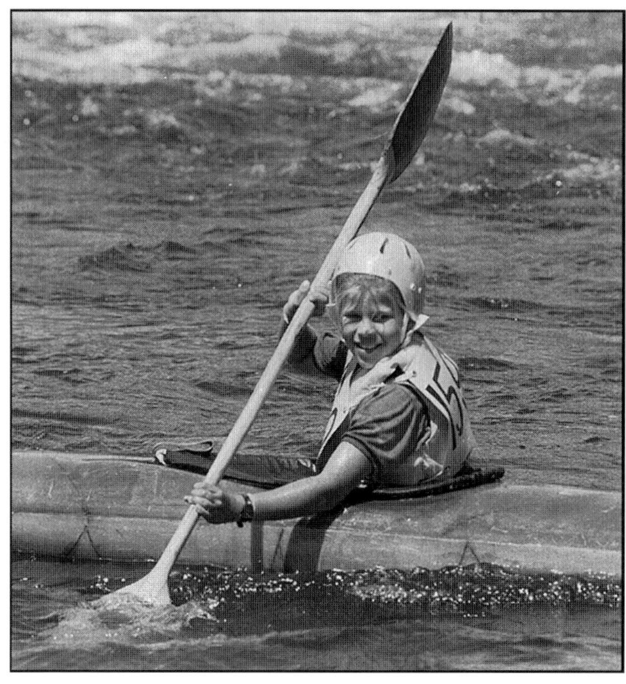

pastime that can be immensely fulfilling. It is also one of the most photogenic of all outdoors sport activities, providing you with countless opportunities for great pictures.

Making a fine collection of portraits of many different whitewater paddlers is but one of those opportunities. The photos do not have to be masterpieces; they can be simple ones like these two, or they can be elaborate pictures with all the bells and whistles of whitewater racing attached. Whatever you choose to do, making portraits will give you a thorough training in seeing and recording fine paddling pictures.

It is important to be careful not to antagonize the people you photograph. Most will be quite pleased to have their pictures taken, and all the more so if you send them a copy of the photograph for their own collection. But there are bound to be some paddlers who do not like to be photographed, especially if they are in what they think are somewhat embarrassing situations, such as swimming behind their recently swamped canoe or having just crashed into the riverbank. Fortunately, most paddlers accept accidents as being part of paddling, and do not object to such photographs.

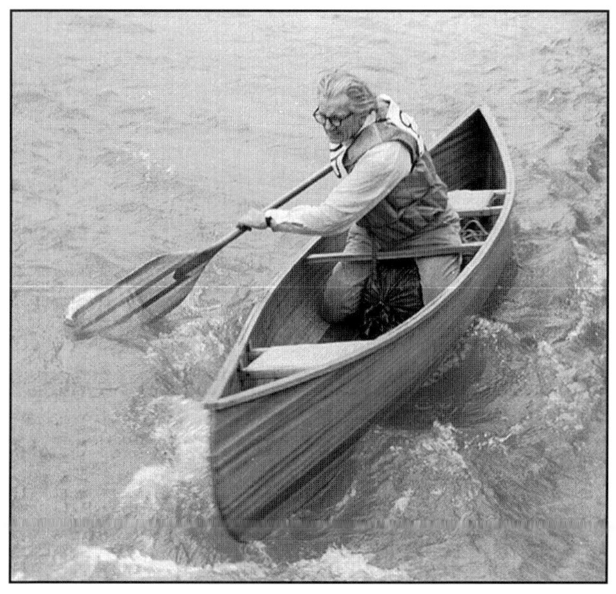

Current—Competition

The obvious lack of sharpness of this photo, not caused by camera movement but by bad focussing, could have been avoided had some simple precautions been taken.

When I abruptly decided to take a picture of the canoe coming down the racecourse, my camera was still in the equipment case hanging from my shoulder. In order to get the shot I wanted of the quickly changing scene, I had to work swiftly. Therefore, in one movement, I opened the carrying case, grabbed the camera, swept it in front of my eye and took the picture, all without proper focussing and accurate framing.

Because the camera was apparently still set at close focus, the picture is not sharp at all and I would have rejected it except for the fact that it is the only shot I have of these two paddlers. To avoid this sharpness problem in situations where you can expect to have to shoot very quickly, keep the camera ready close at hand with the focussing pre-set at the distance you expect the subject to be when you click the shutter. Should you be using an automatic point-and-shoot camera that cannot be adjusted, there is no problem, of course: you just point and shoot.

In general, it is wise to try and make your photographs as sharp as possible. But if for some reason the picture turns out not to be sharp, do not worry too much. Just accept this as a fact of a photographer's life, as long as you know what to do about it in the future. You can learn much by analyzing your less successful pictures.

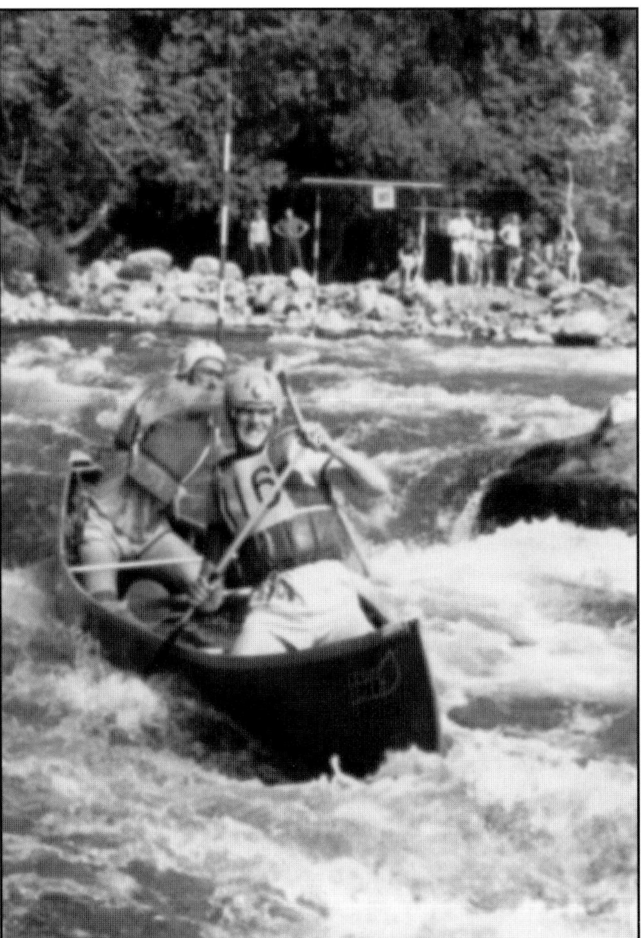

The composition and the vertical framing of this photo are surprisingly good, given the fact that I hardly had time to look through the viewfinder properly. The shoreline in the background is a bit crooked, but the position of the canoe in the picture is fine. The boat nicely fills the wave-filled foreground while coming at the viewer, and the backpaddling person in the bow is clearly shown.

The picture presents an acceptable record of a moment in a slalom race for open canoes, with the main elements well illustrated: river, canoe, spectators on the shore and a gate in the background.

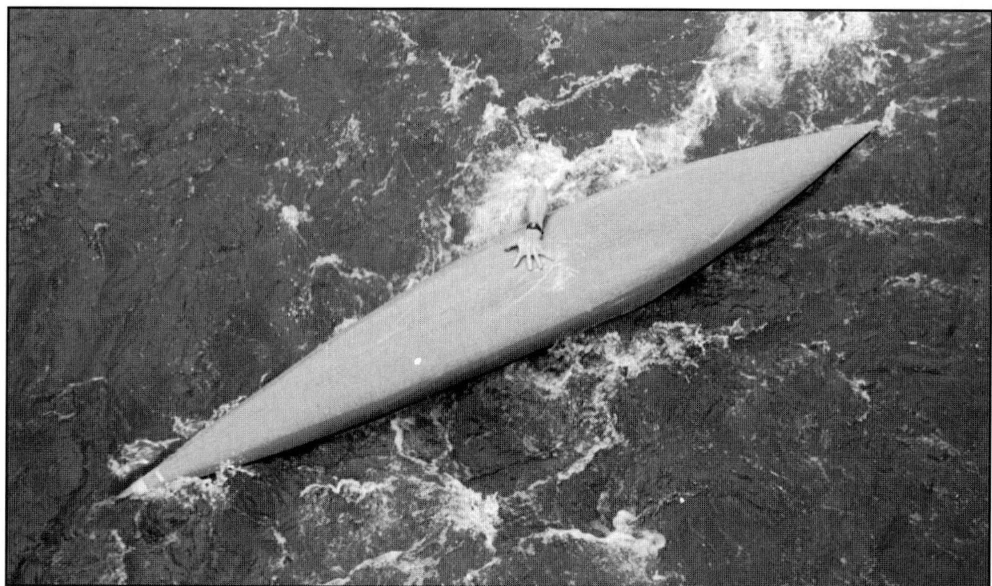

Even more than most other paddling disciplines, whitewater slalom competition sees its fair share of overturned craft, with the occupants in the water after having bailed out, going for a swim. These accidents provide wonderful opportunities for fine action photography; if you can combine it with a touch of humour, all the better.

The charmingly simple picture of the overturned kayak has only three elements: water; craft and hand with spread fingers. This is indeed a hilarious shot, one that would be a sure-fire prizewinner at a photo competition. It tells the whole story of the unhappy kayaker fighting for his dignity after having been unceremoniously swamped. The photograph was made from the same bridge and with the same equipment as the photos on page 93, again proving that once you have found a good location from which to shoot, it is wise to stay there and wait for the images to come floating by for you.

The vertical shot is one of a series of 30 made of this open C2 stuck on a rock near the very bottom of the racecourse. It was having a very difficult time getting free from the obstacle. I had just loaded my camera with a fresh roll of film and was lucky to be standing on a rock jetty a few metres from the boat when it all happened. For ten minutes I was in photographer's heaven!

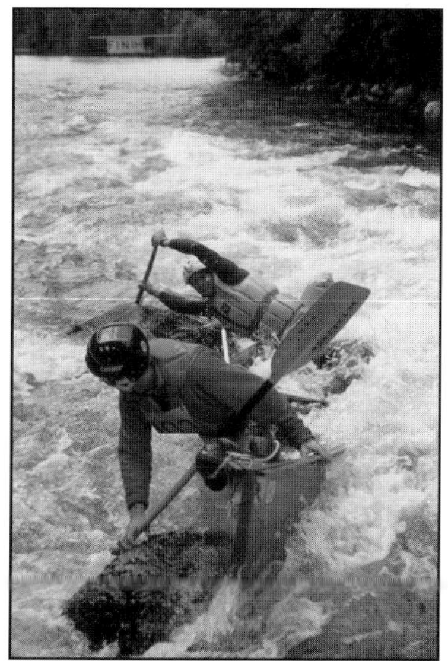

Both these pictures show that you have got to have luck on your side, because these things just cannot be forced to take place. So, be there at the right time, be alert, be prepared; keep your eye and your camera ready at all times. Of course, you need more than luck; you also have to *see* the pictures and frame them correctly, such as the top one where the kayak is set on an appealing diagonal line.

Suddenly the race is over; the tension is gone and you can relax while friends come to congratulate you on a superb penalty-free run. I had observed this playful dog do just that at the end of each run made by this boat, and I could not resist going down to the finish line to record the touching scene. Because it always happened in the same location, I could anticipate the dog's action and shoot the picture at the exact moment the dog and the man were closest to each other, registering the tender intimacy between true friends. I was also careful to completely include the bow paddler and not cut him off through the head or so, because he is very much part of the scene. I love this picture; it feels good to see such positive interplay between animal and man.

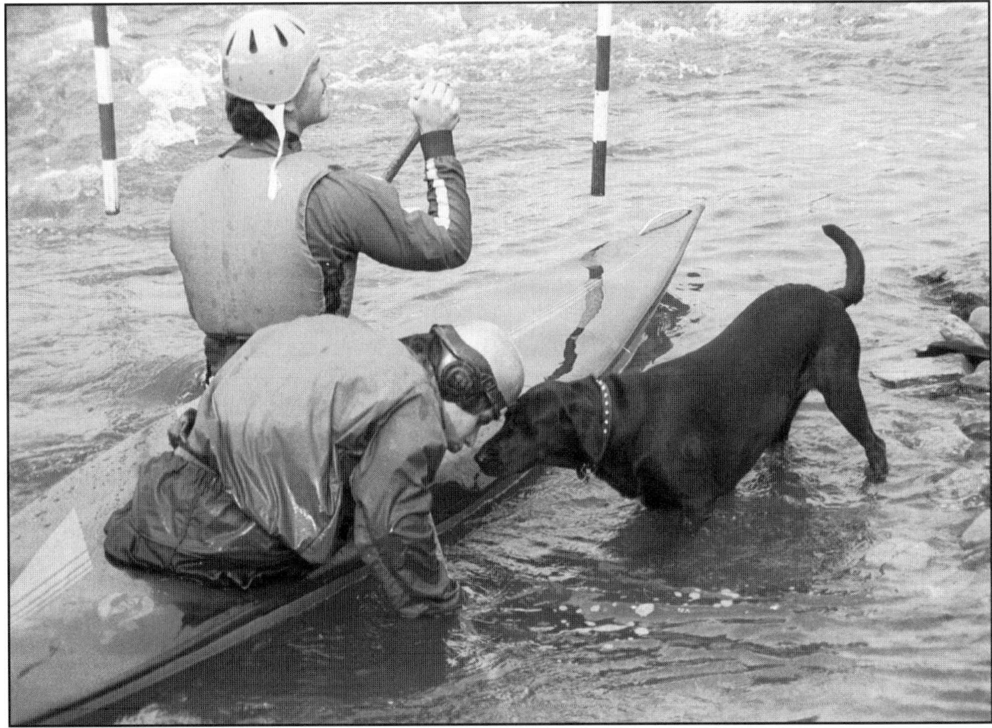

As much as making photographs at whitewater slalom competitions can be an absorbing hobby, it comes with a rarely realized danger. When you are concentrating on photographing a paddler and running around from place to place, trying to find the best spot from which to shoot, it is quite easy to loose your footing on the numerous rocks lining the river racecourse. Furthermore, these rocks are quite often wet and therefore slippery, making it extra dangerous. Running over them is not only risky for your physical well-being, but you could easily drop your camera on the hard rocks or maybe even in the water, thoroughly ruining it. So be extra careful in these circumstances. Wear flexible, non-slip shoes, and keep your camera in a shockproof carrying case with a wide shoulder strap when you are moving around. Maybe even ask an assistant to help you carry the more unwieldy equipment such as the tripod and extra lenses. Study the banks of the racecourse beforehand and remember where the most dangerous and tricky obstacles are located. A damaged camera or a damaged photographer are of no value to anyone.

RAFTING

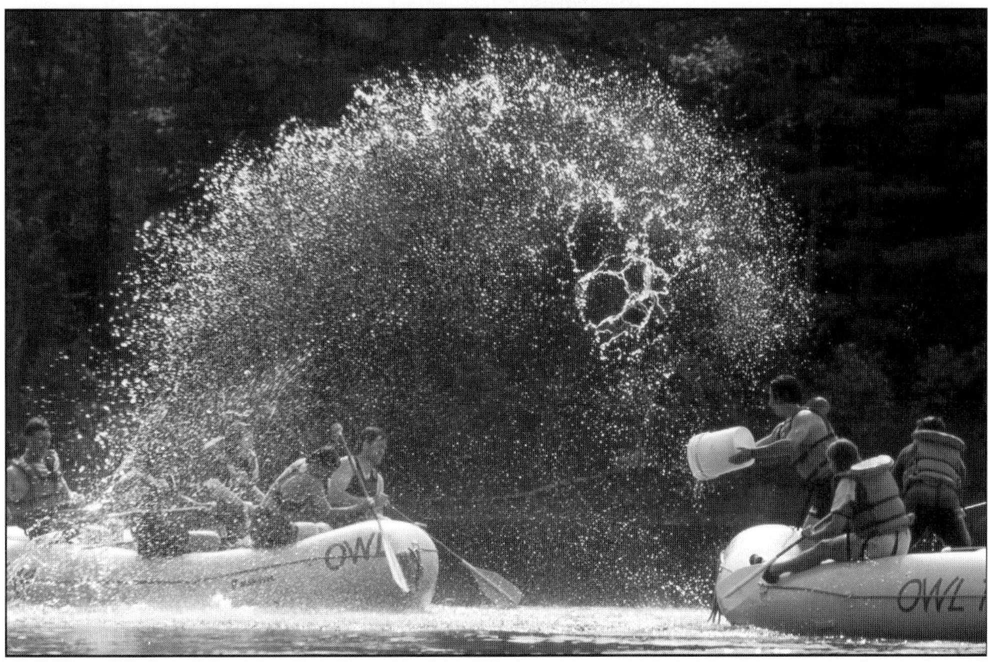

Maybe more than the other paddling disciplines, rafting is synonymous with having outrageous wild fun. While you are getting the ride of your life with jets of adrenaline rushing through your body, the rapids may nearly scare the pants off you. When you are a member of the crew of a modern inflatable raft, you can run rapids and falls, or take trips down wilderness rivers that would be lethal when tried in regular canoes or even most kayaks. By staying within your capabilities and being protected by a life jacket and helmet, you can safely run big whitewater, even if you have never paddled before.

Rafting photography is primarily focussed on recording this fast-moving action and can therefore be difficult to perform. When you are sitting in a raft going down a wave-choked rapid, you and your equipment are not only exposed to an unpredictable deluge of water, but also to constant movement that makes it impossible to hold your camera steady. But, like so much action photography, rafting photography can also be most rewarding. One should be prepared to learn from experience as to when and where things are going to happen, when the best moment will be to shoot.

Although made in calm water, this photograph is also full of action, the activities of several people throwing water at each other out of sheer childlike exuberance, possibly to release the tension after having run some heart-stopping rapids. The centre of interest is the beautifully curved stream of drops suspended like a halo over both rafts. The background is dark, which shows off the water arc well. To 'freeze' the spray, I used a short exposure time of 1/1000th of a second with IS0 100 slide film. There is nothing to distract from the main action; all people in the photo look towards the centre, and everything is taking place within the confines of the picture frame.

Current—Rafting

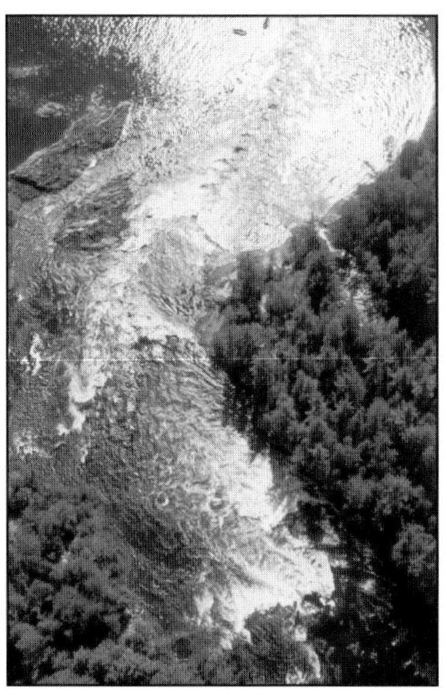

Because rafting takes place for the most part in whitewater, it is essential to be as informed as possible about the nature of the rapids you are going to run. Even familiar rivers show markedly different wave patterns depending upon water level. Scouting the river is therefore one of the crucial safety measures of river running.

An excellent way to study and photograph the layout of the river is from a low-flying airplane. Try to get a ride in a high-wing one, or maybe even a helicopter, where the pilot permits you to open the window on your side so you are not hindered by optical distortions caused by the plastic window pane. Aerial photography is a specialized discipline that can be very demanding, but even with rather simple equipment you can make acceptable photos for your collection. Do not let the camera or your arms touch the airplane, allowing the camera to be as free from vibrations as possible. Using high-speed film may enable you to shoot at short exposure times, which may compensate to some extent for the movements of the plane.

Also check out the situation at ground level. The bottom photo is a typical record shot without many photographic merits. It is crowded, the people on the right are cut off, the horizon is slightly crooked and, regrettably, there are no rafts going down the waves. But it serves its purpose as an overview of the whitewater scene.

Like all other photographs in this rafting section, these two were made at the famous stretch of rapids in the Ottawa River near Beachburg.

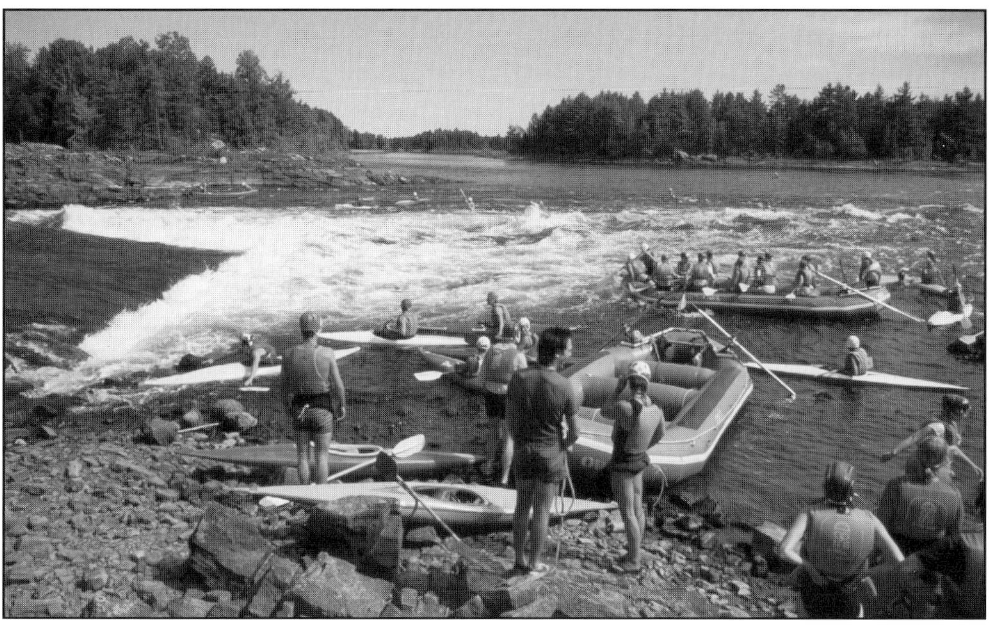

Current—Rafting

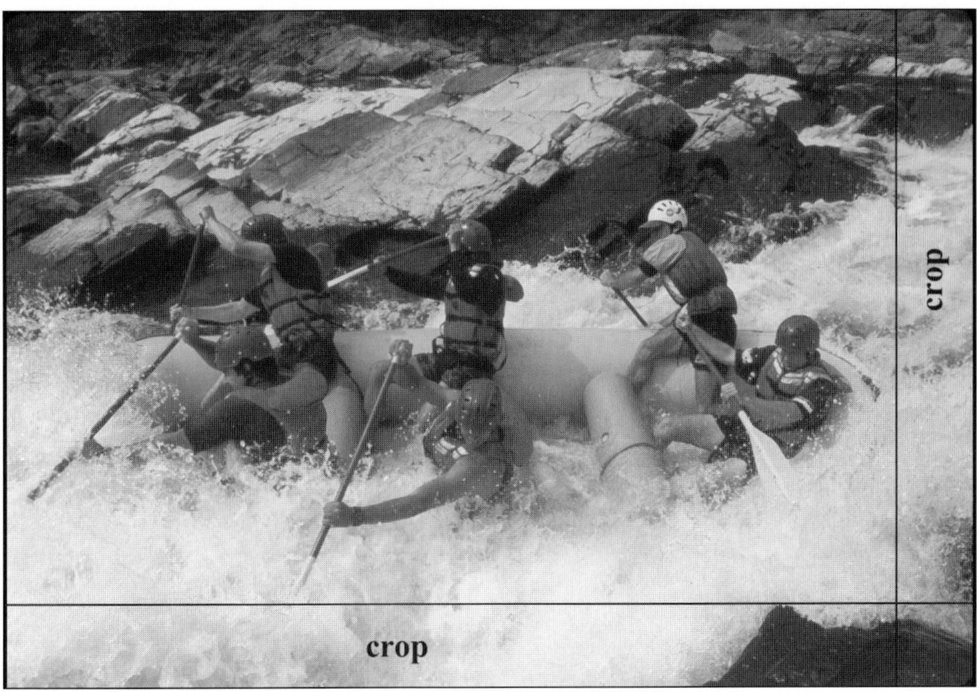

If you are on shore and get an opportunity to be close to a raft when it goes down a narrow channel, for instance, grab your camera and go there immediately. Try to find a shooting position somewhat above the water level. This is your chance to show what really happens in the raft as it speeds down the waves, partially filling with water and threatening to throw its occupants overboard.

Although this scene looks chaotic, everything is, in fact, under perfect control. You are the lucky one to record it! But you have to be prepared, standing in the right spot with camera ready to make photographs quickly because it is all over in a second. Pre-focus on the exact spot you want to shoot the passing raft, and select the correct field of view if you are using a zoom lens. It is always good to make a series of photographs of an exciting scene like this.

With all that water rapidly filling the raft, it looks as if these six paddlers are bound for disaster, but actually they are in no danger. Many modern rafts are self-bailing, so the water will drain out quickly. An interesting visual element is the contrast between the foamy water and the smooth hard Canadian Shield basalt rocks in the background. Notice the guy in the stern 'playing it safe' by sitting on the floor.

The photograph printed above can be improved considerably by some judicious cropping. If you cover the areas marked 'crop' with some pieces of white paper, you will see the important difference this makes. The obnoxious black rock at bottom-right disappears as does a piece of whitewater on the right-hand side. The photo is now much more balanced and concentrated around the raft, without that distracting element at the bottom. Cropping is a fine tool and should be used often. Ideally, you should do the cropping 'in the camera' when you are looking through the viewfinder, but this is not always feasible when everything is happening so rapidly.

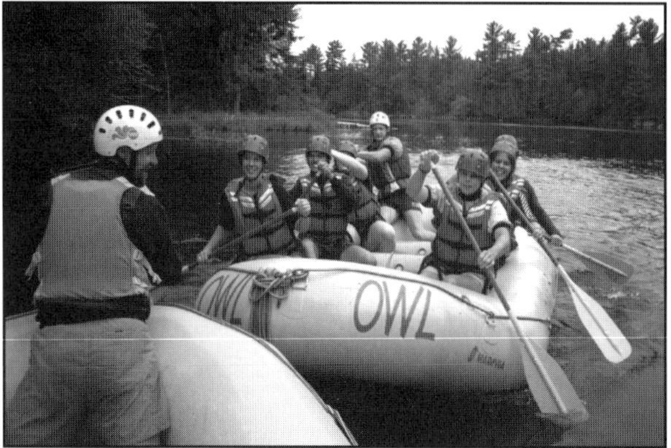

Do not dismiss these five photos just because they are crooked, badly composed, off-centre, unevenly exposed and generally not great from a purely photographic point of view. True, but if these pictures are all you have of this fascinating event, they should be invaluable to you. The important aspect of these shots is that they tell a little story, with a beginning, middle and end, like all good stories. It is the story of a raft going down a sharp drop while being preceded by a backwards-going raft carrying noted sports photographer, Henri Georgi. He is leaning over the upstream-pointing bow, trying to photograph the people in the following raft while it is moving in the big waves of the rapid. Maybe not much of a story if you just read it, but quite a big deal if you are also sitting in that leading raft, attempting to make a meaningful photographic record of what is happening in both rafts at the same time.

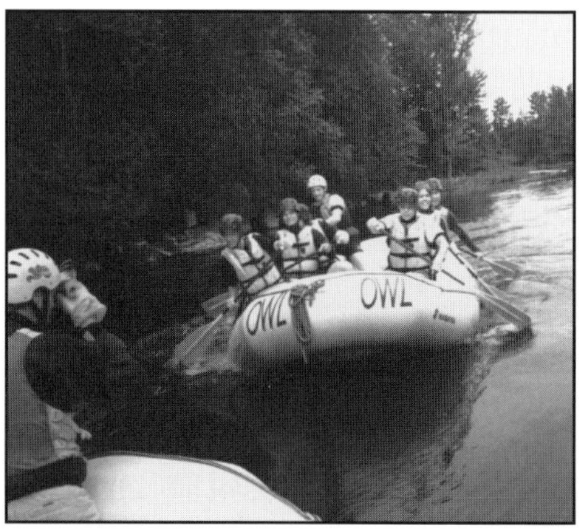

While we were rushing down this rapid, I was hanging on for dear life, with my left hand grabbing the tube-frame of our violently bouncing leading raft. In my right hand, stretched out high over my head, I clutched a small waterproof automatic point-and-shoot camera loaded with high-speed print film, trying to photograph Henri doing his job while also keeping the second raft in the picture. I could, of course, not look through the viewfinder and had to aim the camera as best I could in the direction of the sub-jects. That this would result in severely crooked shots was most likely. Indeed it did.

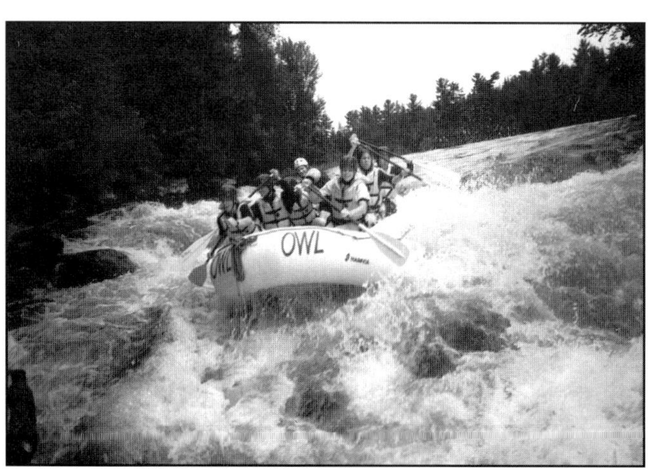

Of the 12 photos taken in the few seconds the run lasted, I selected these five to tell the story. The first one opens the account by showing all players in a properly horizontal shot. But then, as the rafts go down the chute, everything

Current—Rafting

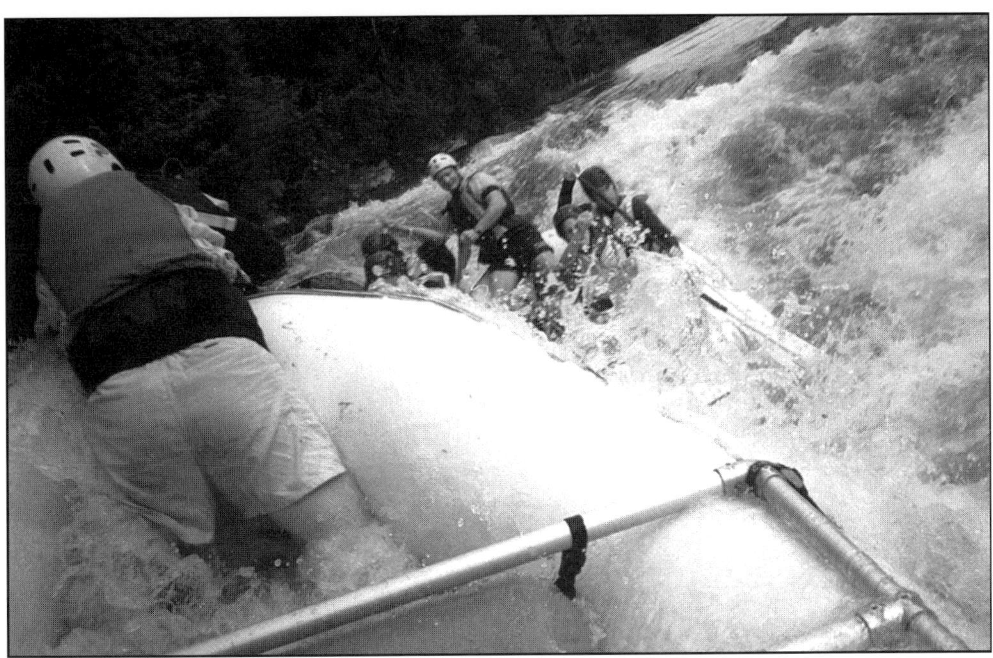

starts to move and I have to take the camera away from my eye. Photos two, three and four form the main body of the story, showing what is happening; the crucial shot, of course, being number four where Henri is standing knee-deep in the water-filled leading raft and the second one is diving in the waves. The final shot shows the satisfied photographer as well as his waterproofed motorized camera, ending the story on a positive note.

Obviously, this is not the greatest of reportages, but if you succeed in getting a sequence like this, shot under very difficult conditions, you have done a good job. Better to have technically bad shots than no shots at all. Photograph mainly for your own satisfaction.

By doing such action sequences a number of times, you build up experience in pointing the camera in the correct direction without having to look through the viewfinder. But do not neglect the safety aspects of this work. Wear a life jacket and a helmet, and hold on tight to your seat. You, the photographer, should not fall out of the raft, let the others do it!

Always attach the camera to your body by means of a strap or a piece of string, so you do not lose the camera should it slip from your wet hand. Far too many of them are resting on river bottoms.

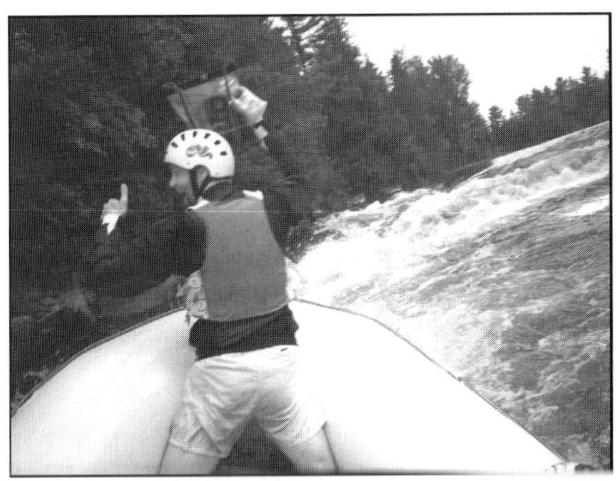

Current—Rafting

Rafting in really big water is an absolutely exhilarating experience, even when viewed from a distance. The wildly bouncing raft, sliding down a slope of raging water with clouds of spray flying over it, seems about to disappear between gigantic waves. Such images are a delight to look at, and a dedicated photographer should find many great opportunities to record superb pictures in whitewater rafting.

I had set out to take some photographs showing the raft surrounded by a sea of waves, attempting to invoke a strong sense of danger—that the crowded raft could sink into the unforgiving waters if the control over its movements were somehow lost. I therefore climbed a 10-metre-high platform on the side of the river and used a 75-300 mm zoom lens with the camera mounted on a tripod. By deliberately selecting a vertical image and placing the centre of interest, the raft, approximately in the correct one-third position according to the rule of thirds, I succeeded in demonstrating the wonderful interplay between river and raft. You can see how these boats can run roller-coaster waves through amazingly heavy water. But never take the river for granted; things can go wrong in an instant. The waves can turn the raft upside down without any warning.

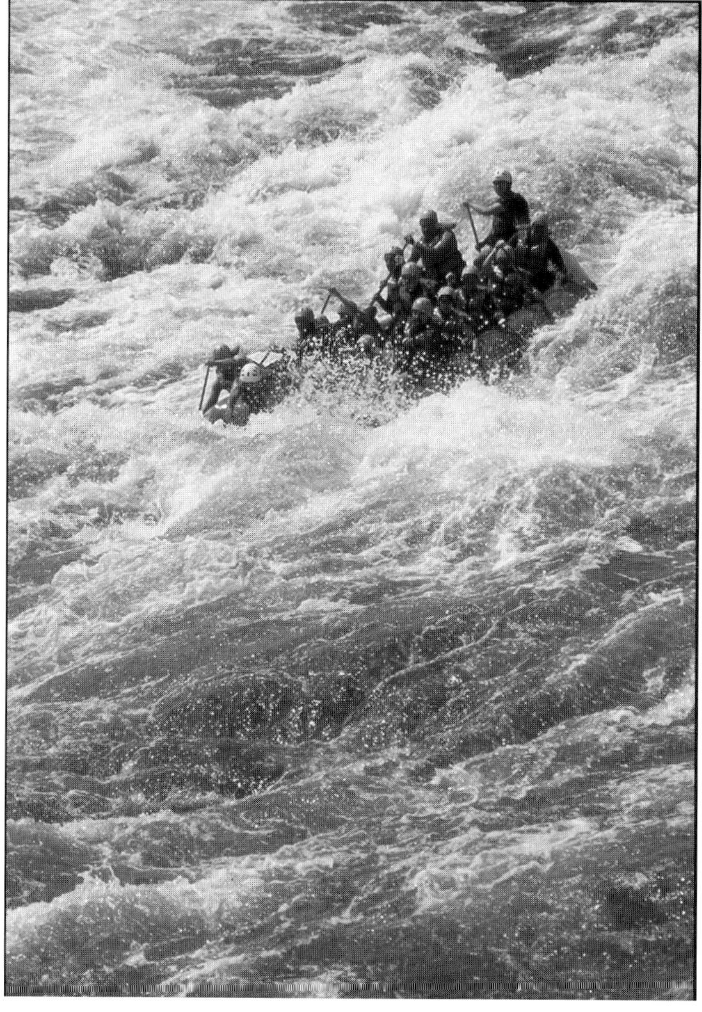

Current—Rafting

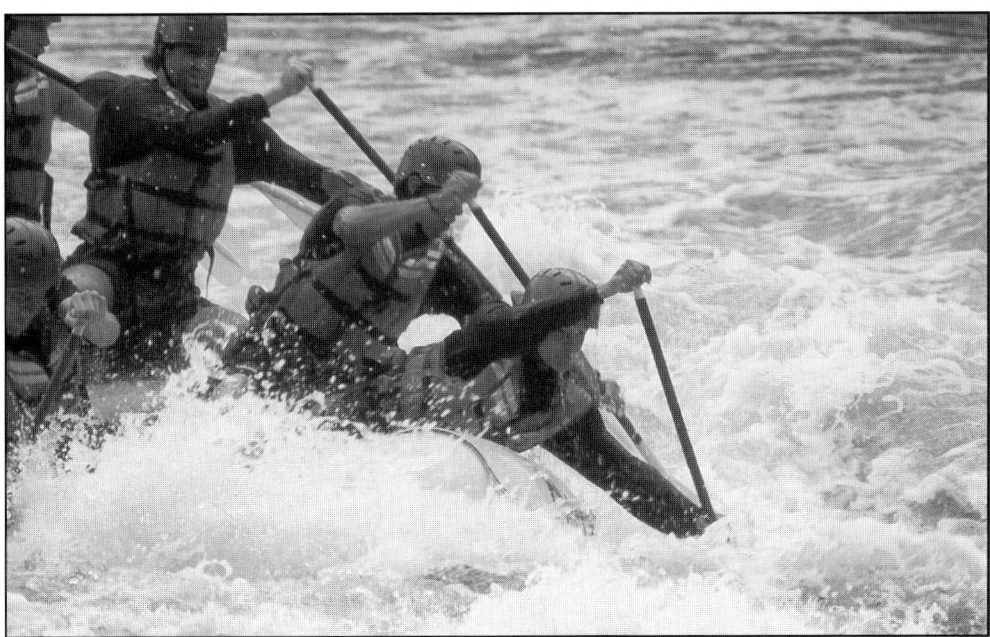

An interesting challenge is to try and make photos that are not just record shots (no matter how important these may be) but rather have a more artistic flavour where content is less significant than style and where the image conveys something timeless; something that has beautiful lines, enchanting angles, unexpected views, mesmerizing light, a special feeling—all expressed in a way that touches the heart. These images become something to have enlarged and hang on your wall, providing enjoyment to viewers for their own aesthetic reasons.

You could attempt this by simply shooting a number of photos, more or less indiscriminately. Then, do the selecting at home, and afterwards you may discover that you have produced a few masterpieces (happens all the time in the world of photography). Or you may want to be really creative instead and try to photograph a specific image that you see happening on the water—or in your mind's eye—and that struck you as special. This is far more difficult but much more satisfying.

Although this photo is by no means a great work of art, it demonstrates a few features that set it apart from many other paddling photos. I particularly like the fluid motion of the four arms holding their paddles and descending smoothly into the foaming waves. It gives me a feeling of a choreographed ballet, a graceful dance performed by armoured warriors 'conquering' the churning waves. Many of such 'water-ballet' photos are there for you to discover; just go out and learn to really *see* them.

It is, of course, always necessary to remain critical, especially of the shots that have a cherished place in your heart. In this photo I am not too happy with the partially cut-off heads of the two top-left paddlers. But it is more important that their faces are still in the photo, including the face of the paddler lower down on the left side. Whether you find or create them, trying to make artistic photographs will enrich the creative side of you. Hunting for such photographs is endlessly fascinating.

Current—Rafting

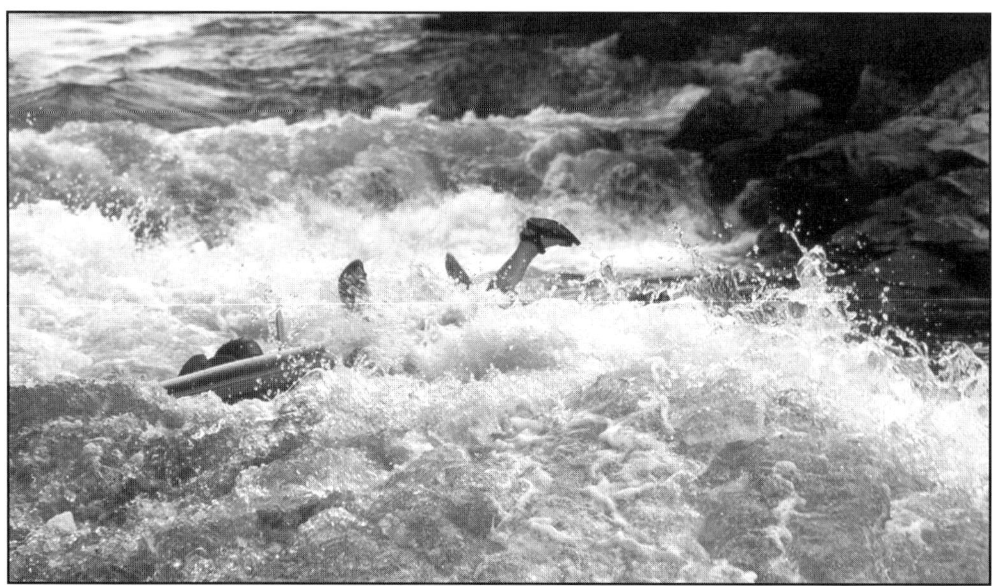

When I saw the inflatable kayak, the little sister of the raft, go down the short but rough drop, I sensed trouble coming and prepared to shoot whatever might happen next. I was rewarded with this hilarious shot of a sandal-clad foot sticking out of the water, which again shows that interesting photographs are there for the taking, if you just keep your eyes open and the camera ready.

In whitewater rafting, accidents such as falling out of the raft and having to swim are not only inevitable but also a big part of the sport's attraction. You, the photographer, can also suddenly be thrown out of the raft by its violent and unpredictable movements. Of course, this will be when it is least convenient, right at the time the camera is in front of your face and you need one or two hands to hold it there. In most cases, there is no real danger when you fall out of a raft, provided you are wearing proper safety equipment. But be sure you know how to swim when clutching a (waterproof!) camera. It is best to have the camera attached to you by a short strap.

When accidents happen, your first reaction may be to try to help the unfortunate paddlers get safely to shore or back into the raft. In some cases, your help may indeed be needed, but otherwise your first priority should be to make photographs of the event. Later you can show the swimmers how much fun they, in fact, had and how safe this sport really is, in spite of the ferocious water

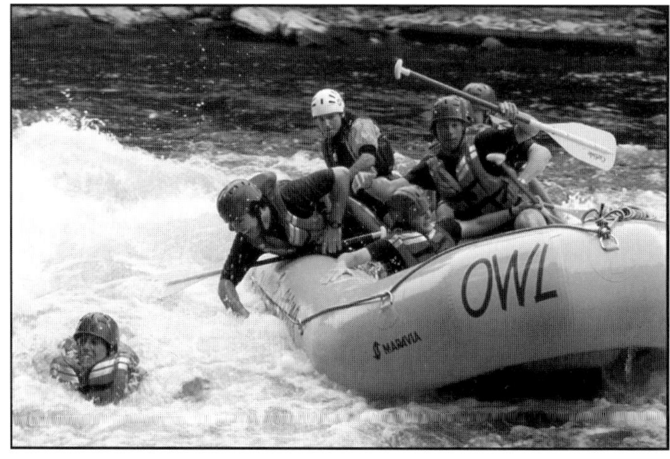

Current—Rafting

This raft flipped over in a split second and, although I had my camera ready, I missed the actual mishap because of not paying enough attention. But I kept on shooting anyway and recorded the efforts of the raft personnel to rescue each other (and the paddles, if at all possible); a rescue quickly pulled off without any casualties. If you have made a series of shots of an event such a this one, but have space in your album or presentation for only one shot to tell more or less the whole story, select a representative one with lots of action and with all or most of the people involved. Consider this photograph: all nine rafters are there, seven of them in the water and one on top of the overturned raft trying to help a buddy get up on top too. One shot instead of a series to tell the story is a compromise, but it can still do a fine job.

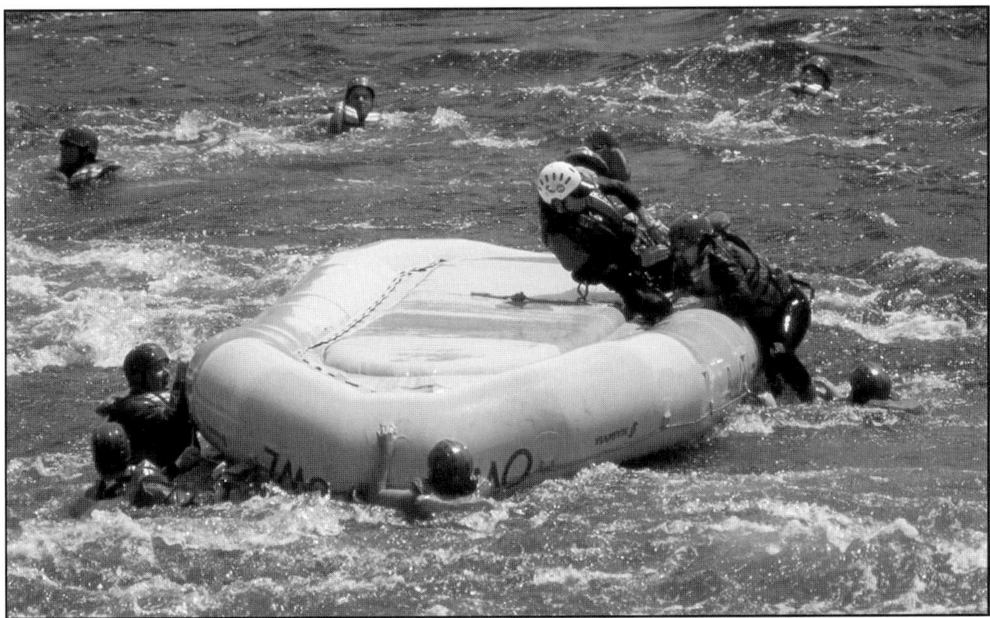

Whitewater rafting is by its very nature a team sport where excited groups of likeminded thrill-seekers occupy oddly shaped pumped-up vessels that have very little in common with the venerated and often breathtakingly beautiful canoe. There is little elegance and magic displayed by a raft riding the big waters. Instead, all is sudden movement, a wild and powerful crashing through mighty waves, generating huge curtains of water drops. The wilder and higher the waves, the better. No wonder so many people start yelling excitedly when running rapids in this watercraft.

Because of the special nature of the raft, a photographer is somewhat restricted in the kind of photographs that can be made with the raft as the centre of interest. Its admittedly unglamorous lines make it hard to imagine a raft being used as a prop in a tender photograph about a sunset in the wilderness, or a fog-shrouded rainy day. But for action shots of group activities in fabulously rough wildwater, the raft is the right subject for you. Get yourself a waterproof camera, secure it to your person, climb in the raft and let the waves come where and when and how they may. There are superb photographs to be made in this bucking water bronco. Take the challenge and go for it.

Current—Rafting

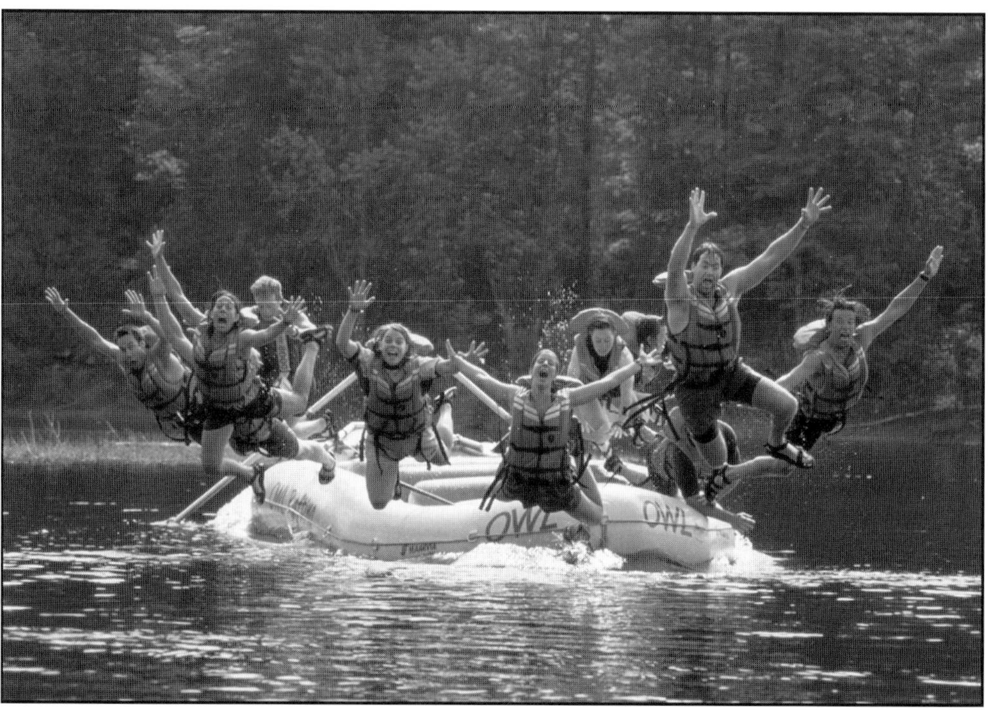

This photo was made in the same location as the one opening this section, showing again how much exhilarating innocent fun the challenging sport of whitewater rafting can be. All participants in this shot were standing on the rim of the raft and, in response to a signal, jumped forward into the water, screaming their lungs out and creating a fine picture in the process. This is an excellent well-thought-out photograph. The background is quite dark and without too many details, allowing the paddlers to stand out clearly against it. There are no hands or paddles or pieces of the raft sticking out of the photo, everything stays in. It is 'complete.' The shot is made at the very peak of motion; almost everybody is looking at the camera, giving the viewer a feeling of direct involvement with the action. Originally, the photo was made in colour and, although above black-and- white reproduction is quite effective, the colour print shown on the next page is obviously much livelier.

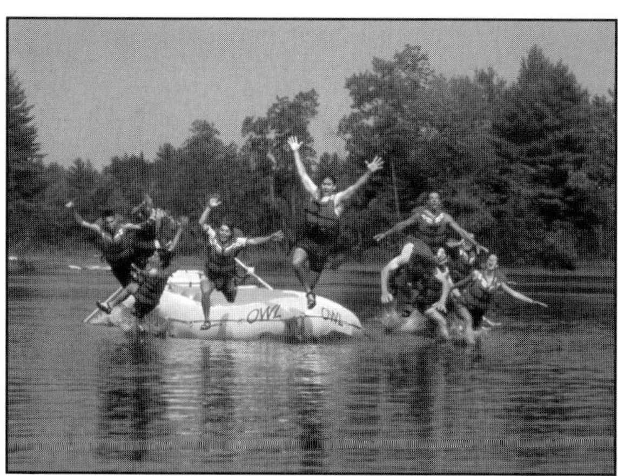

To illustrate the importance of a good background in photography, the same action was shot against another, less uniform background. Note how the light sky distracts the viewers' attention away from the central action. Also, not all the people are 'frozen' at the peak of their jump, making the group less cohesive. This is, without a doubt, a far less interesting photograph.

COLOUR

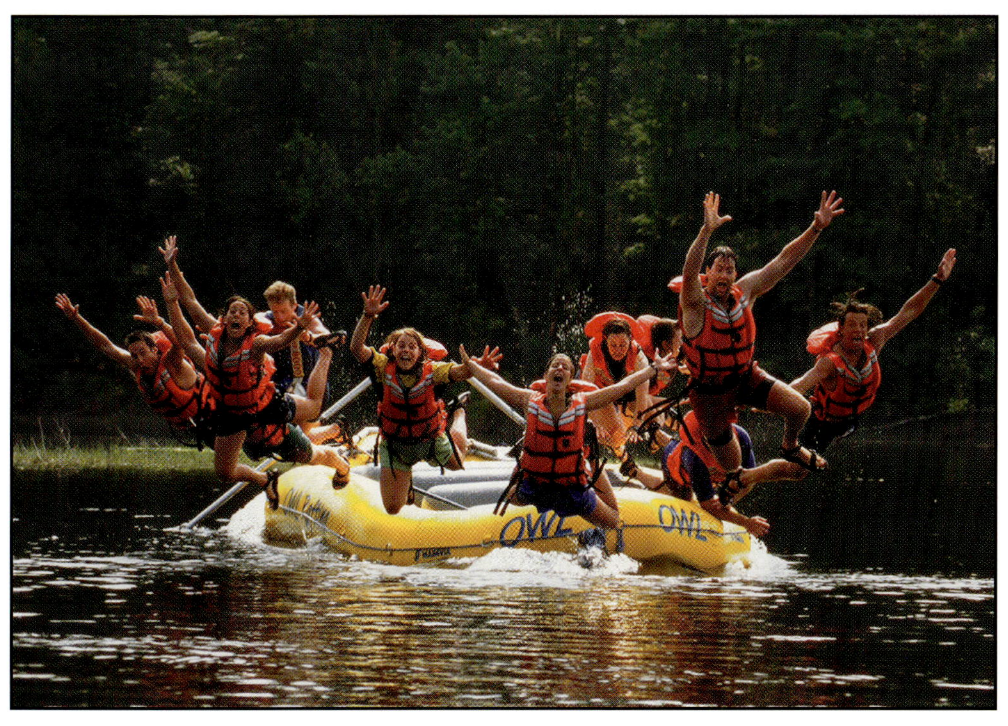

plate 1

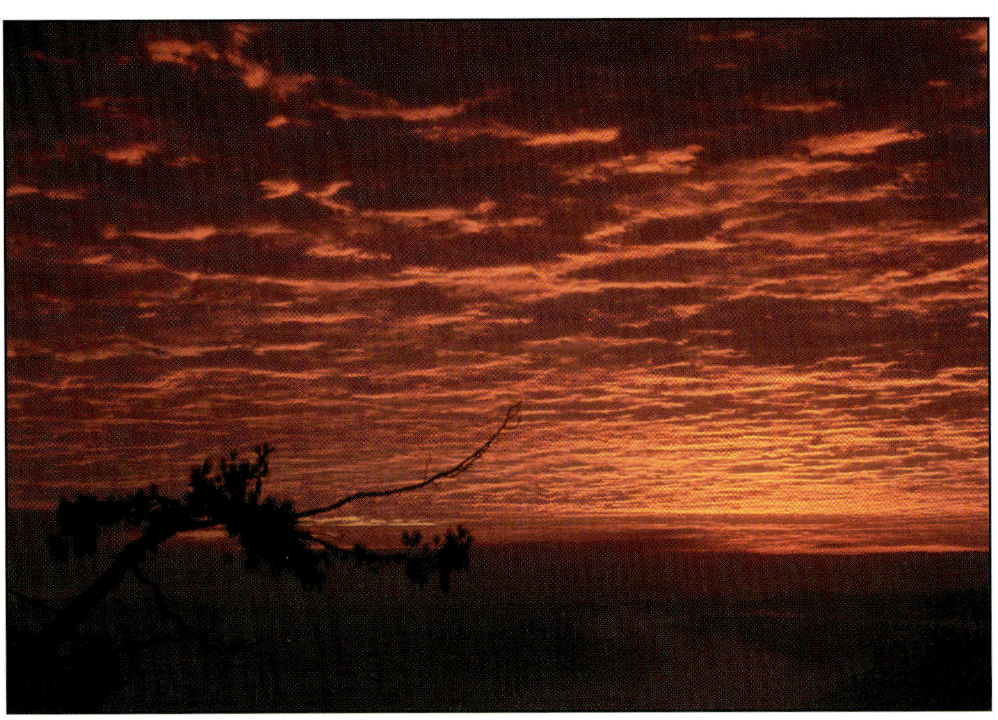

plate 2

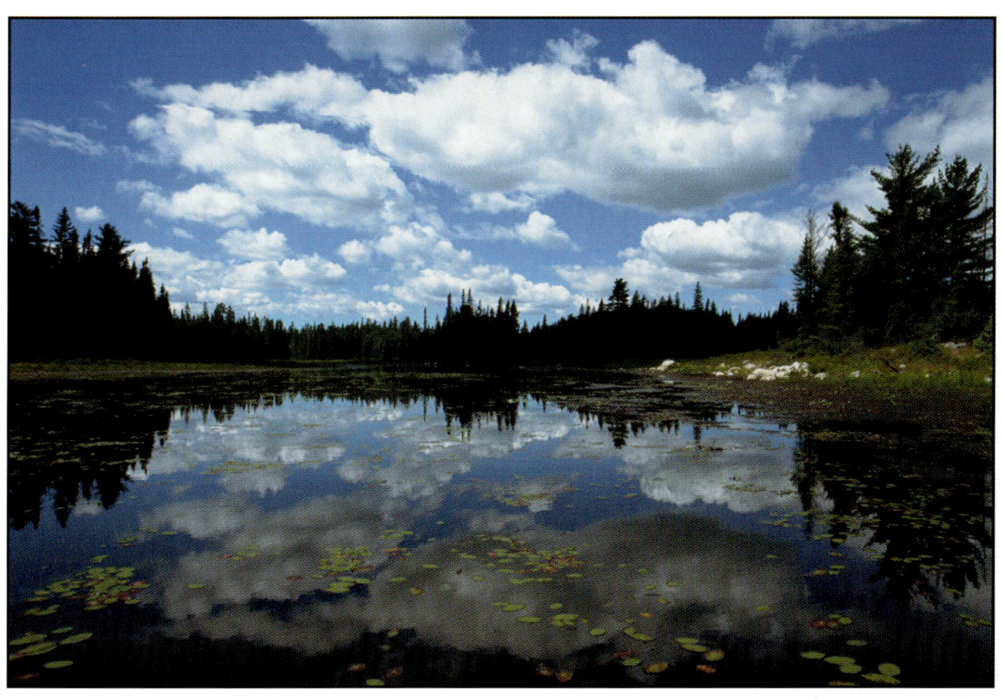

plate 3

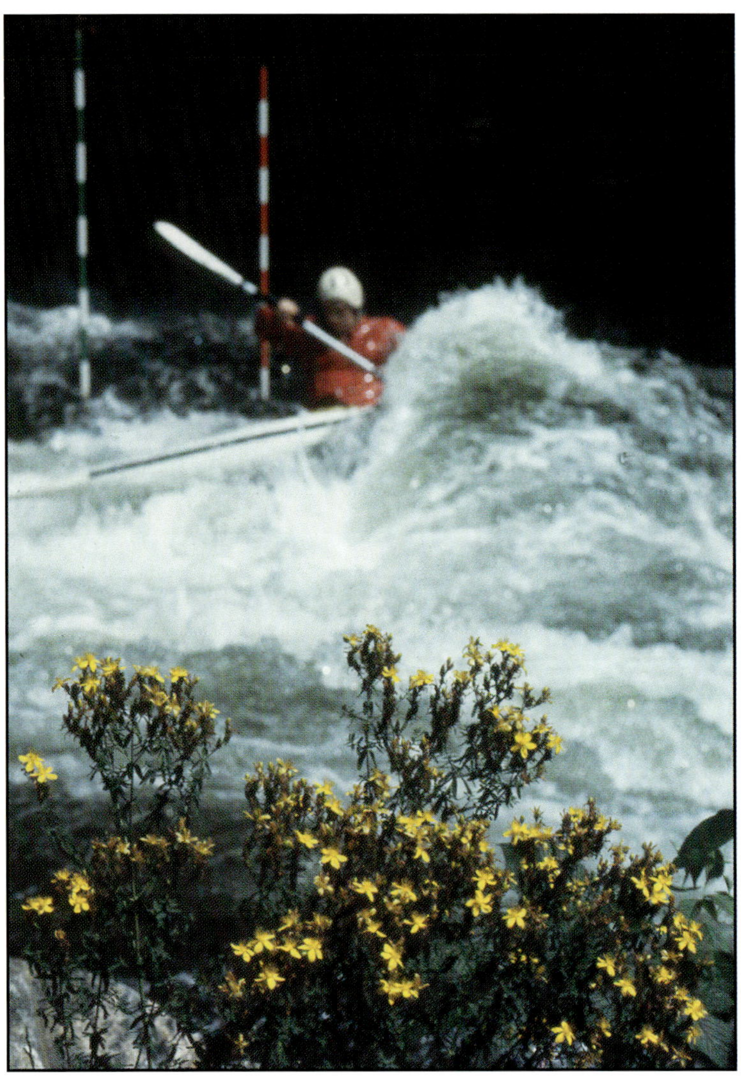

plate 1

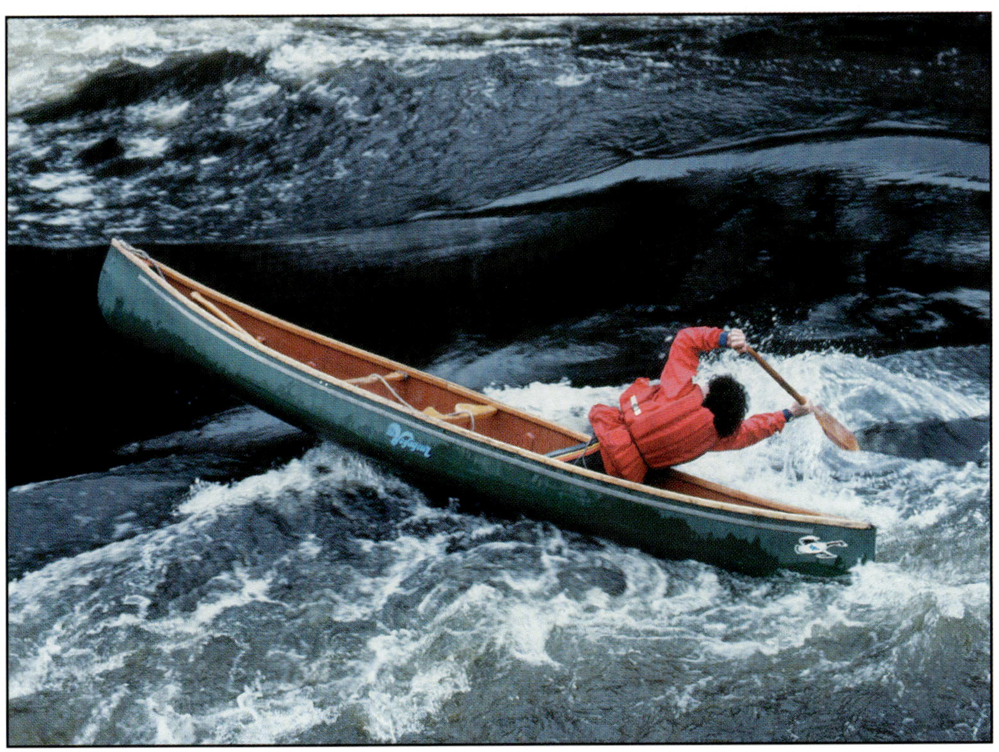

plate 5

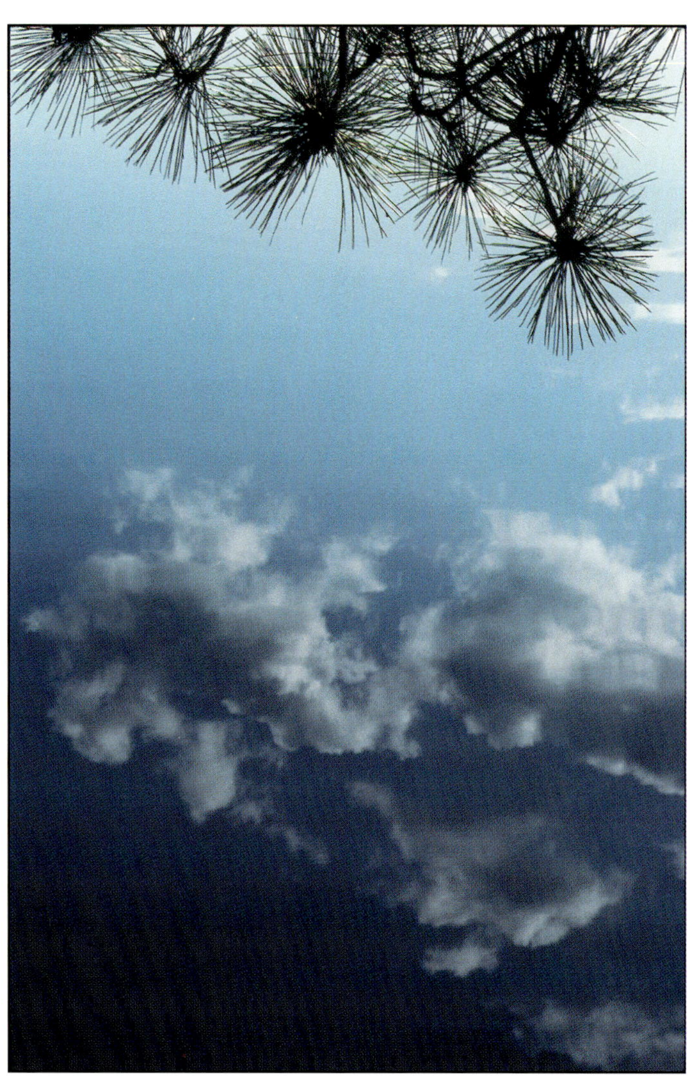

plate 6

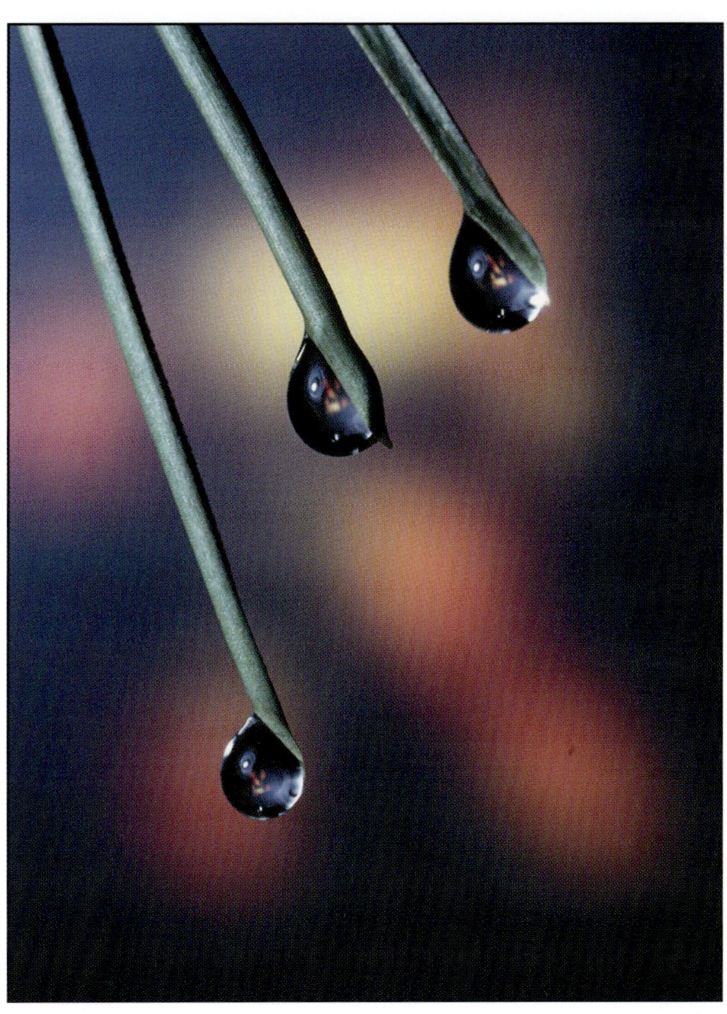

plate 7

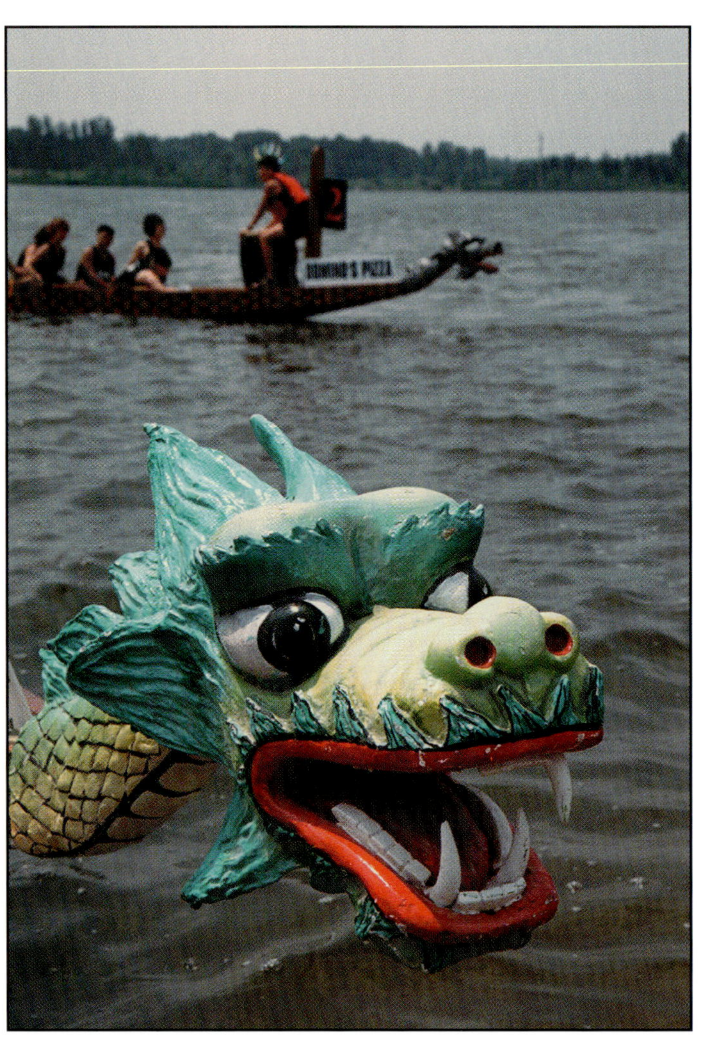

plate 8

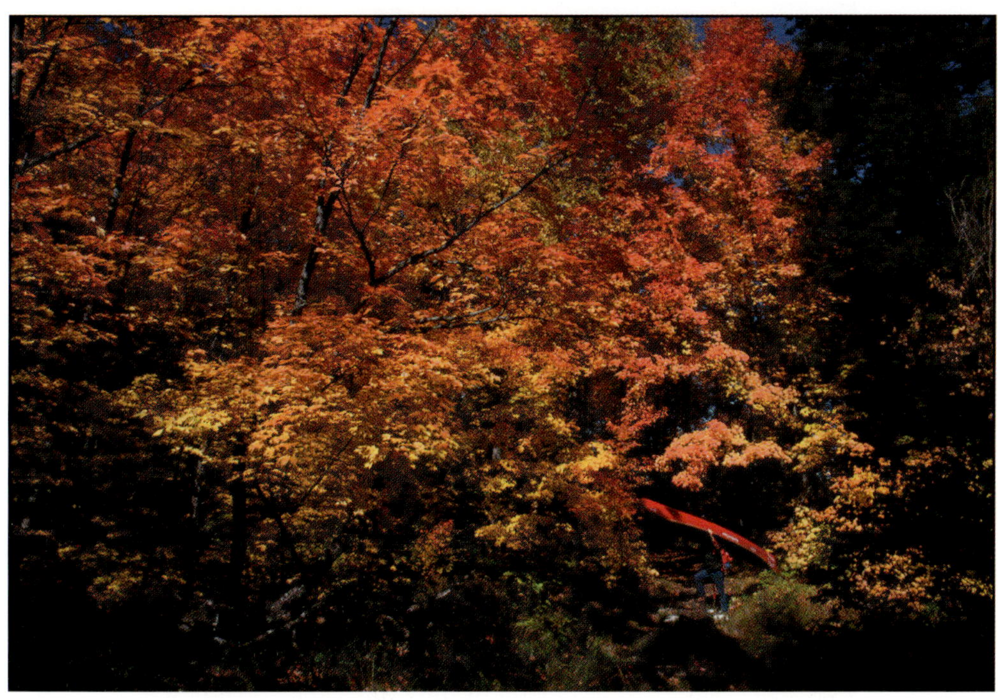

plate 9

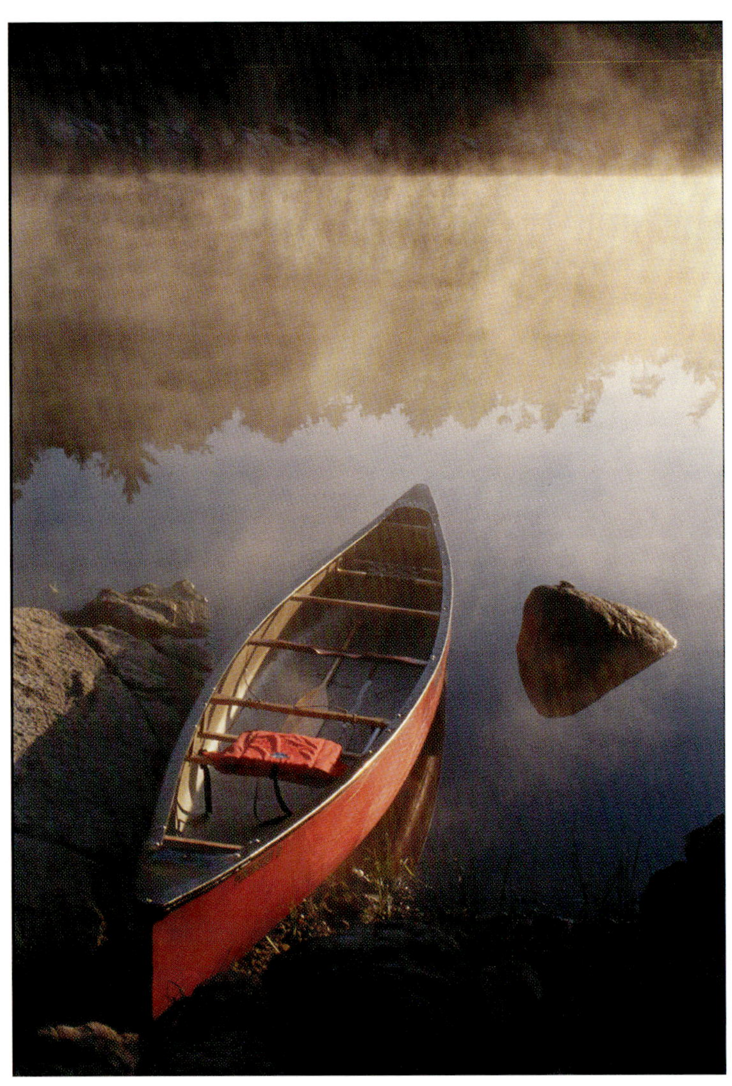

plate 10

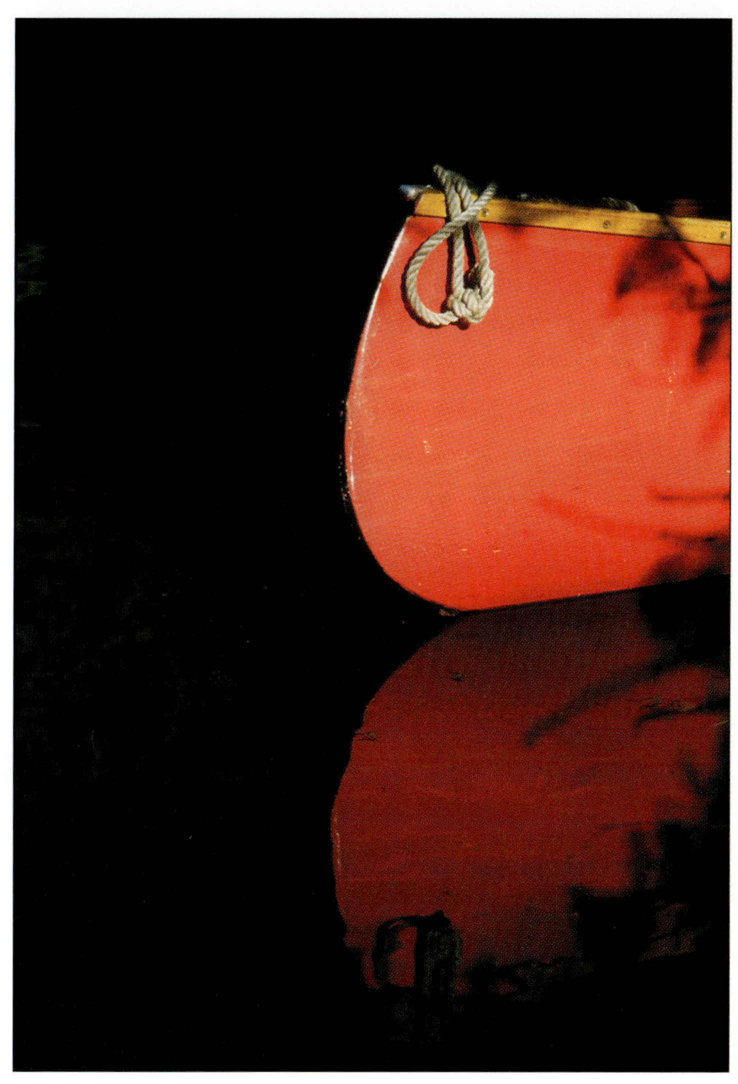

plate 11

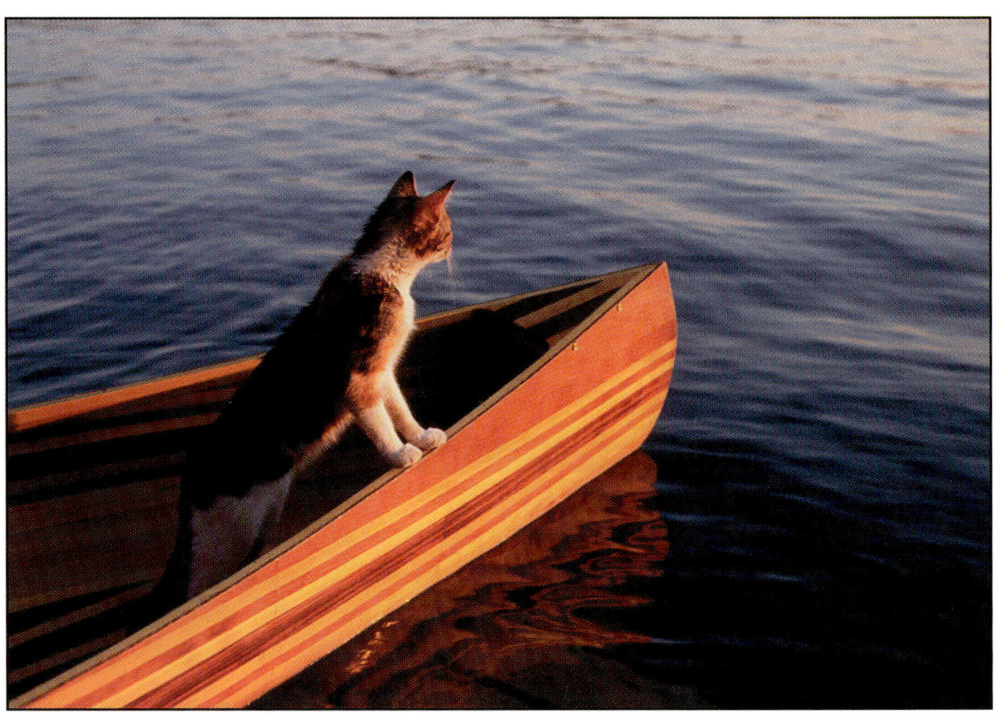

plate 12

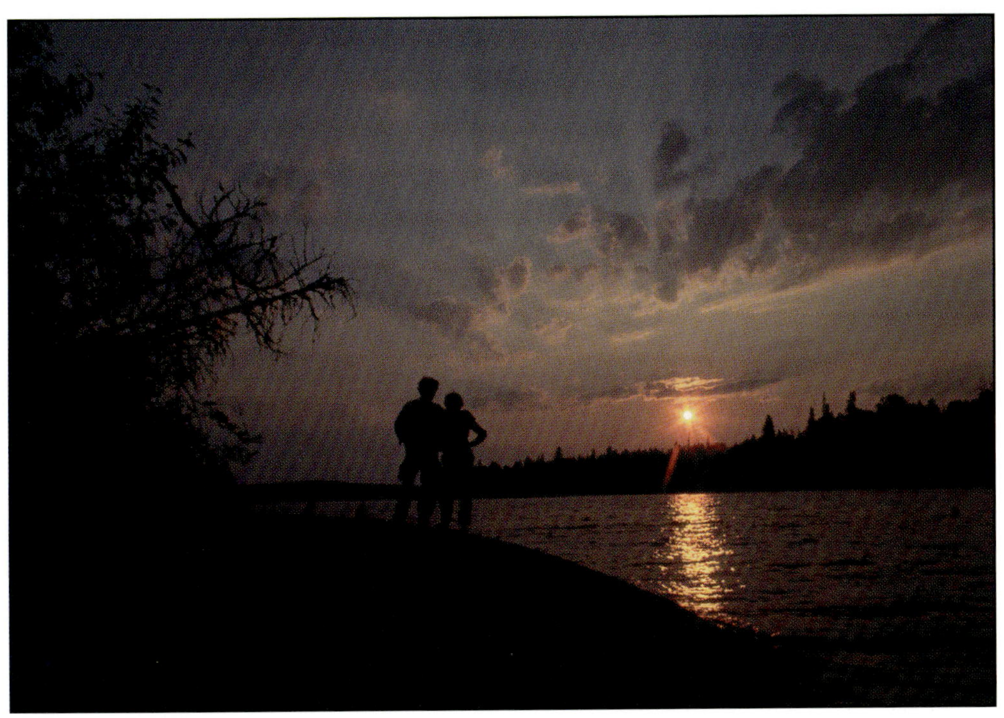

plate 13

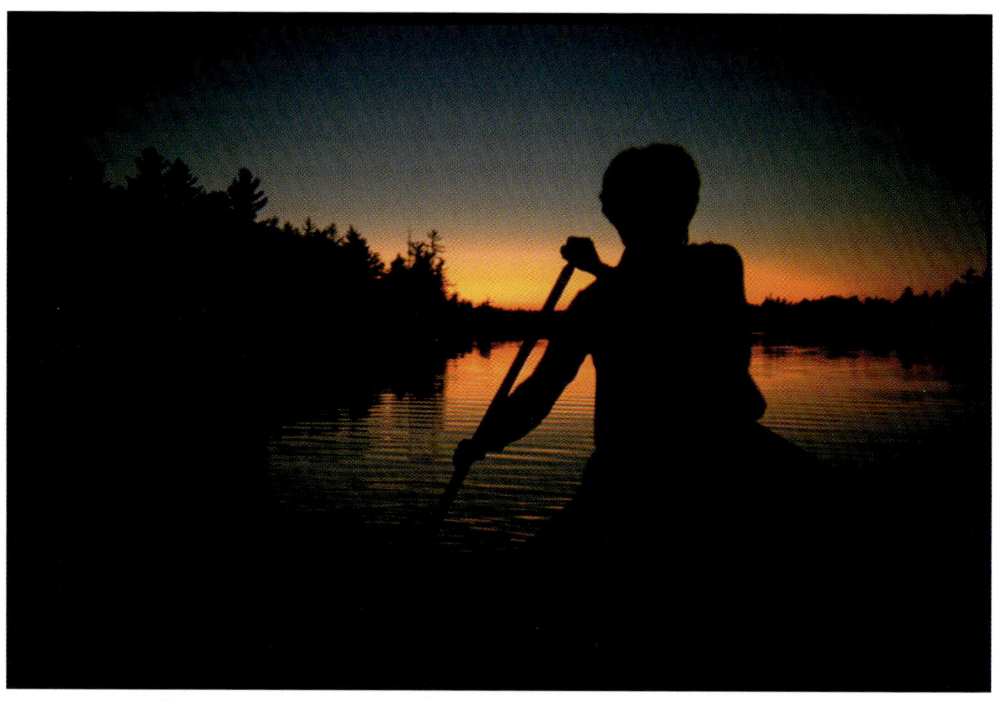

plate 14

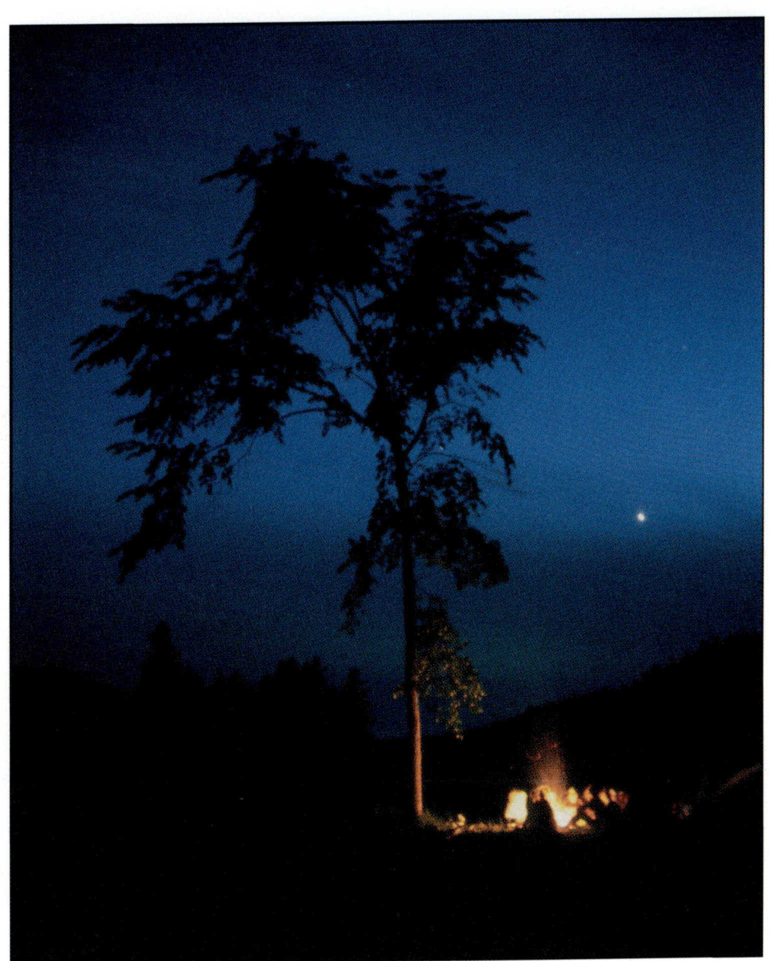

plate 15

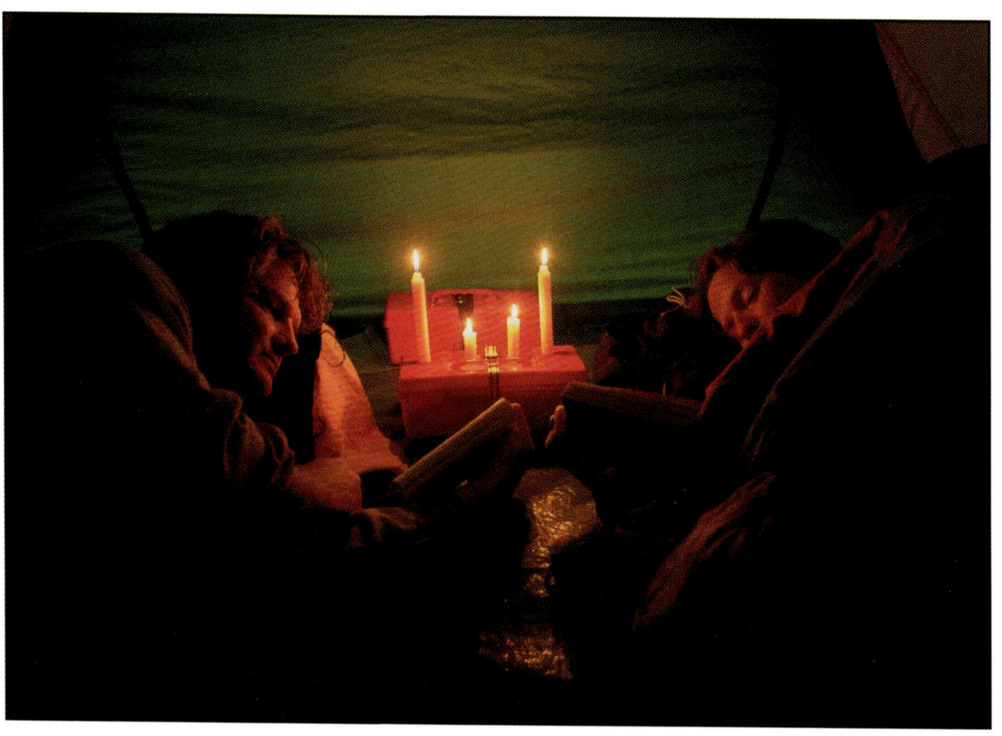

plate 16

COLOUR COMMENTS

plate 1

Of all the elements in a photograph, colour is often the most conspicuous. Although black-and-white photography can be amazingly effective with its emphasis on lines, shapes and textures, colour, especially the bright hues, immediately attracts the attention. That becomes evident if one compares this colour print with the black-and-white rendition on the previous page. The people, all dressed in vivid red, stand out very clearly against the contrasting yellow raft and the green-grey trees in the background, much more so than in the non-colour print. Thus, a compelling image is created, filled with pure visual excitement.

plate 2

The magic hour of predawn twilight, before the sun rises above the horizon, is filled with wonderful picture opportunities. In this one-colour image, made at the Barron Canyon in the same location as the photo on page 153, the gorgeous crimson clouds fill the whole sky with sculptured backlit waves. The silhouetted tree branch is quite small but still plays a role in defining the mood of the picture. By putting the camera on a tripod and shooting the same picture a number of times, in 10- to 30-second intervals and without adjusting the exposure setting, an intriguing series of images of the gradually changing colours in the sky can be taken.

plate 3

This is another example of a picture where one colour dominates, although there is some green present in the leaves of the water lilies in the foreground and the trees to the right. The composition shows vertical as well as horizontal symmetry, producing a rather static but still eye-catching image. It is, above all, the majestic collection of white clouds suspended in the blue sky that attracts the attention. The photo was made from a canoe with a hand-held camera equipped with a 20 mm wide-angle lens and loaded with ISO 100 slide film. We had to sit very still for some time so as not to disturb the mirror-smooth water surface reflecting the sky and the trees.

plate 4

Seeing a picture before the event that you want to photograph actually happens can produce some interesting results. At the Minden Wild Water Preserve I had noticed this yellow-flowered bush on the shore, as well as the standing wave and the gate poles in the background. I then imagined a photo that would create an artistic impression of a kayak race, using those elements. Next, I waited for a paddler wearing a red life jacket to appear in the right position. By purposely focussing on the flowers in the foreground, and leaving the other compositional elements in the back somewhat less sharp, the desired effect was created.

plate 5

This solo paddler, playing in the Blue Chute of the French River, is observed from a position several metres above the water level, which creates attractive opportunities for fine action shots. In this photo the canoe is positioned along a diagonal and the paddler, hanging out of the boat in an impressive high brace, is well placed against the white foam of the waves. There are only two colours: red of the paddler and the inside of the canoe, and blue-green of the water and the outside of the canoe. Obviously, the centre of interest is the red life jacket. To capture the beauty of an action picture like this one, the photographer must be knowledgeable about paddling whitewater and be able to anticipate the movements made by the canoeist.

plate 6

Many pictures have hidden inside them other pictures that can exist very well as images on their own. An interesting example is this one, which consists of the central section of the photo on page 157. It was found by using a zoom lens to experiment with different compositions. The surreal image, showing the cool blue sky and white clouds reflected in the water surface, creates a rather unsettling feeling because the clouds are below the tree branches. The photo, which has great impact because of that confusing reversal, is also quite believable when viewed upside-down. This is an excellent picture to help improve your visual perception.

plate 7

Close-up photography opens up the extraordinary world of tiny treasures, letting one savour the beauty of details rarely seen by most people. This shot of three pine needles carrying drops of water on their tips could only be made in the absence of any wind, and with the use of a tripod to support the camera. The needles were stabilized by holding them against a stick by means of a small clamp. The warm diffuse colours in the background were provided by several out-of-focus wildflowers. For photos like this one, good equipment and a solid technique are required, as well as much patience. The results can be truly spectacular. Experiment by taking the same picture with different backgrounds.

plate 8

One of the reasons that photographing dragon boat races can be such a treat is that the vivid colours of the boats, and especially of the dragon heads, are among the most remarkable sights in all paddle sports. This vertical image has considerable impact because it concentrates on just the head, showing part of another boat as a secondary element in the background. The appeal of the photo, which was made with a hand-held camera on ISO 400 print film, obviously comes, to a large extent, from the colours painted on the intricately shaped dragon head. By being observant, you will see beyond the shape and colours, and note that in this head a tooth is missing in the upper jaw.

plate 9

In the fall, nature writes its own poetry in colour, painting the world with light of many hues. For the nature photographer, this is the time of great visual excitement. When I saw these wonderfully coloured branches hanging over a portage trail in Algonquin Park, I waited until somebody carrying a canoe came by and then asked the person to stand on the trail below the trees. With the dark red canoe well lit by the bright sun and turned sideways towards the camera, the boat became a small but strong centre of interest in the field of red and yellow tree leaves surrounded by dark foliage. I felt intuitively that a red canoe would create a more interesting picture than a yellow or green one.

plate 10

When I encountered this canoe, caressed by the low morning sun and with the swirls of mist rising from the smooth water surface behind it, I knew this image was something special. I took several vertical shots of the scene, putting the dark section at the top and the clean section filled with soft tendrils of mist lower down, letting the canoe occupy the prominent space in the middle and at the bottom, making this a perfect cover shot. Indeed, it was used on the cover of the book *The Canoe in Canadian Cultures*. The quiet mood of the scene, with the canoe under a slight angle and the rock on the right filling in the empty space there, providing necessary balance to the rocky shore on the left, is captured very well in this image.

plate 11

This is perhaps the simplest, yet one of the best photos I have ever made of a canoe. It is called *Red Reflection* and its unpretentious single-colour design is set against an almost featureless dark background. The canoe is lit only by the late-afternoon sun, creating a powerful image of emotional impact and timeless beauty. The rope hanging over the gunnel and the bits of shadow from foliage on the shore are small but important elements in the picture, providing subtle breaks in the smooth surface of the boat. This is the kind of image that makes the canoe lover's heart sing, aching to go back for another healing adventure in that enchanting country filled with countless waterways.

plate 12

This is a 'grabber,' a picture that immediately seizes your attention because of the impact of its extraordinary subject matter. A cat in a canoe, looking intently at something across the water (in fact, her friend the dog, blissfully sitting in another canoe some distance away), is obviously such an attention-grabbing photo. But there is more than the uniqueness of the main subject that makes this picture special. The low late-afternoon sunlight illuminating the beautiful canoe, which is distinguished by the long horizontal lines of its wooden strips, gives the picture a lovely golden glow and tenderly touches the soft fur of the cat.

Colour Comments

plate 13

To most people, the jewel in nature's crown of colours consists of sunrises and sunsets, whose breathtaking beauty can be truly awesome. Photographs of such events are always among the most cherished memories in anybody's trip collection. In this sunset picture, the silhouette of the two people is important because the shot was made to help tell the visual story of their first trip in this part of canoe country. Without the people, the photo becomes a different kind of picture, a landscape shot. This Lake Missinaibi scene was taken on ISO 64 slide film, with a 24 mm wide-angle lens and using a tripod (set close to the ground) as well as a self-timer.

plate 14

To photograph sunsets from within a floating canoe can be a daunting task because the rather long exposure times required can cause an annoying lack of sharpness when a hand-held camera is used. However, if done with care and by setting up a tripod in the canoe in front of the sitting photographer, it may be possible to take sharp pictures, such as this one. Because the canoe was constantly moving a little bit, I did not lock the ball head on the tripod but kept it floating. I could, therefore, keep the camera horizontal, even when the canoe was moving, still providing sufficient support for sharp pictures. The afterglow of the sunset needed an exposure of 1/8th of a second, but by being careful and holding very still, it was possible to make a successful photo.

plate 15

Photographing the sky when most of the afterglow has disappeared, so that only a faint veil of light is left in the darkening sky, requires long exposure times in the order of several tens of seconds or even minutes. A tripod to support the camera is, therefore, an absolute must. What makes this picture so fascinating is the blue sky, which appears to be more intense in colour in the photo than when seen with the naked eye. The dominant tree silhouette is pictured quite sharp because of the absence of wind. This is another useful example of how effective silhouettes can be in colour pictures. Because of the long exposure time, the flames and smoke of the campfire are blurred and over-exposed, as well as the faces of the people sitting beside it. Still, the photograph captures the essence of an evening at the campsite very well.

plate 16

The story of a canoe trip can be told with pictures of many different subjects. This one was made inside our tent during a two-day period of almost constant rain, which we spent mostly reading and talking and sleeping. The illumination for the photo was provided by four candles placed on a red plastic box, creating a warm yellow light that was strong enough to take pictures with, using a tripod-supported camera loaded with ISO 64 slide film. Obviously, this kind of illumination should never be attempted in 'normal' situations because it is far too dangerous to have open flames in a tent! After making the photo with great care, we read some more, using battery-powered flashlights. Then we slept.

Colour Comments

TRAIL

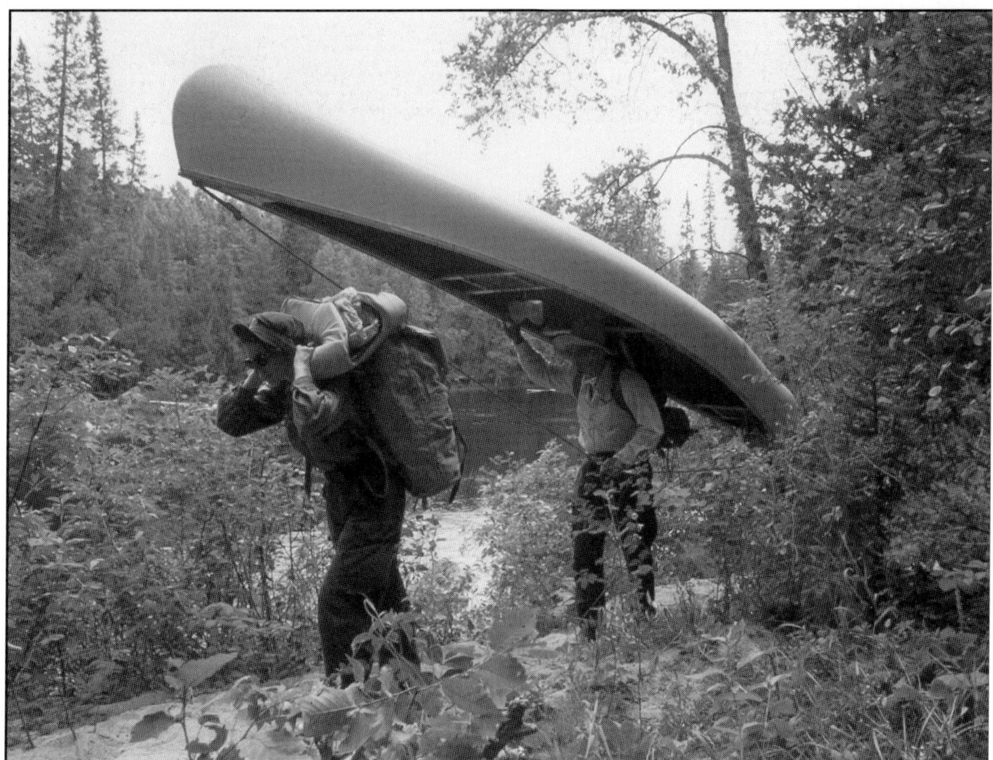

For many trippers, portaging is the least enjoyable part of the adventure: nothing but muddy or rocky trails, sore shoulders, sweat in your eyes, pestering bugs everywhere. Indeed, it can be sheer torture. Others consider portaging a sometimes welcome opportunity to stretch cramped legs and take in some fine views offered by the trail. Whatever it may mean to you, portaging is an inescapable part of wilderness tripping and some good photographs showing you doing that hard work should be an integral part of all trip reports. (How else would you be able to brag about it?)

When part of a group, you can always ask a friend to make a shot of you carrying the gear. However, in the case of the above photo there were only two people, so the camera was set on a tripod and the release button triggered via the built-in self-timer activated by the person who could move around easiest, the one carrying the pack. A wireless remote control (such as radio or infrared) and a motorized camera would have made it possible to take several shots without having to re-set the camera.

The result is a simple, natural-looking action photograph, quite effectively illustrating some elements of portaging, such as the use of a tumpline to carry the large Duluth pack and the way the canoe is supported on the shoulders. The locale also comes into play: the Missinaibi River in the background, the bush and trees, the trail around Split Rocks Falls. Because of the somewhat diffuse overhead sun, both faces are a bit dark, but not enough to really spoil the picture. One could try to use fill-flash to lighten the faces somewhat, but good results are far from guaranteed. By all means, experiment; that is how you learn to make good photographs.

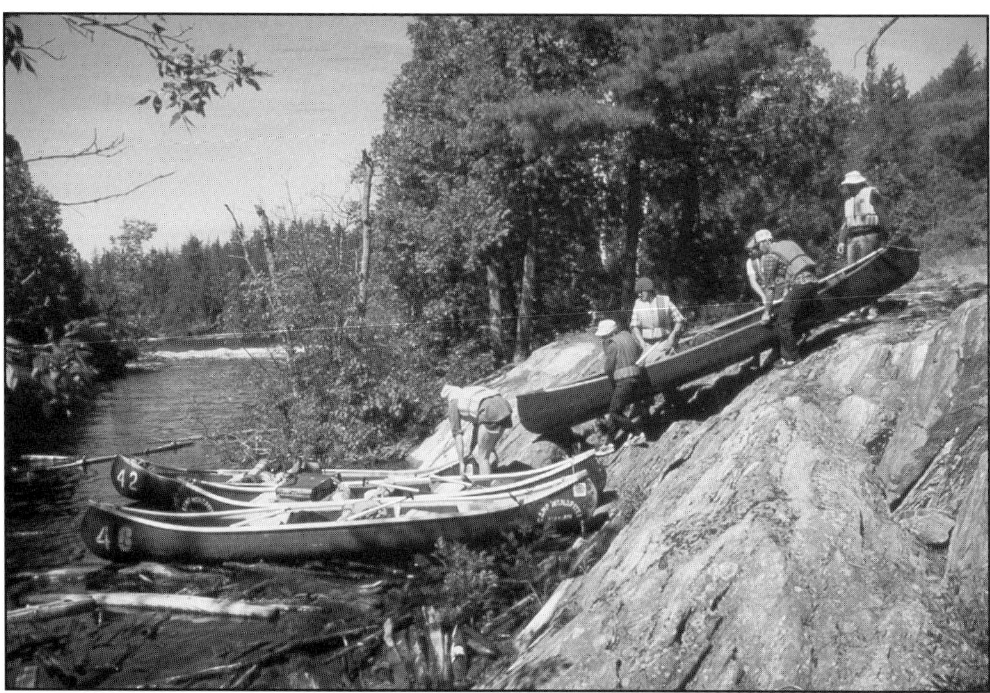

When travelling with several people, photographing portaging activities is, of course, much easier than when there are only two. After having helped carry canoes and gear, you can grab your (easily accessible!) camera and find a good spot from which to shoot. Try to find the best angle for your photos, one that shows the whole scene with all the trippers doing their bit. When you are still helping with the portage, look around (and behind) you to discover different shooting possibilities. You may also want to consider taking close-ups such as hands gripping the gunnels, sweaty faces glistening in the sun or the bow of the canoe resting on the rocks. These secondary shots will make your story really come alive.

In this photo, taken on the Temagami River, the whole group (except for the photographer, of course) is recorded while bringing the last canoe to the put-in point, featuring the importance of team work in canoe tripping. In the background, the outflow from the rapids is just visible, and the patch of light sky in the top-left corner is partially covered by an overhanging branch, making the sky somewhat less conspicuous. This kind of snapshot obviously does not need to be taken from a tripod, unless you want to be in the picture too. (Paddling photographers are always the least-photographed members of their group. That is a law of nature.)

The shot was taken at high noon with the blazing sun shining from a cloudless sky, producing a harsh light that make the people's faces all but invisible in the shadow under their hats. But that is quite acceptable in this case, because the people are photographed from a distance and appear small anyway. When tripping, there is very little you can do about the quality of the light available for your pictures. You have to work with the available light; you just cannot wait for the better softer light that can occur early in the morning and at the end of the day.

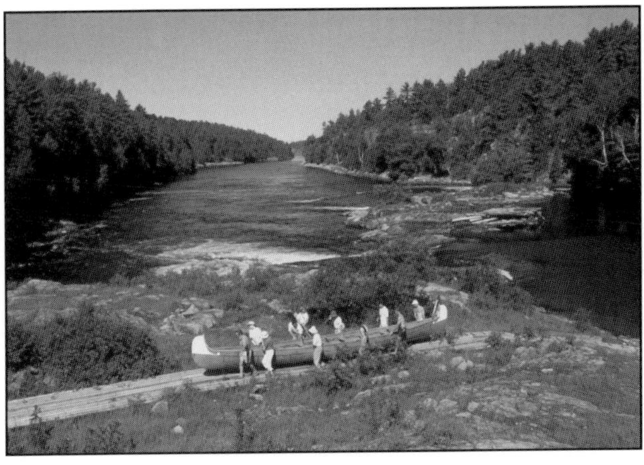

One of the many intriguing aspects of travelling in North American canoe country is the opportunity to follow some of the routes the fur-trade voyageurs used in the 17th to 19th centuries. Recollet Falls on the French River is one such location where modern trippers can walk the exact same portage trail (only now covered by a modern wooden boardwalk) used in the past.

Visiting and photographing such places provides the opportunity to develop some understanding of what life on the river was all about so long ago. The top photo, showing a modern Montreal canoe being carried over the Recollet Falls portage trail, is a valuable record shot that gives an adequate picture of what the situation looks like at present.

However, the picture becomes visually much more interesting if the sky, empty in the first photo, is filled with magnificent white clouds as shown in the large picture. Together with the receding shorelines and seemingly narrowing river, these clouds generate a strong feeling of depth. By positioning the camera in such a way that the boardwalk becomes hidden in the foreground, and therefore unnoticeable, this photo shows practically the same scene observed by the travellers canoeing these waters centuries ago.

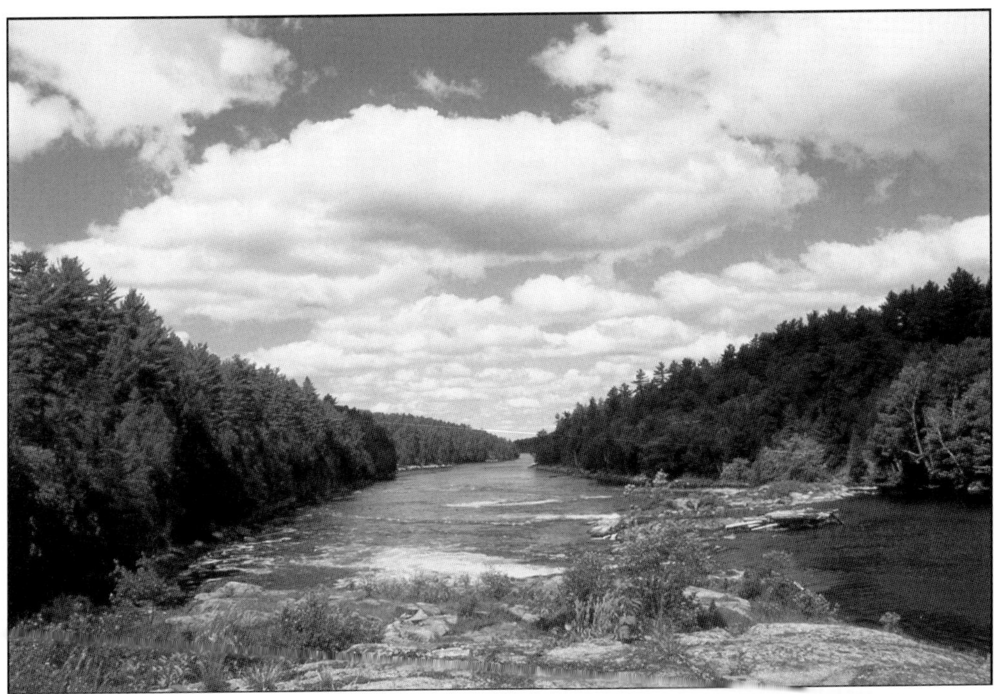

Trail

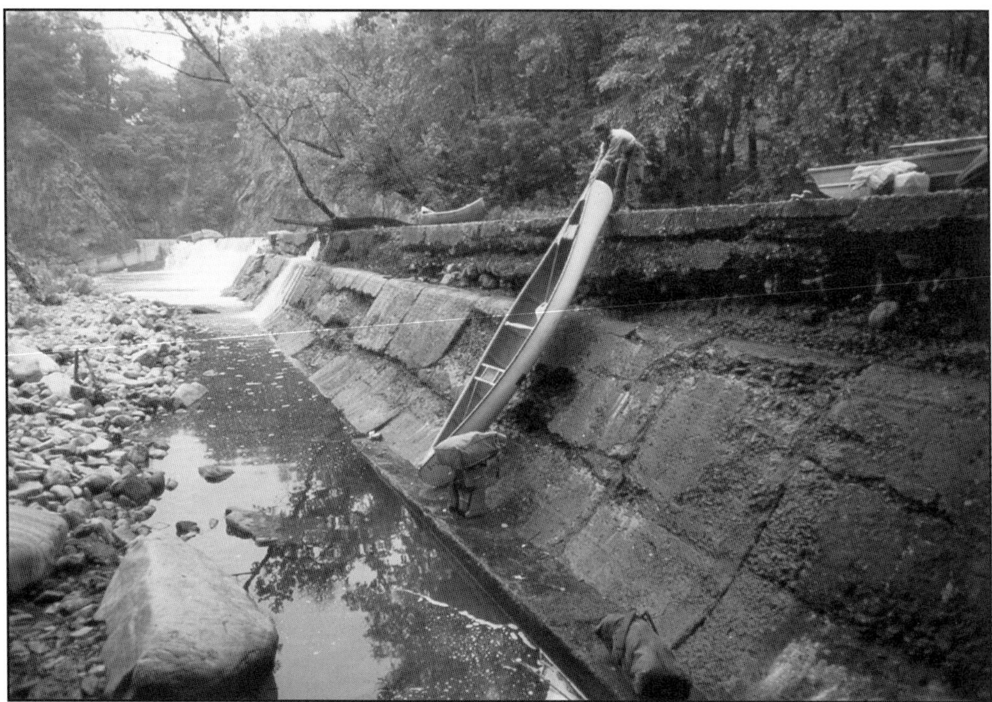

Unfortunately, it is no longer all happy unencumbered paddling on many North American rivers. Over the years, too many previously wild waterways have been 'tamed' by dams; power-generating stations proliferate and a great number of rivers large and small are no longer easily accessible to canoe trippers.

When we encountered this old dam on the Cacapon River, I photographed it with the canoe as the centre of interest, clearly showing the crumbling concrete of the structure. I wanted good record shots of all significant locations on the river and this obviously was one of them. The powerful diagonal lines of the dam lead the viewer directly to the whitewater in the background, and the uncommon position of the canoe immediately catches the eye. A rather unusual shot to have in a collection of wilderness canoeing photos, but nevertheless it is one that portrays exactly what we encountered.

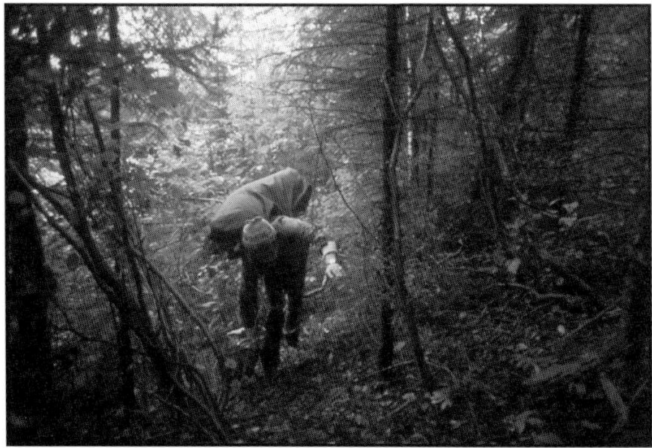

The bottom photo proves that using flash to illuminate dark scenes is not always the best solution. This man, struggling up a steep slope (it is hard to see the steepness in a two-dimensional photograph), would have looked much less natural if lit artificially. Such light would have overpowered the sombre atmosphere of the dark forest. This shot was, therefore, made by available light only on high-speed ISO 400 film.

Portage trails can be endlessly fascinating. Many have been used for countless years, first by the Native peoples after their invention of the birchbark canoe centuries ago, then by missionaries, explorers and fur traders beginning in the early 17th century, and, finally, since the second half of the 19th century, increasingly by recreational canoeists like ourselves.

The trail on this photo winds its way around the Paresseux Falls of the Mattawa River and is part of an old trade route that has to be followed by every paddler travelling between the Ottawa River and Lake Nipissing. It looks exactly the way it has done for many centuries; the rocks are the same ones that numerous earlier travellers must have cursed as they banged their toes against them. (Surprisingly, it is hard to find evidence of any traveller having attempted to improve the trail by moving big rocks out of the way.) Only the trees and bush are different, being part of nature's constant cycle of renewal. For certain, the blackflies and mosquitoes were as much a nuisance then as now.

Because I wanted to document the transportation of a large canoe over this trail, I followed members of the Barrie Canoe Club around while they carried their North canoe on the shoulders of six people, trying to avoid stumbling over the rocks on the uneven trail. As it was quite dark under the forest canopy, I used high-speed ISO 400 film (and no flash because I wanted everything to look natural). There was no time to

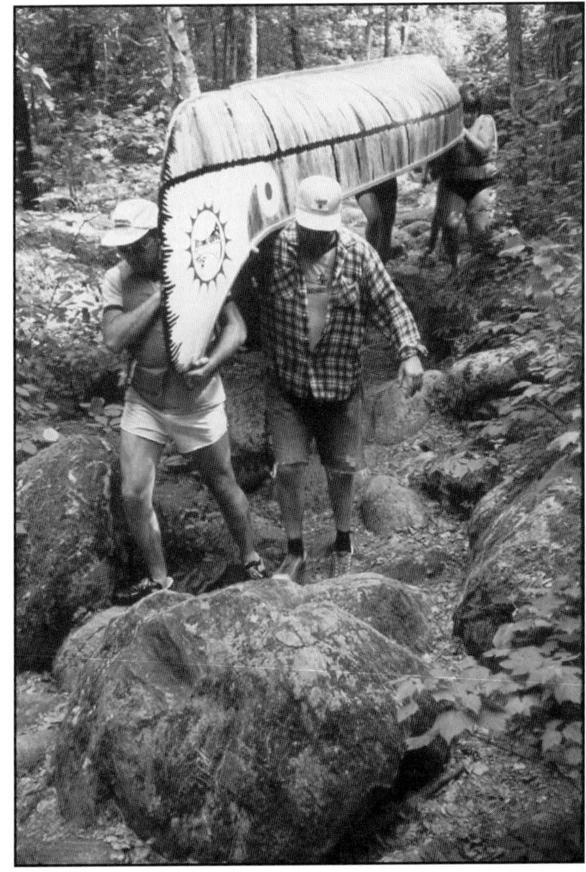

set up a tripod in the constantly changing scene so, in order to be able to shoot at a long exposure of 1/30th to 1/60th of a second, I had to stand very still, press my elbows against my body, hold my breath and push the release button slowly. A monopod would have been of considerable help. Fortunately, the sky was overcast. The absence of direct sunlight coming through the canopy eliminated irritating spots on the forest floor.

Of the series of photos made, this vertical one with the big rock in the foreground and the canoe at the top, takes the viewer's eye into the picture along a leading line and illustrates best what it means to carry large heavy canoes over rough trails. Not always an easy task but one that has to be performed over and over again.

Trail

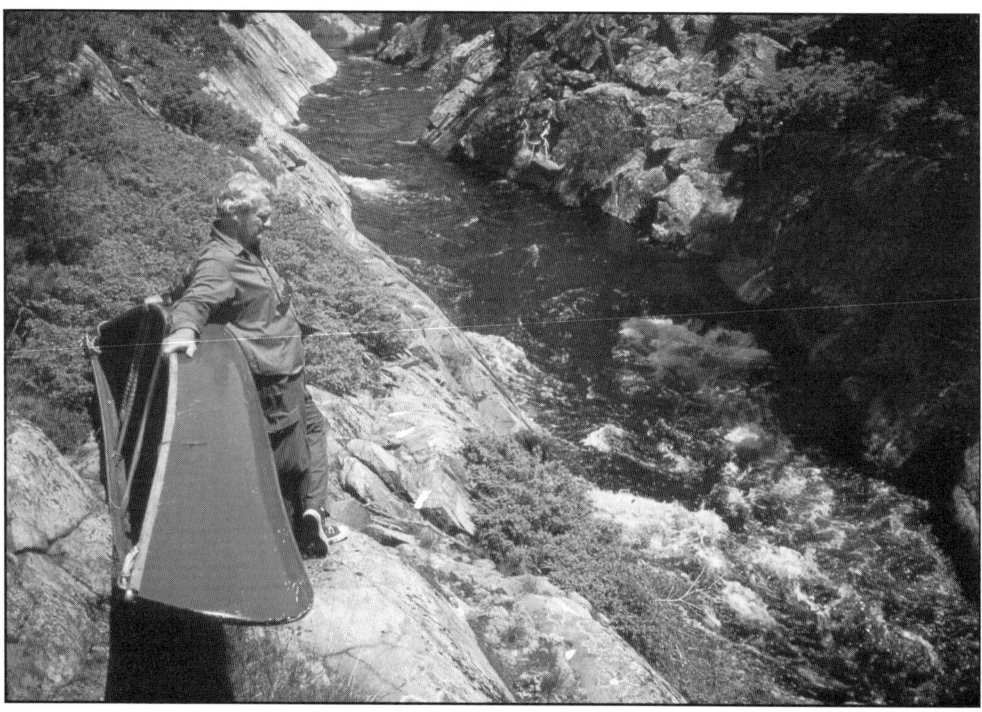

Better than verbal descriptions, photographs are the best way to document places or events. So, if you encounter something worthwhile on your portage, put your load down for a moment and take some pictures, even if they are just simple record shots. They will greatly enhance the quality of your trip report.

You can, of course, only do that if you have easy access to your camera. While on a portage, keep the camera on your person, safely protected by a shock-resistant carrying case, and not hidden away in a pack with the rest of the equipment. The camera Ria

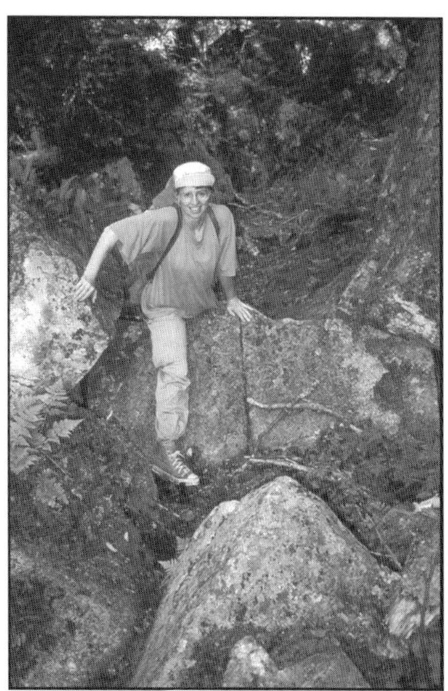

and I carry with us on most portages is a completely automatic point-and-shoot one that does not require any special settings and is instantly ready for use. The two photos on the next page show the camera case hanging from a strap around my neck, accessible at any moment.

All four photos on these two pages were taken with that camera. They show important portage moments we are very happy to have recorded photographically. The first portrays the famous La Dalle, a narrow section of the Old Voyageur Channel on the French River, extensively used by express canoes and other craft during the fur-trade years. Although the portage trail was not clearly visible, we decided to carry around the channel anyway as we were without life jackets and did not want to risk an accident in the swirling waves.

Only later did we discover that this is a clean channel without hidden rocks; running it would not have posed any real problems. The photo is well composed, with the channel itself on a pleasing diagonal and the canoe with the man providing visual balance on the left.

The small photo on the previous page shows the aptly named Crotch Cruncher, a rather intimidating but unavoidable wedge-shaped rock in the upper section of the trail of the infamous Diablo Portage of the Steel River loop. The two photos on this page were made at the steep part of that portage with the intention of showing, not only the angle of the trail, but also to illustrate the fatigue portaging can cause.

A big advantage of our camera, shared by many other point-and-shoots, is the built-in automatic flash, which makes

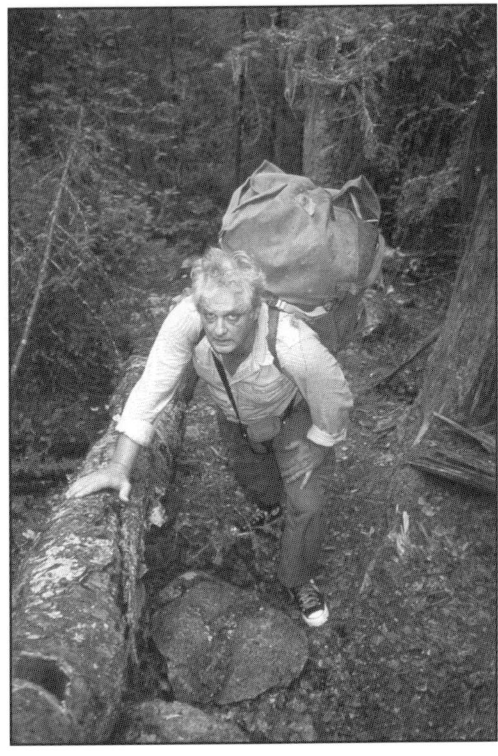

lightening up dark scenes very convenient. Without the flash it would not have been possible to make the last three pictures; the lack of natural light on the trail would have rendered the people much too dark and lacking in detail.

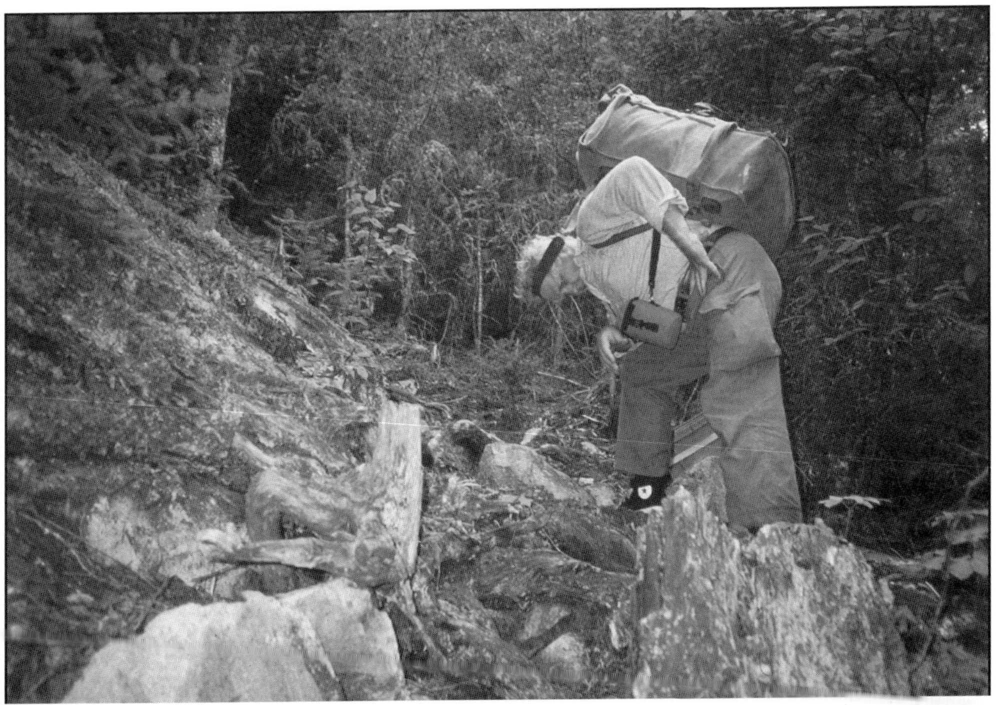

Trail

Portages are there for a reason. If you take the time to find out what those reasons are, you may discover some interesting images. For instance, the river may be blocked by a log jam consisting of a huge collection of tree trunks and branches, brought down by the current, over many years, to an impassable place in the river. There, they are pushed together, only allowing the water to seep through between the logs and causing the river to be blocked to traffic. This photo was taken using a wide-angle lens, with the camera tilted downwards to emphasize the foreground and create a strong perspective. The diagonal logs form an eye-catching pattern of shapes and lines.

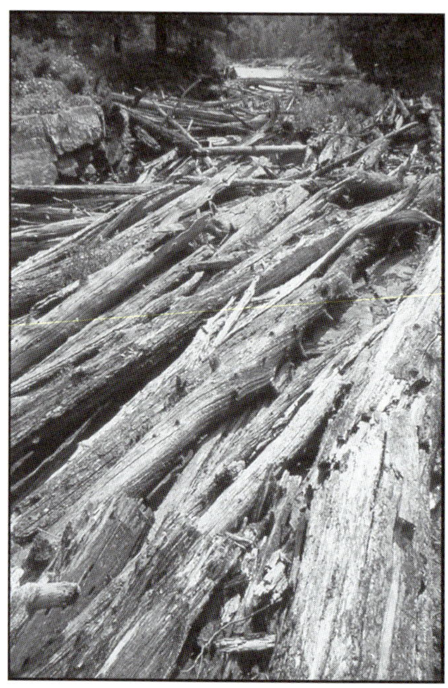

Other frequent reasons for having to portage are waterfalls. You should spend time and energy to discover these beauties. Falls can be photographed in various ways, from the straightforward 'freezing' of the water drops (see page 69) to the delicate soft, even ethereal, rendition in the photo below. This effect can be achieved by putting the camera on a tripod or other support (here, my arms with the elbows resting on my knees as I sat on a low rock) and using a sufficiently long exposure time (from 1/15th of a second to several seconds) to blur the rushing water.

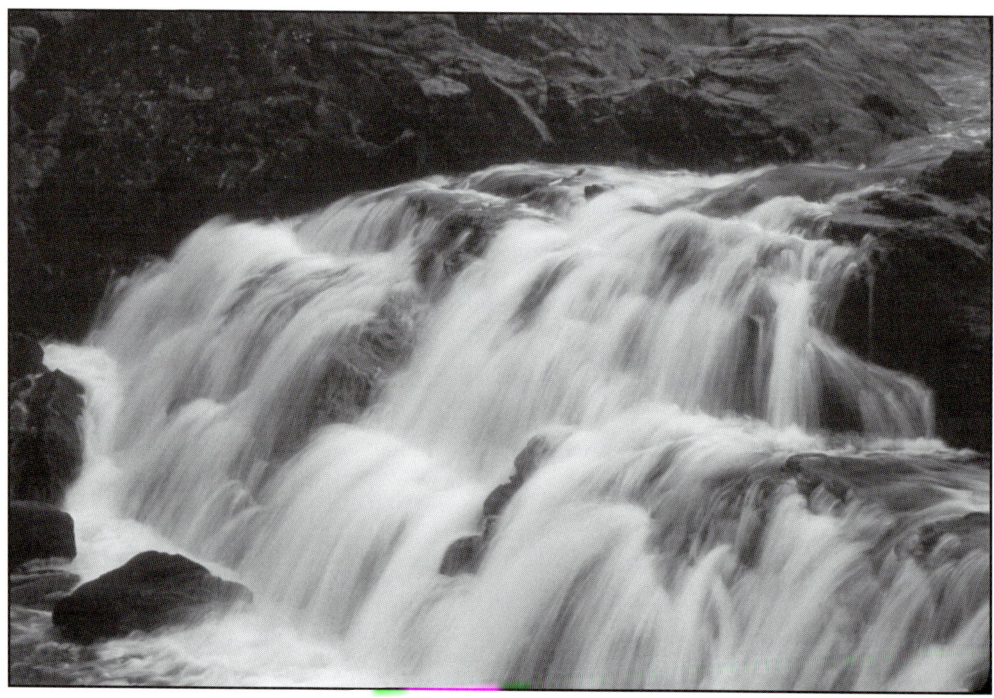

Trail

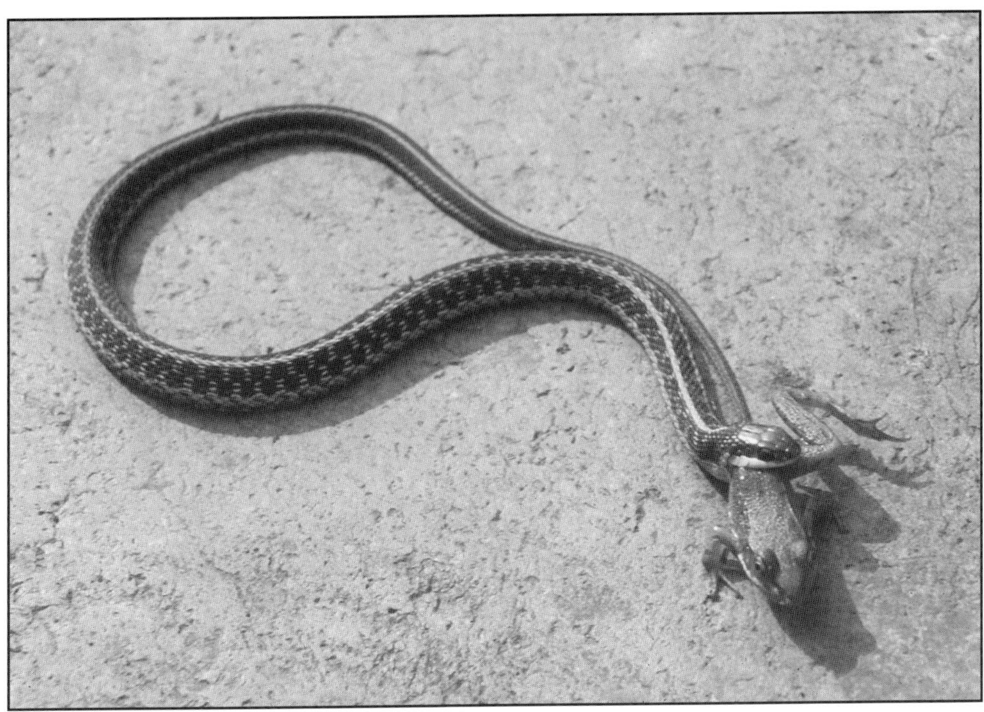

A good reason to always carry a camera when on the trail, portaging or just hiking for fun, is that you may have unexpected encounters such as the ones shown in these two photographs. The frog-eating garter snake, only about 20 cm long and beautifully patterned along its back and sides, completely oblivious to everything around it, was feeding on a flat sun-drenched rock close to a swampy area. It took a long time to swallow its meal, giving me the opportunity to make several photos and record a simple absorbing drama that occurs regularly everywhere in nature. Fortunately, the sunlight was softened somewhat by a slightly overcast sky.

In case of the loon's egg shell, on the other hand, the sun bore down on the scene in full force and the shadows are therefore very dark and undetailed. By placing the egg in Ria's hand to provide scale (coming from a medium-size bird, these things are really huge) and her holding it so that the light struck it slightly from the side, the rounded egg shape comes out very well. This was, of course, an abandoned nest with just the empty egg shell fragments in it. Never approach too close to a bird's nest; if you want to photograph it, use a tele lens and shoot from a distance.

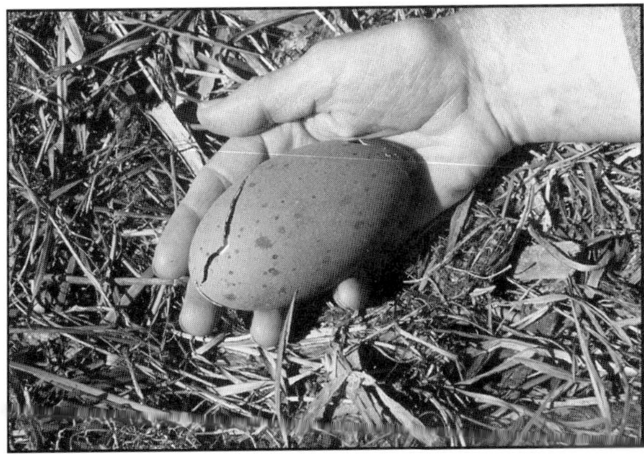

These are just two examples of the many treasures you can find on the trail, if you keep your eyes open and your mind receptive to the beauty round you. Learn to *see* and recognize them.

Trail

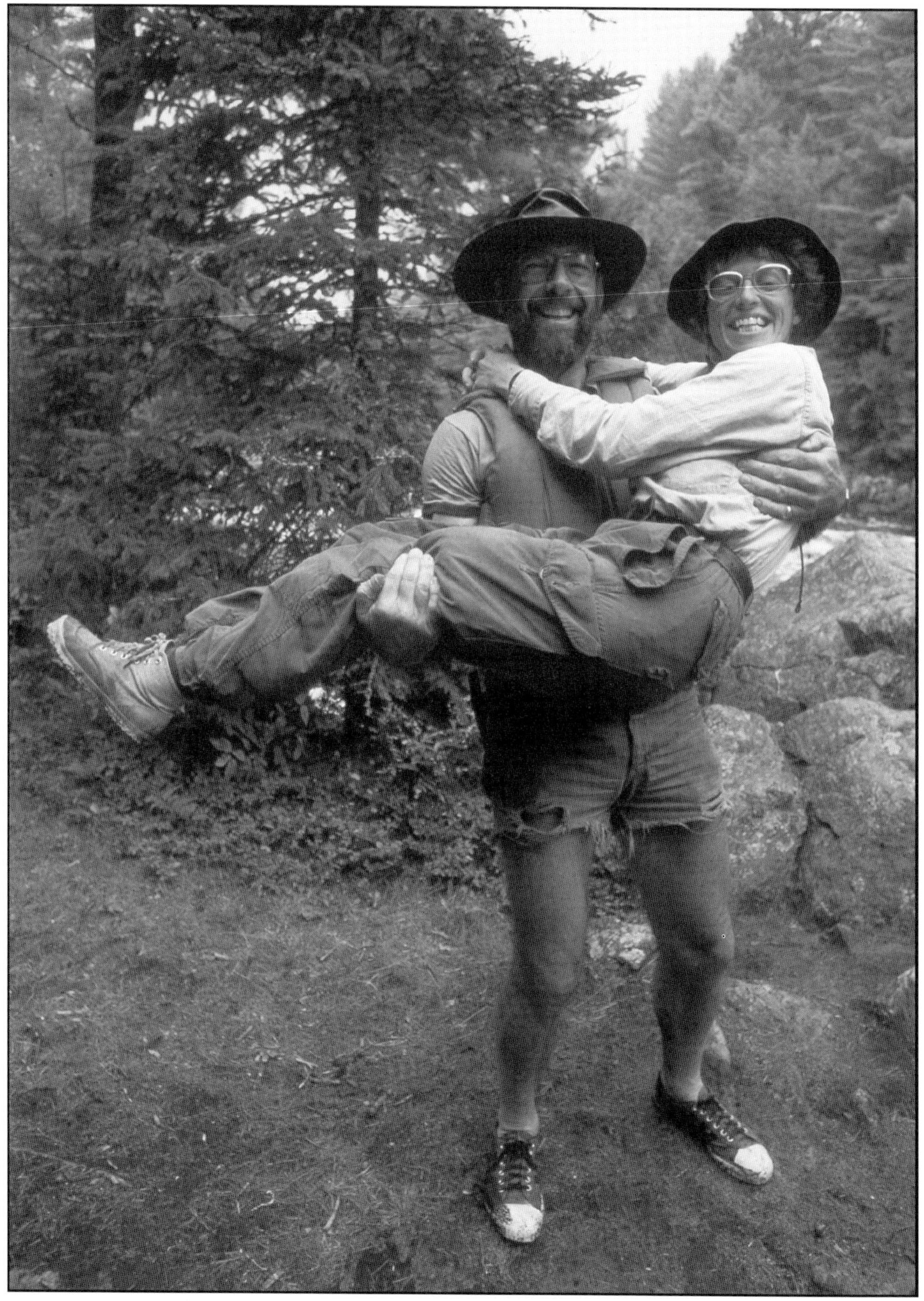

... and look what I found on the portage trail...!

CAMPSITE

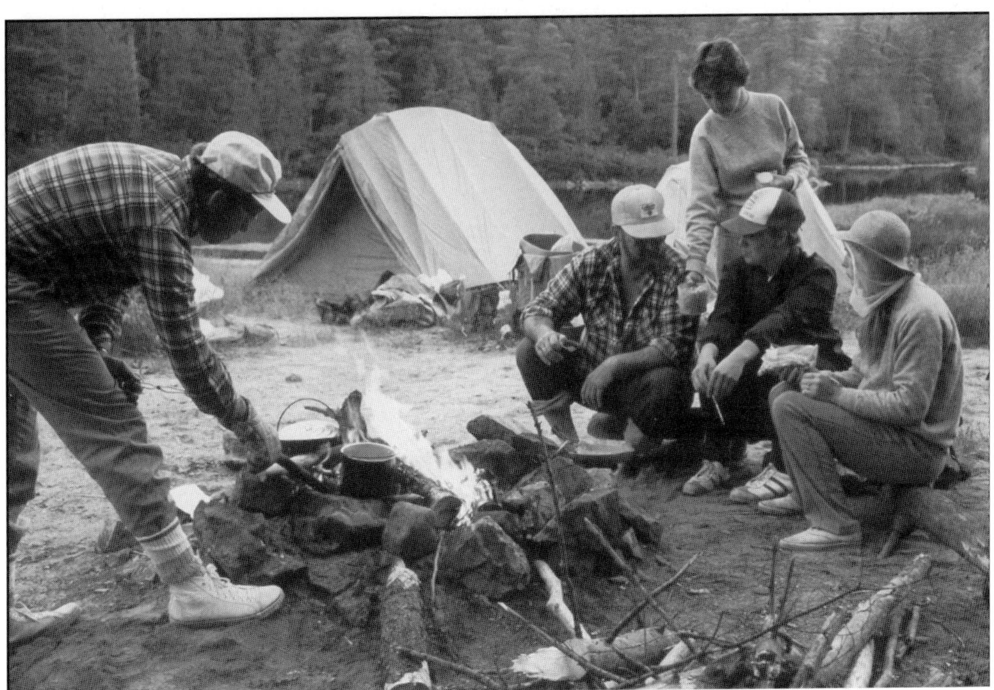

There you are then, finally at the campsite. All team members have performed a hard day's work filled with paddling and portaging. Now it is time to relax around the campfire, waiting for the meal to be cooked, while enjoying the peace and quiet of Mother Nature. Try to set up camp at a site that provides good opportunities and backgrounds for photographs. A rock wall or a tree would be great for making overviews of the campsite from a high viewpoint.

For you, the ever-vigilant photographer of the group, there should be no time off. You know that life on and around the campsite offers many opportunities for great photos, essential documents of the trip. A good practice is to carry your camera with you as much as possible. This way people get used to you making photographs of them and stop being self-conscious.

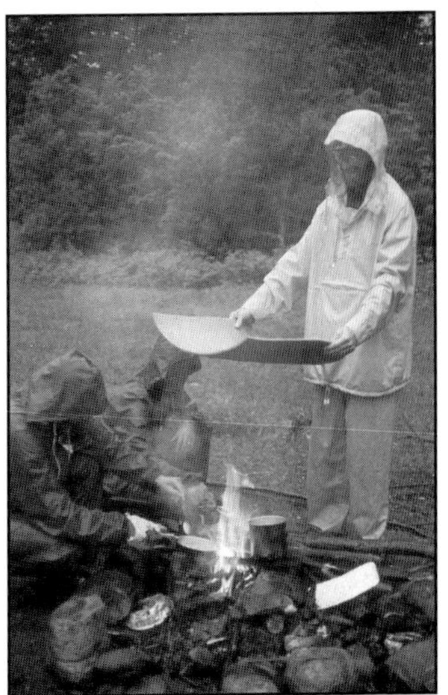

Even when the skies open and rain threatens to douse the fire, do not stop shooting. There is bound to be some interesting material there that will give you and your friends a lot of enjoyment and fond memories. For instance, it is interesting to see how this inventive man keeps the rain away from the fire by holding up a sheet of blue foam plastic. Keep the camera out of the smoke and have an umbrella or a plastic bag or so ready to protect it from the rain.

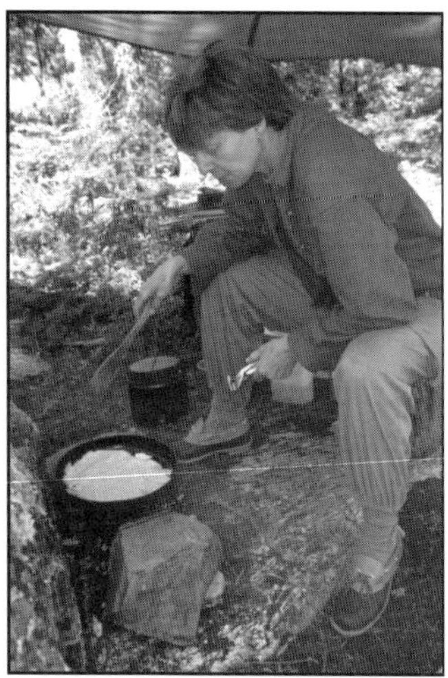

If there is one food with a true outdoors appeal in the world of wilderness canoeing, it is bannock, the unleavened Indian bread that is a staple food on many a canoe trip. Every outdoors cook has her or his very special private recipe for this food created by the gods of paddling. Making a series of photos illustrating the creation of an irresistible bannock bread should be high on your list of obligatory campsite photos.

These three pictures are from a series of eight, made to show the life of one such bannock bread, from preparing the dough through the actual cooking to the final tasting. The first photo shows how the wood fire was placed out of the wind behind a big rock and how small

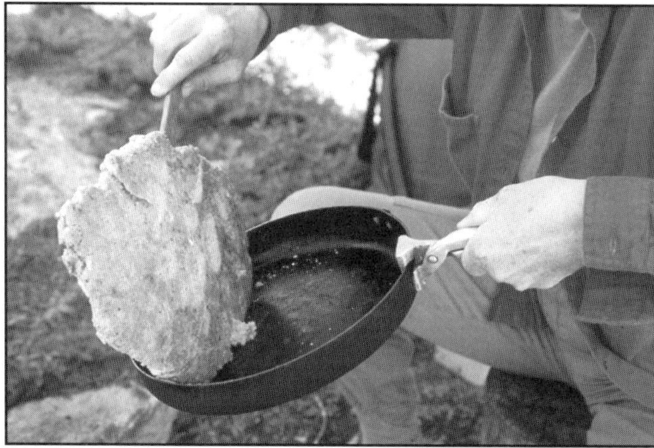

such a fire only needs to be. The photos then gradually get closer, with the final one making direct eye contact, drawing the viewer into the experience of biting into the delicious bannock. Close your eyes for a second and you can surely smell the aroma rising from this product of culinary cratfswomanship. How true, indeed: "Happiness is a warm bannock!"

The photos were made using fill-flash, which was necessary because of the lack of light under the tarp, set up to keep an occasional drizzle away from the fire, the cook and, of course, the bannock. The series was done with a hand-held camera, following the cook around under the tarp and selecting the images as they came along. Producing a series of pictures is a very effective way to tell a story, where each shot leads to the next one in a natural progression.

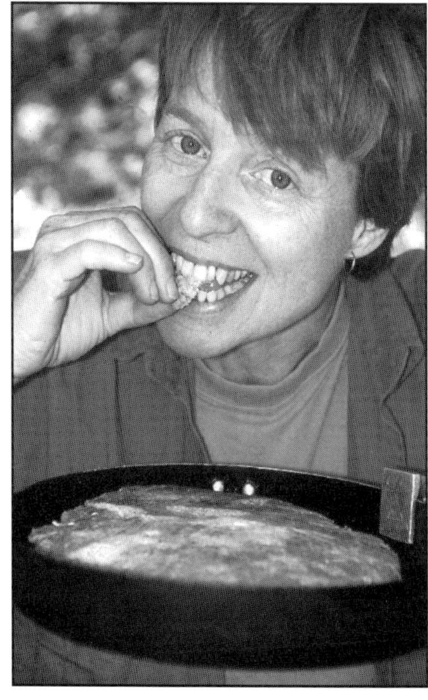

Campsite

In canoe country, the little animals are often the real scene stealers. The big wildlife such as bear, moose and wolf are captivating to encounter, but potentially dangerous and very hard to get close to without disturbing them. The little ones, on the other hand, sometimes venture right in the campsite, keeping a watchful eye and waiting patiently for an opportunity to grab something to eat.

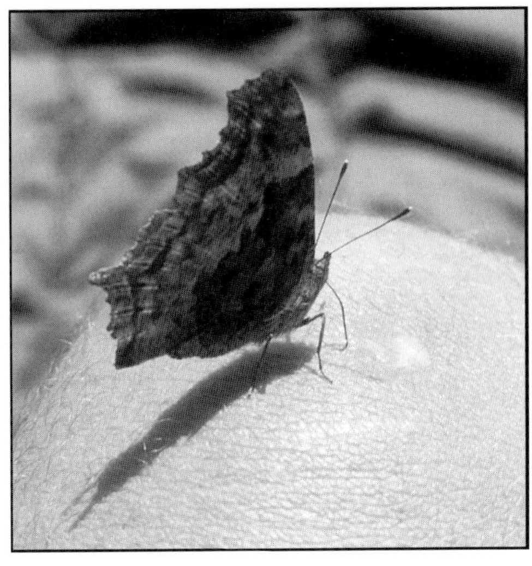

This butterfly was one such enchanting visitor I could photograph with the help of a close-up lens. The fluttering beauty had landed on my knee, looking for some nice salty sweat but not finding any. Carefully, I deposited a few drops of milk beside the butterfly. It started drinking through its long proboscis, while I kept very still. Often these unaffected pictures of little creatures are truly enchanting.

After we had set up camp, I discovered a snapping turtle laying her eggs on the gravely beach about 50 metres from where we were. She was labouring hard, first digging the hole and then carefully depositing her many eggs. The slight drizzle marked her carapace with tiny dark spots. I stayed a good distance away, so as not to disturb her, photographing the animal with a 300 mm telephoto lens.

We never try to attract and feed animals directly, but they are welcome if they appear of their own initiative. Remember, no photograph is worth risking the welfare of any animal.

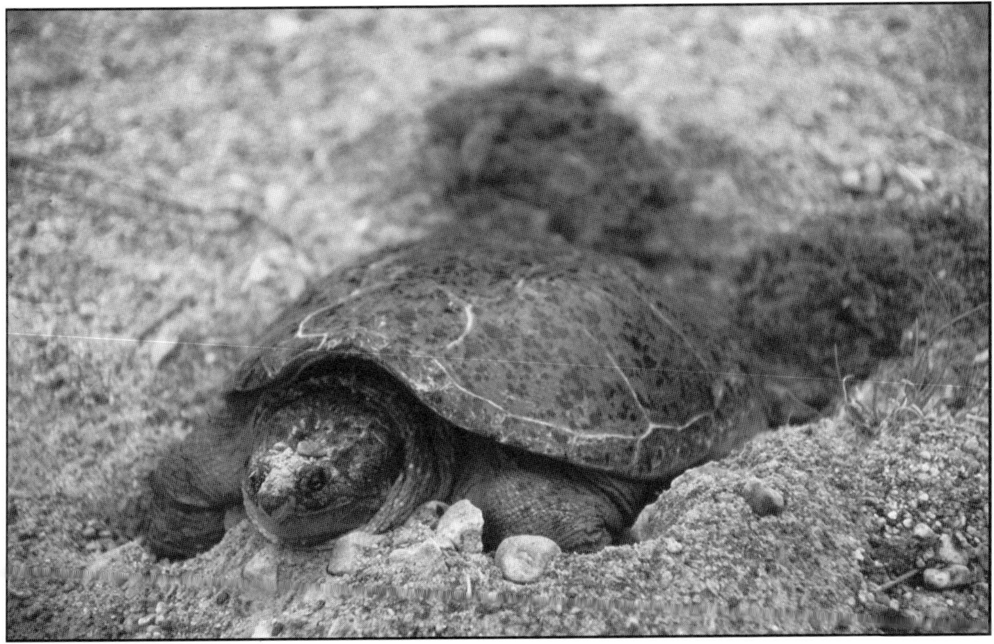

Campsite

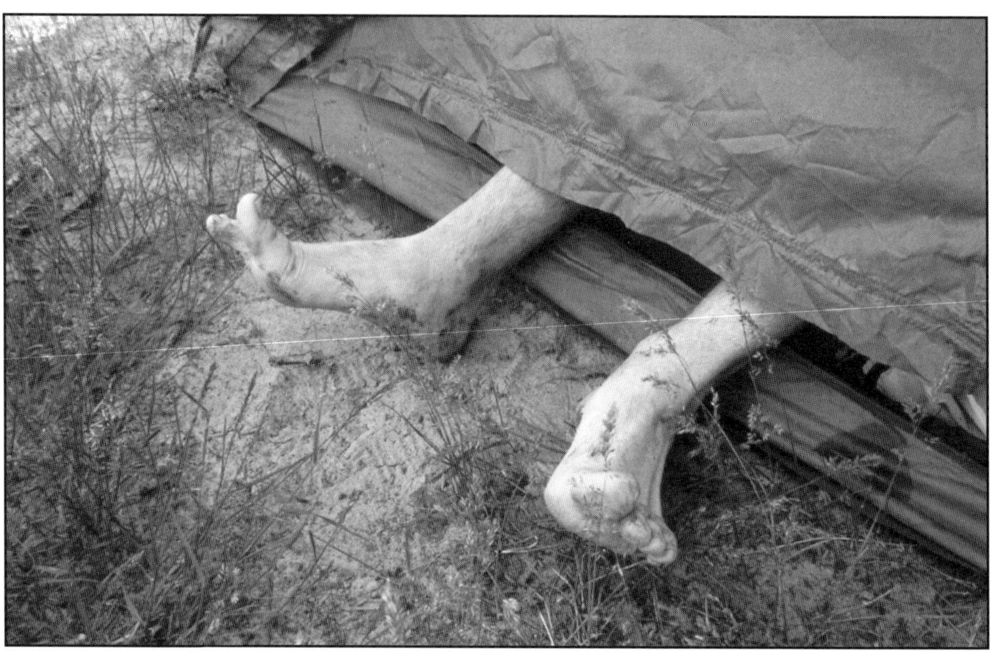

At the campsite, successful photos can be made of the simplest, most unexpected of subjects. For instance, when walking around early one morning, I came across this pair of rather dirty feet sticking out of a tent, obviously belonging to someone apparently a bit too long for his sleeping quarters. At my question if he was happy lying there, exposed to black flies and who knows what, he wiggled his toes in silent response, allowing me to make this offbeat photograph. Not the kind of picture you see every day. This gives a good idea of the many interesting images that can be found everywhere when you keep your eyes open and your mind alert.

The multi-person portage below was shot while the subjects were unaware of being photographed. The group of young campers, learning the ins and outs of portaging, had no idea of the funny image they were creating while trying to carry the canoe all at the same time. Note the one on the left going the other way. I had observed them learning different lifting techniques and was waiting patiently until the one telling picture would show up to best illustrate the story.

When creating the account of your canoe trip in pictures, include as many humorous situations as you can find. Everybody loves to see funny things happening, and your

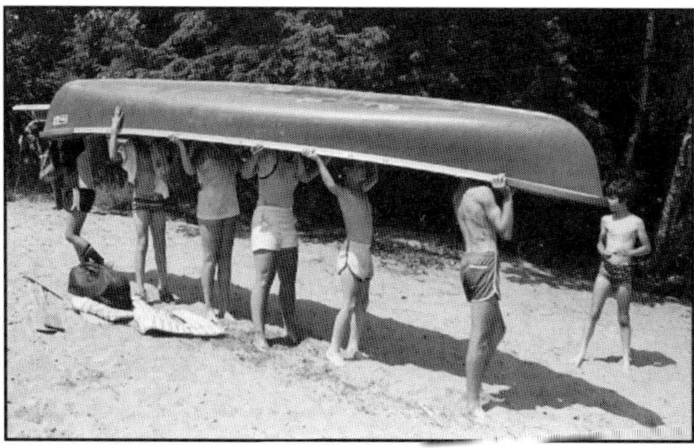

slide show or picture album will be all the better for them.

A good camera for this kind of see-and-grab photography is obviously the simple point-and-shoot. It is easy to carry around at all times and you can also shoot quickly and unobtrusively, a great advantage when documenting scenes like these.

Campsite

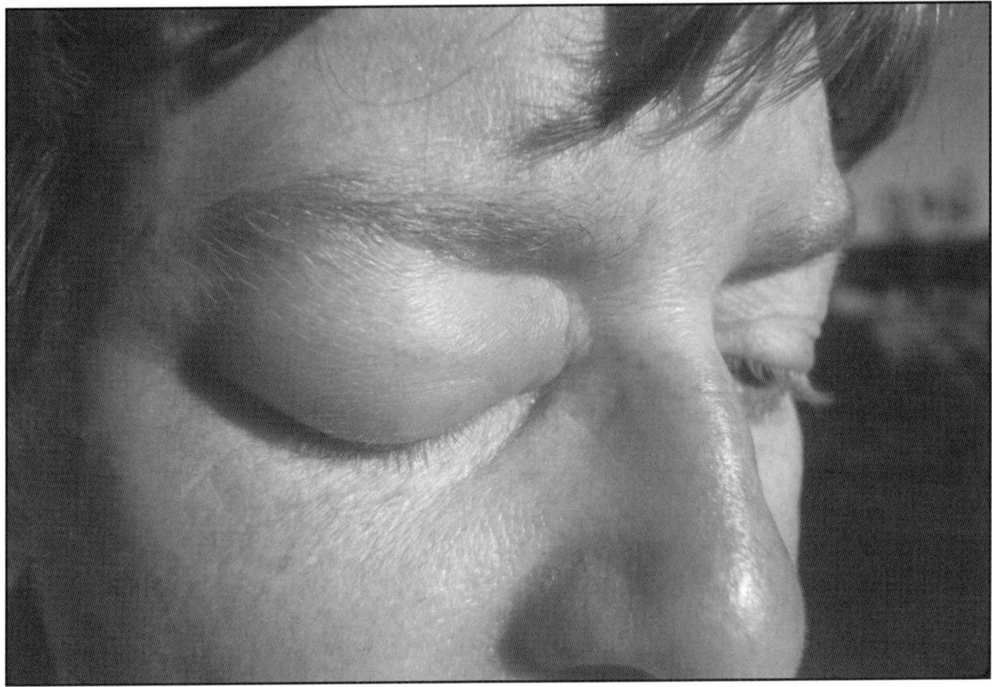

Many photographs of canoe country bugs, such as blackflies and mosquitos, show the small or large groupings of these animals settling on tents, clothing or gear or trying to crawl into various unprotected places on your body, as they look for blood.

I was searching for something different and was therefore very grateful when Ria obliged me by letting herself be bitten involuntarily near the outside corner of her right eye. Just one blackfly bite led to a formidable swelling that completely shut her eye, showing very effectively what these little pests can do. And this from a tiny blackfly only about three millimetres long.

A folk remedy used to lessen the impact of such an attack prescribes pressing a soaked tea bag to the swelling and letting the tannin in the tea do its work. It takes about an hour for most of the swelling to disappear without unpleasant side effects.

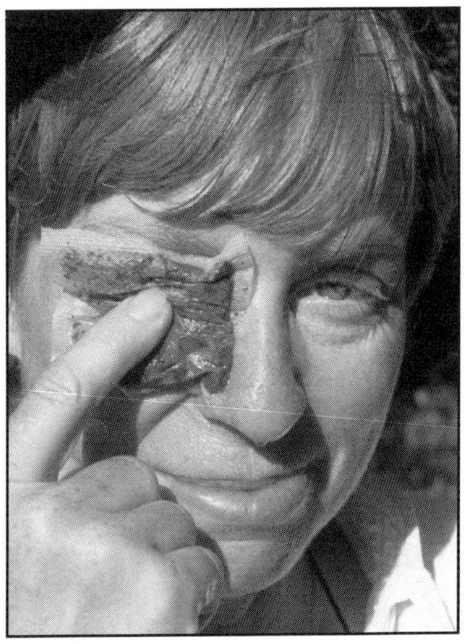

Both photos are tightly cropped close-ups, concentrating on the affected part of the face, thus adding to the impact of the images by eliminating much of the surrounding area. Because the midday sunlight was hard, I positioned Ria in such a way that the light illuminated her face without creating too many dark shadows.

These shots are good examples of the power of seeing and recognizing everyday happenings missed by many less observant people.

Campsite

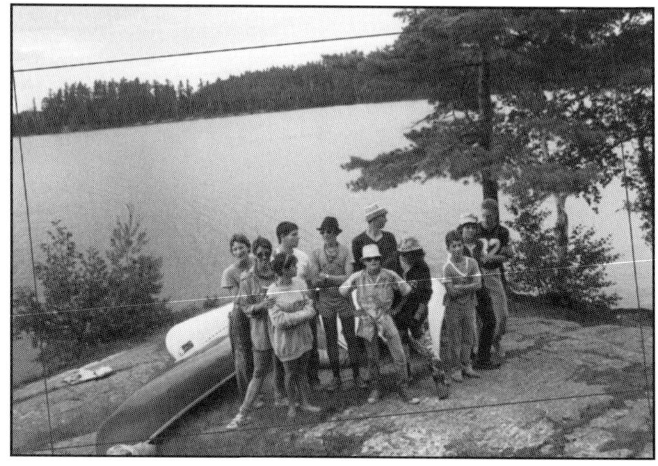

This irritating 'crooked-horizon' shot can be rescued by some carefully executed cropping. Cover the strips outside of the black rectangle with a few scraps of paper, and immediately you will see how much this simple procedure improves the quality. Therefore, take a paper cutter or a pair of scissors and cut the print along the black crop lines. The resulting picture will look less distracting and much more natural. This hassle could have been avoided in the first place by keeping the camera, and therefore the horizon, straight when I was looking through the viewfinder, but ... (fill in an excuse).

The photo shows several young paddlers posing for their group shot on the campsite they have just established. Especially in the case of young people it is very important that a good photographic record be made of what is happening throughout their canoe trip. These shots will be of great value to them in their later lives. Notice that this photo includes much of the surroundings as well as several of the canoes, and not just the group of people (posed rather stifly, I must admit).

The picture below illustrates another problem, but one that is not so easy to remedy. These people were preparing lunch on a large flat rock on the north shore of Georgian Bay. Although the group was nicely placed in a semicircle around the open wanigan, and everybody was busy cutting, cleaning and cooking the food, it was one o'clock in the afternoon and the bright sun was shining down with a hard unforgiving light that created black shadows everywhere, making good photography a bit difficult.

Conceivably it might have been possible to lighten up these shadows somewhat by using a reflector to bounce sunlight into the dark areas, but who has this kind of equipment available on a leisurely trip in far-away canoe country? (Even fill-flash was not an option as there was no flash of any kind available.)

The photo was taken anyway, because having a less-than-perfect picture is much better than not having one at all. Sometimes compromises have to be made.

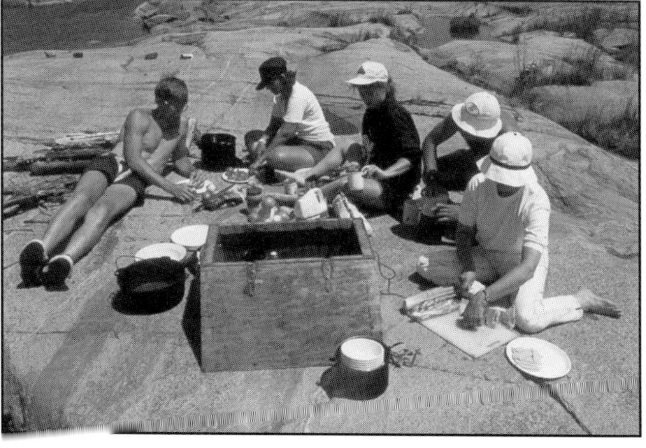

Campsite

This photo documents a group campsite located at the confluence of the Missinaibi and Mattagami rivers. I made it a vertical because I wanted to include the big rock in the foreground and accentuate the shape of the foam-lined edge of the water. The rock adds a strong feeling of depth and the sunlight coming from the top of the photo provides interesting backlighting.

When camped close to the water's edge like this, it is not likely you will drop your camera in the water, but you still must be aware of the dangers your equipment can be exposed to in this environment. The wind can blow water spray mixed with sand and foam all over you and your equipment, and the wet sand on the rock-strewn beach makes it easy for you to trip and damage your camera.

An example illustrating how easily things can go wrong without one realizing it, is given in this photograph. The fuzzy spot just below the right-hand tent is caused by a grain of sand that had stuck to the front of the lens. When looking through the viewfinder, the grain was almost impossible to see. Its presence only became evident when the slide was projected at home. Regularly checking your equipment for cleanliness, the front of the lens included, is obviously very important.

There are a few more weaknesses in this photograph that should be discussed. Although the backlighting on the rocks and tents is visually quite attractive, there is some unpleasant flare in the picture, caused by the sun shining directly into the lens.

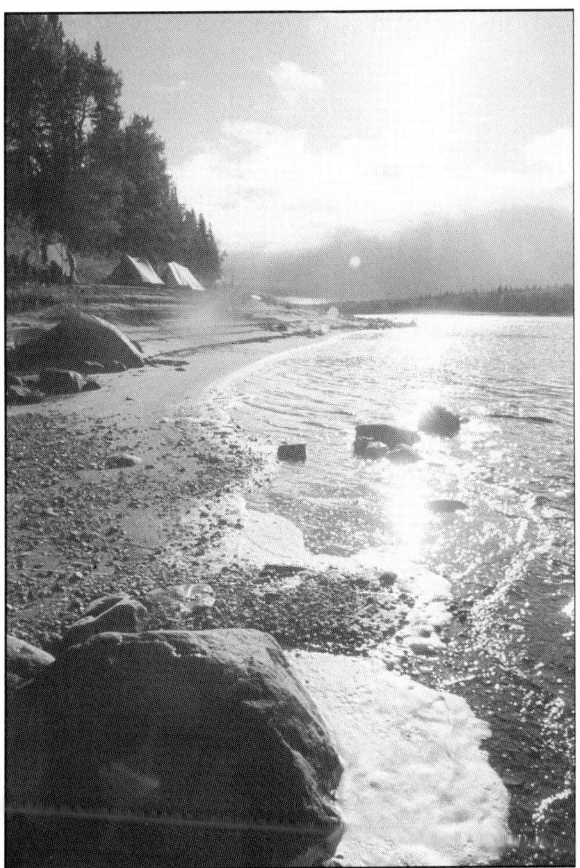

Parts of the right-hand side, therefore, look somewhat washed out. Furthermore, the composition is rather awkward. All the 'weight' of the picture (rocks, shoreline, tents, trees) is concentrated on the left-hand side, whereas the right-hand side only contains the quite undetailed river surface and sky. It feels as if the photo might tumble to the left. It would have been better if, by stepping one metre to my left, I had placed the big rock in the right bottom corner, thus creating a more balanced image. In spite of its shortcomings, I decided to keep this in my collection, because it was the one photo I had of this place.

By carefully analyzing your pictures, especially the ones that have shortcomings, you can learn much about how to improve your photographs. It would be time very well spent indeed.

Campsite

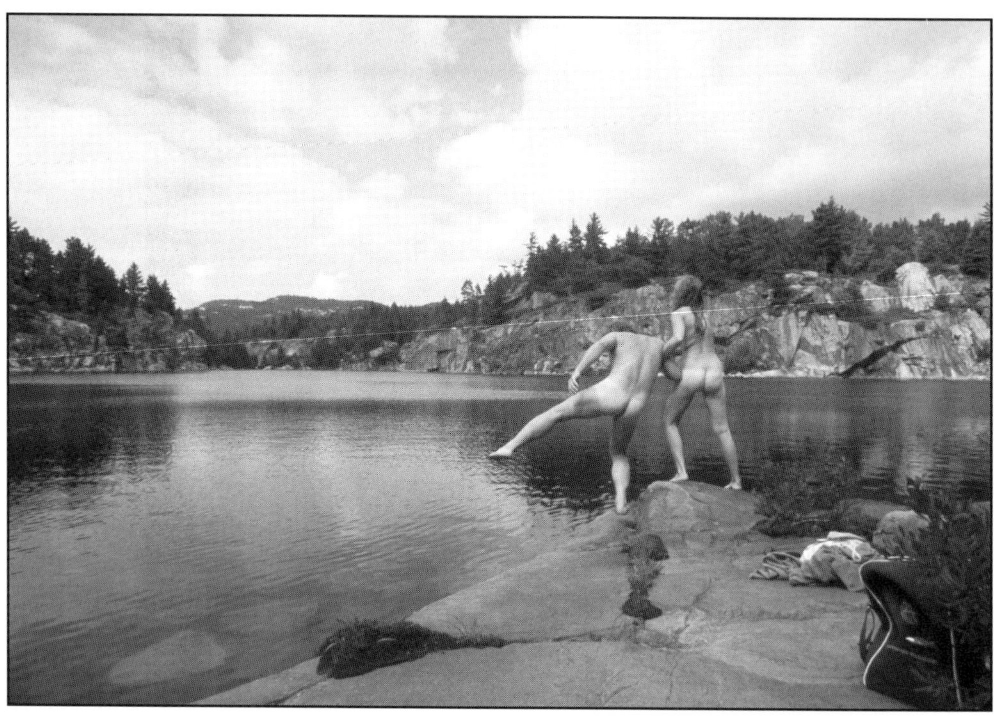

What is more delightful, after a day of hard sweaty work in the canoe, on the trail and the campsite, than finally taking off all your clothes and jumping into the lake for a well-earned refreshing swim? What indeed! It is one of the supreme joys in our tripping lives, this daily ritual we gratefully call "the blessing of the waters."

And how lucky you are as the photographer of such an intimate event to have friends who do not object to being photographed in the nude, just as they are under their grimy tripping clothes (obviously worn not for decoration, but only for reasons of practicality and protection against the bugs and the elements). Nudity and nature go hand in hand,

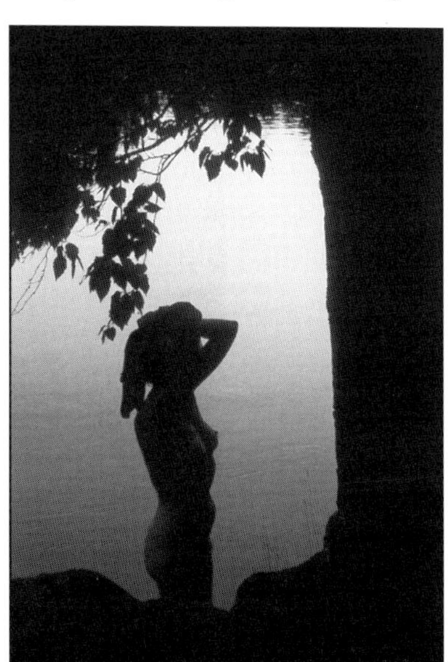

inseparable as canoe and paddle. It is so good to see these two grown-ups enjoy their precious freedom, and play like children having innocent fun trying to push each other into an out-of-the-way lake in Killarney Provincial Park.

Some people have problems accepting nudity as an integral part of the outdoors, but few can deny the beauty honest images such as these can provide. This woman, drying her hair with gentle gestures, creates an innocent and appealing silhouette, the tree tenderly reaching down and caressing her with its leaves. An enchanting image.

Make such photos discretely and *always* consult the people about their intended use; get permission if you want to show the pictures to others.

Campsite

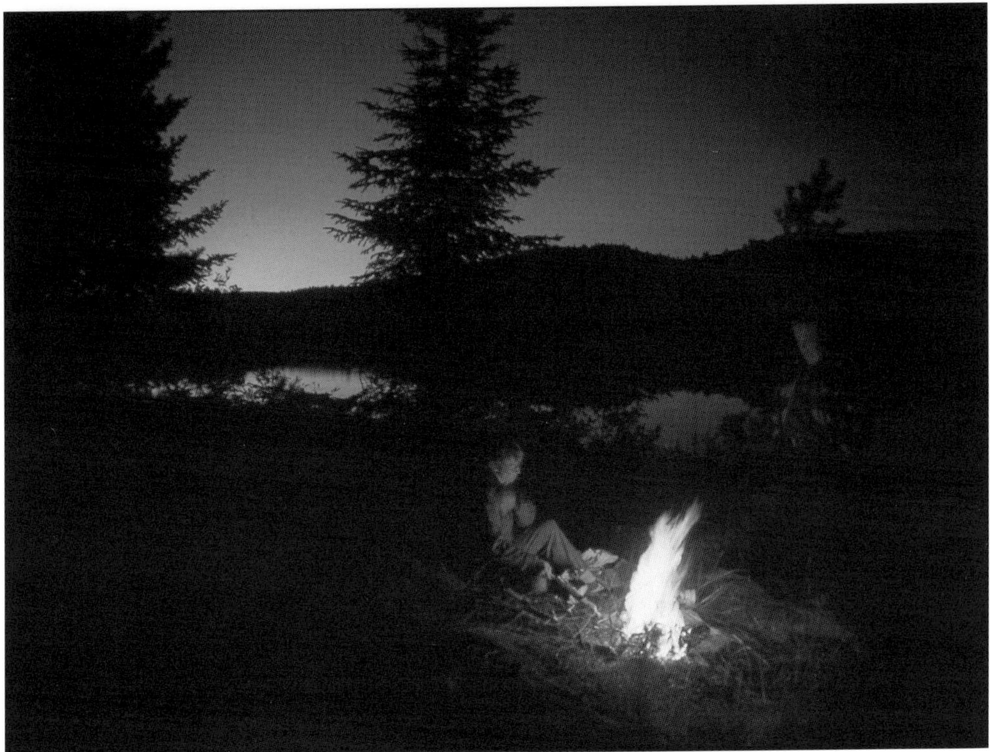

It is every canoeing photographer's dream to make a good shot of a campfire with people around it and crowned by a sky ablaze with glorious sunset colours. This is quite a technical challenge as there are three distinct areas requiring attention as far as correct exposure is concerned: the sky, the fire and the people.

If you have a limited or no understanding of the technique behind correct exposure, and/or you use a camera without possibilities for adjusting the settings, just put your camera on a tripod or another means of support and make the photograph (preferably several), letting the automatic camera do all the measuring and setting. The modern camera is an amazing creation and can often take fine photographs of difficult subjects without human input.

If, however, you understand what exposure is about, your best bet is to make a spot meter reading of a representative section of the sunset sky (the afterglow in case of this picture) and use that for your photograph. This compromise will lead to a correctly exposed sky (the most important one of the three areas mentioned above), overexposed flames and probably somewhat underexposed people. Make a series of photos around this measured setting, write the technical information down in your notebook and then at home select the most successful picture for future reference.

It is a good idea to make several photographs in succession, to show the changing colours as the sun continues setting. Using adequate support for your camera is most important, because the exposure times may run in the seconds. But all the effort you put into this photographic challenge will be worth it; few campsite photographs are more captivating than these. A similar kind of campfire photograph is shown in the section Colour.

Campsite

At first, this photograph may look like just another funny picture of a place in the outdoors where humans occasionally do what comes naturally. However, there is much more behind this simple snapshot of a toilet seat nailed to a tree than an easy laugh. It is possibly the most meaningful picture in this book because it emphasizes what we have to do for nature: we should always do our very best to keep it undisturbed and clean as much as possible; protect and preserve it for its own sake as well as ours. That is a formidable and often thankless task, but it must be done, because there is far too much ugliness in canoe country as a result of callous unethical actions by only a relatively small number of uncaring persons.

The picture tells us a bitter story of such neglect and bad environmental practice because this is a harmful outdoors toilet, a place (much too close to the campsite) where the excrement, including the paper, is just dumped and forgotten, left for the animals to disturb and for other trippers to 'enjoy.' Every good outdoors etiquette book says it clearly: make a simple hole in the topsoil, about 15 cm deep and far away from water and campsite, and fill it in after use. Never leave your refuse in the first convenient spot you can find. (Note to some photographers: do not just drop your film wrappers and containers on the ground to become litter; take them home with you.)

By making such revealing photographs of the dreadfully stupid things that can be done to nature, and by showing them to many people, discussing them, publishing them if you can, you will heighten people's awareness. All these actions help in the fight against indifference and abuse. Your photo does not have to be a work of art, a simple record shot will do if it conveys the message. It is how you use such photos that counts, not their technical quality. Do not hesitate to make these important records of some people's harmful actions. Your story can have impact and make a difference for the better.

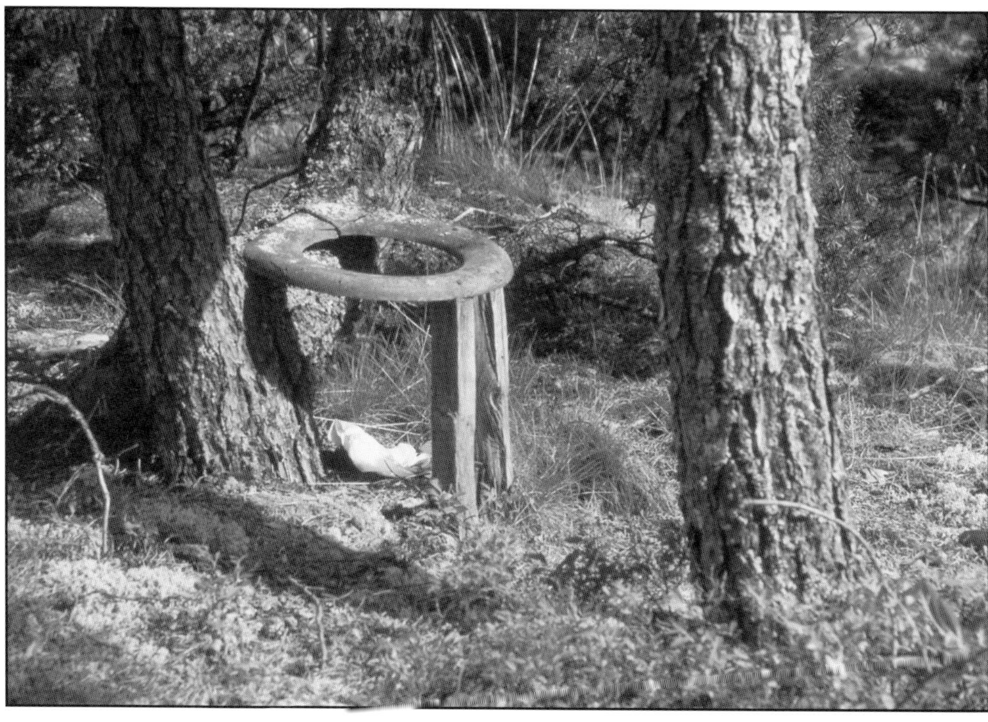

Campsite

SKY AND WEATHER

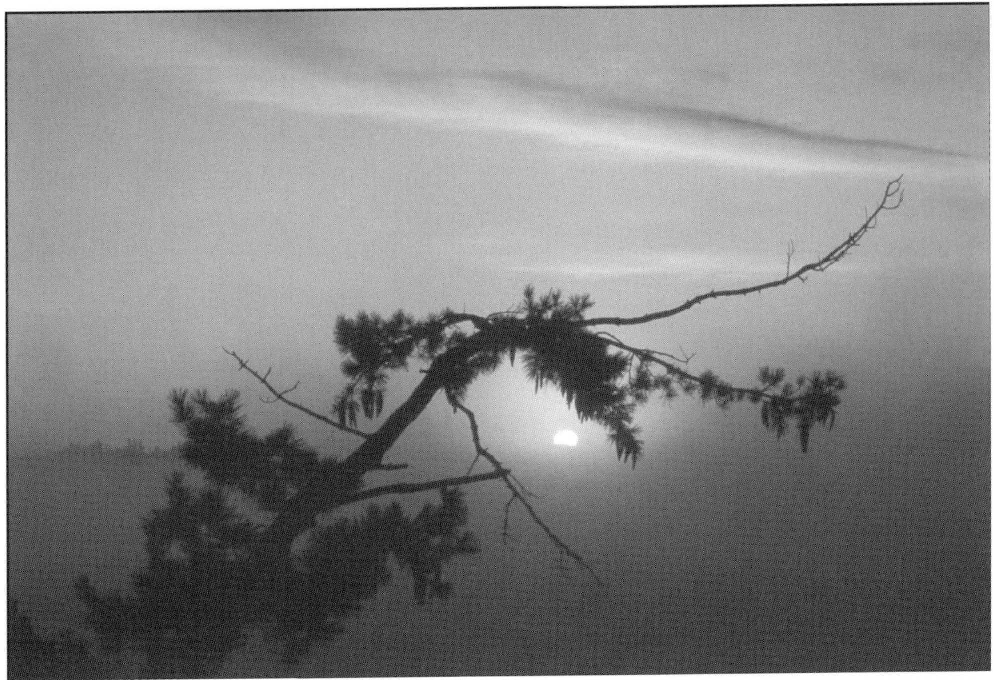

Aaah…! Sunrise…! Sunset…! Blessed are they who have the open mind and seeing eyes to stand transfixed, captured again and again by the mesmerizing displays of some of nature's most sublime beauty. Absorbing those fabulously gorgeous colours overflowing the sky, whose appearance and hues imperceptibly change with the slowly moving sun, our hearts are filled with gratitude for being allowed to treasure these soul-warming experiences.

Obviously, in order to observe the changing light of the sun, one has to be in the right place at the right time to see it all happen. And, in the case of greeting the rising sun at particularly appropriate locations, it can mean having to get out of bed early. For instance, in order to take the above photo (and also the one on page 114, taken on another day), our alarm clock woke us at three in the morning, giving us enough time to get to the top of the north rim of the Barron Canyon by five.

On previous visits to this marvellous observation post, I had noticed the curved branch hanging over the chasm, making a sharply delineated silhouette against the light of the early sun, low in the background. To make several shots of the sun as it gradually appeared out of the slight fog covering the horizon, I put the camera (loaded with ISO 100 slide film) on a tripod and selected a position that gave me a view of the sun being embraced by the branch. In the end, it was all very much worth the trouble of having to get up so early and climb the steep trail in the dark.

Do not listen to those defeatist photographers who say that sunrises and sunsets are visual clichés; just listen to your heart. If you love what you see when the sun performs its magic, capture the photographs as best you can and as much you want. Again and again and again! You will always relish those precious images of pure colour and form.

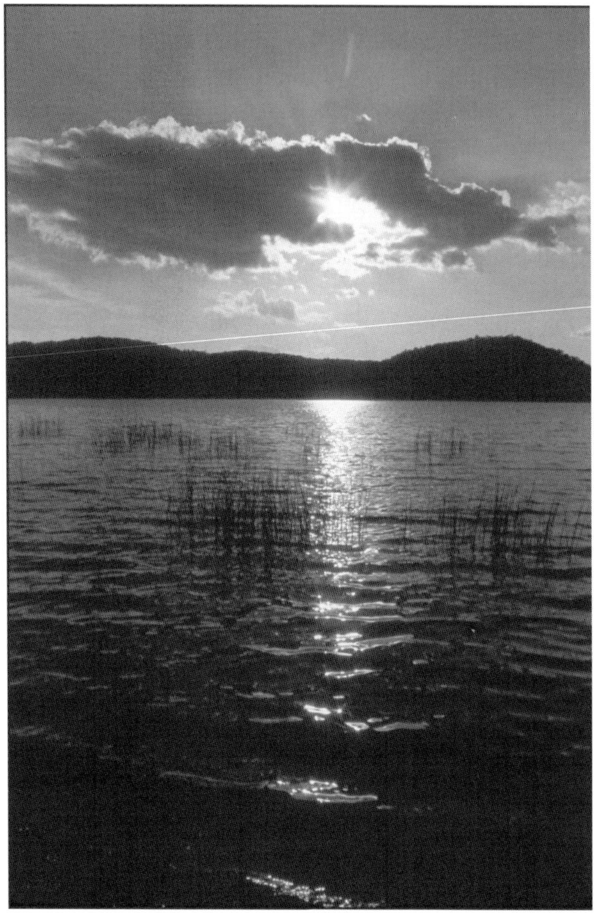

It is endlessly fascinating to study the wonderful lighting effects the sun can create on undulating water surfaces. While standing on the shore with the camera ready for action, observe what is taking place in front of you and think about how you can best photograph these scenes. The opportunities for fine photos are there; you only have to find them.

For instance, notice the subtle interplay between the various elements in this picture—sun, cloud, sky, hills, water, reeds, rippling trail of reflected light— and experiment with their positions relative to each other by moving around and changing your point of view. Move to the side so that the reeds are standing in the sun's reflection, subtly changing its appearance. Consider shooting the picture as a horizontal. Zoom in and out to exclude or include various parts. Put the reflection in the middle of the picture, or more to the side.

Above all, it is the sun-cloud combination that decides the mood of this picture, even though it occupies only one-third of the total area. If the sun gets away from behind the cloud and floods everything with light, you have a different picture. And if the sun is completely covered by the cloud, there are different images still. The more time you spend building photographs from their basic components and analyzing them, the more you will understand about composition (which actually is filling a rectangle with visual elements to create a pleasing whole).

A crucial step in the making of photographs is finding the right rectangle in which to do your composing. A simple but very effective way to help you do that is by using your hands to make a rectangular opening in front of your face, look at the subject and select the correct framing by moving your hands closer to or farther away from your viewing eye, then rotate them to experiment with vertical or horizontal framing. An even easier and more accurate method is to take a 35 mm slide mount and hold it in front of your viewing eye at various distances, vertically or horizontally. Attach the slide mount to a string and keep it in the camera case or on your person, and you will always have a convenient framer available. Experiment, play, enjoy. Get to know your subject, and learn.

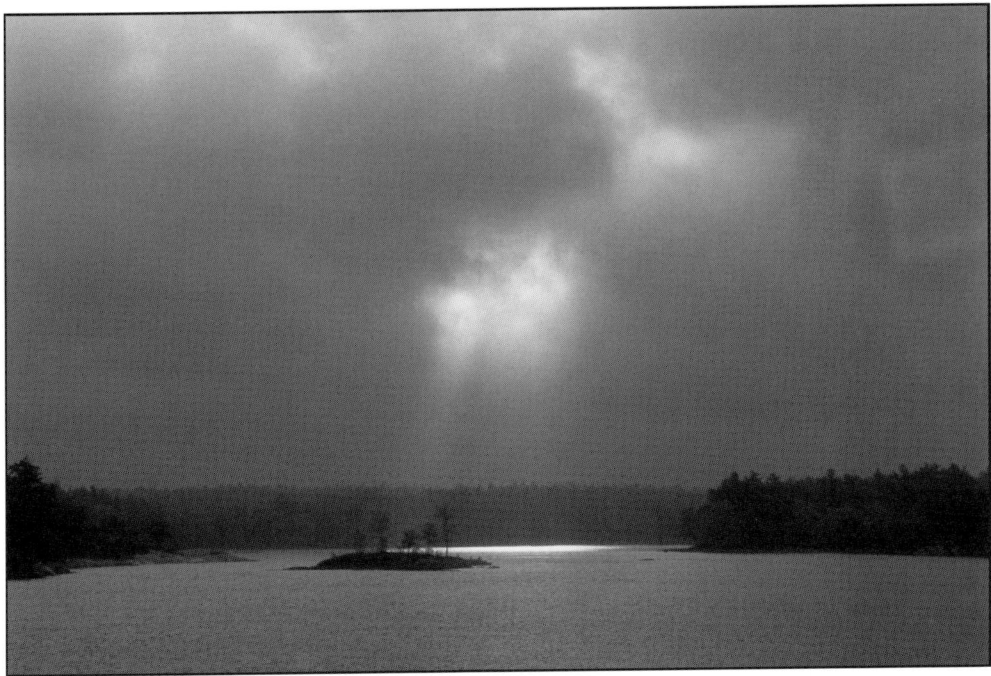

When the world is covered by a thick low-hanging blanket of clouds, there is little colour; everything looks grey. But give the sun one small opening to peek through, and suddenly pure enchantment fills the frame. From a rather nondescript image of a far shoreline, the scene in the above photo is miraculously transformed into a wondrous picture worthy of a fairy tale. What a little shaft of sunlight can do! Be aware of pictures like these; they can bring a romantic mood and mystery to your story.

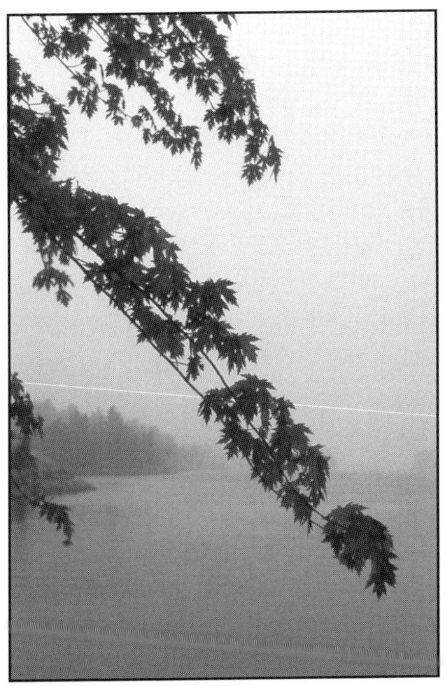

The low-contrast surreal effect of fog, which is a cloud hanging so low you are standing in it, is something to be used to create pictures that have a very distinct atmosphere where everything in the background becomes softened, receding away in the distance. Because of the low level of the diffuse light, use of a tripod is a good idea.

The picture on the left has a dominant, sharply delineated subject in the foreground, giving it a strong feeling of depth.

When photographing in the fog, which is often thickest early in the morning, you should take some precautions to protect your camera from the moisture in the air. The front element of the lens may become coated with a thin layer of water droplets that have condensed out of the mist. Carefully clean the lens with a special soft chamois cloth or a piece of lint-free tissue.

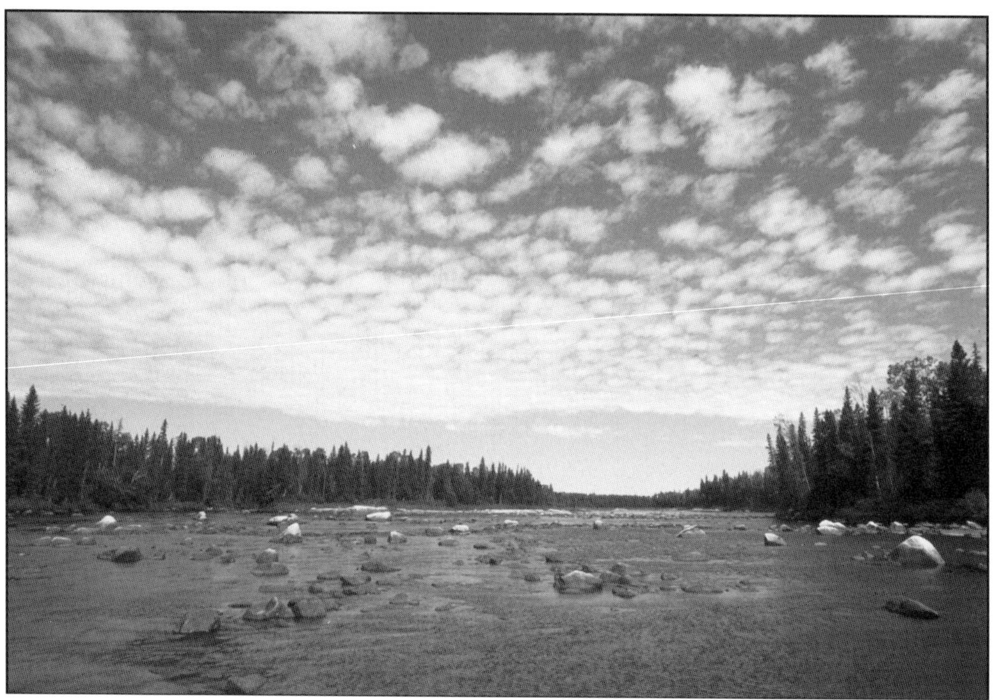

Clouds make the sky come alive. They can be like children playfully chasing each other in a heavenly game of tag. But they can also become monstrous thunderheads, ready to pour millions of tons of water onto the earth, creating great floods. A sky filled with clouds is always a compelling sight, displaying the beautiful patterns, textures, light and colours that can be found only in nature.

For the alert and ingenious photographer, clouds in their limitless but elusive diversity create exquisite shapes that can be turned into fascinating images with a great variety of dramatic nuances. They can be recorded either as sculptures in the sky on their own or together with earth-bound objects such as landscapes. The above photo, for instance, shows the sky covered by myriad little clouds like cotton puffs that are seemingly getting smaller in the distance. The pattern of the clouds is repeated in the extensive rock garden of the Missinaibi River's Albany Rapids. When looking for images like these, experience and a keen eye for beauty really can make a difference.

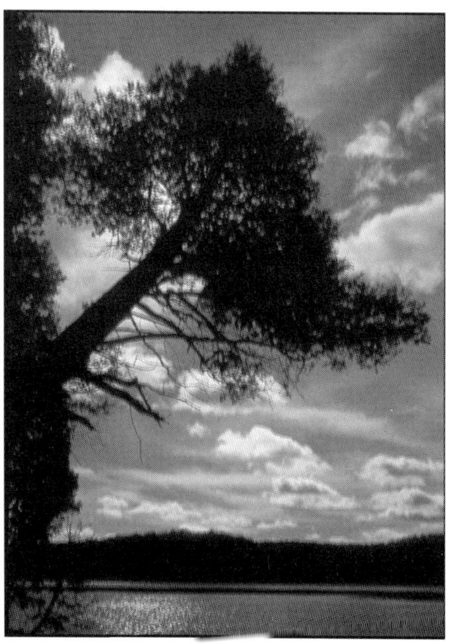

In the picture on the left, although the clouds are in the background and not prominent at all, they still determine the atmosphere of the photo. Without the clouds the picture would be rather uninteresting, in spite of the attractive centre of interest, the curiously angled tree silhouette.

Reflections are purely optical effects generated by light; they do not exist as tangible objects. Still, if the reflecting water surface is very smooth, reflections can look extremely realistic, often creating visually striking images. This symmetrically balanced picture of a cloud-streaked sky was taken from a canoe early in the morning, and shows one such graphic arresting image. When you are paddling, keep your eyes open for reflections of sidelit rocks and trees on the water's edge. They can produce compelling photographs. Particularly interesting are dead trees that have fallen in the water, creating bizarre shapes with their crooked branches.

In the bottom photo, where only a small section of the sky itself is visible, the reflections of the clouds are responsible for the

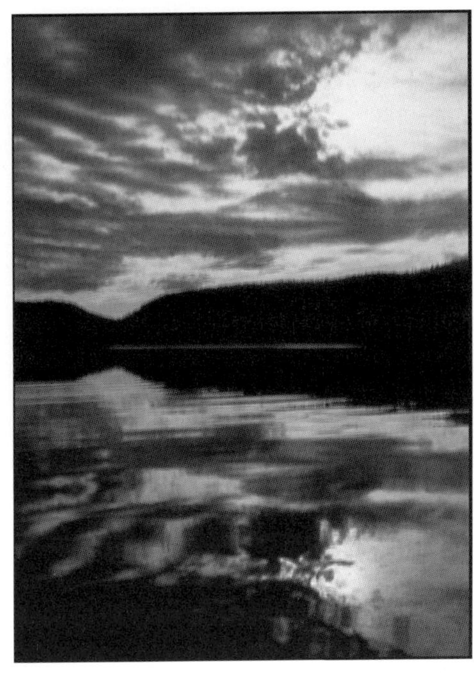

special 'feel' of the image. Comparing this shot with the one on page 40 illustrates the creative fun one can have while playing with the elements in a composition.

Looking for pictures within pictures is a good way to train your visual awareness. For instance, the rather confusing (seemingly upside-down) photo on page 118 only consists of a small central section of the photo below.

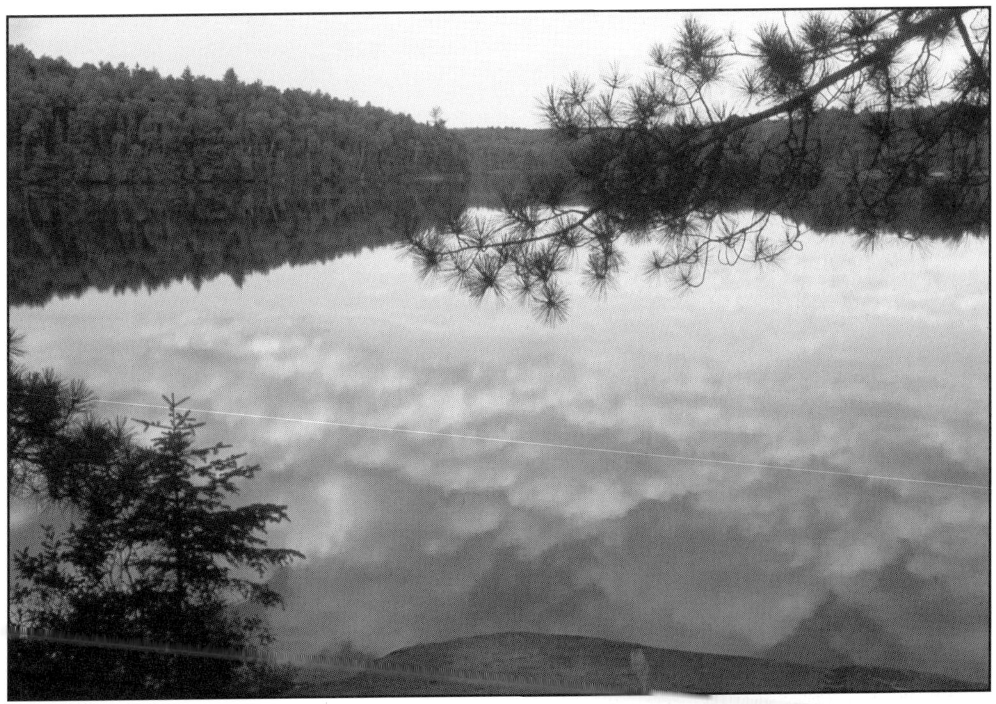

When the sun shines directly into a lens, especially a complicated one like a zoom lens with its many internal glass elements, the result can be a number of disturbing optical images in the picture, degrading its overall quality and often completely ruining it. These unwanted images are caused by stray light bouncing around in the optical system, producing flare and ghosts that, besides the random spots of light, may also result in loss of contrast and sharpness in the picture.

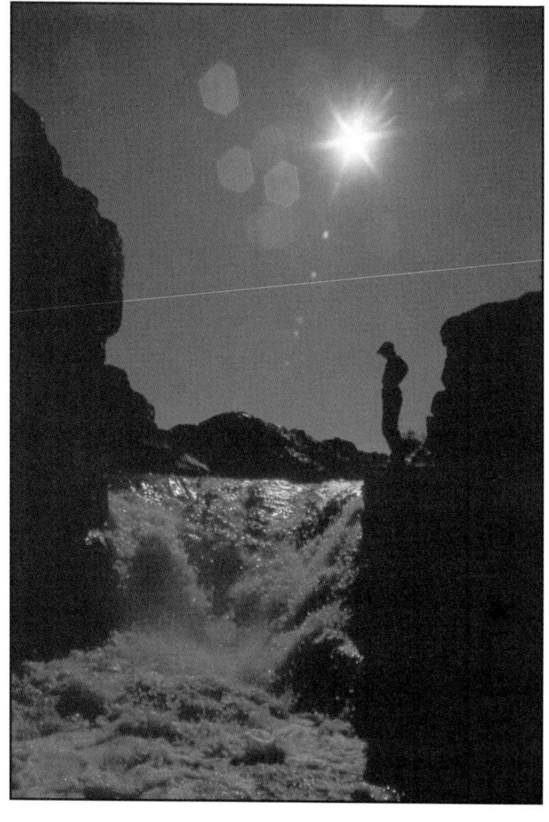

For instance, this photo, taken at the second drop in the Thunder House Falls of the Missinaibi River, exhibits quite a bit of flare and ghosts (the polygons below and to the left of the sun). However, here it was done on purpose, because I wanted to see if I could create striking optical effects that would give the photo something special. Indeed, although often unpredictable, the result of letting the sun hit the lens is, in this case, quite interesting.

The best way to avoid unwanted flare and ghosts is to keep sun from shining directly into the lens. Shield the front of your camera from the sun by providing shade from a hat or some other object. If the sunlight comes from the side, a lens hood may help block it.

(By the way, never look at the sun directly through the viewfinder, or you may seriously damage your eye.)

When shooting the moon, as in this photo, two technical considerations are important: determine the correct exposure and use a tripod because the exposures should be

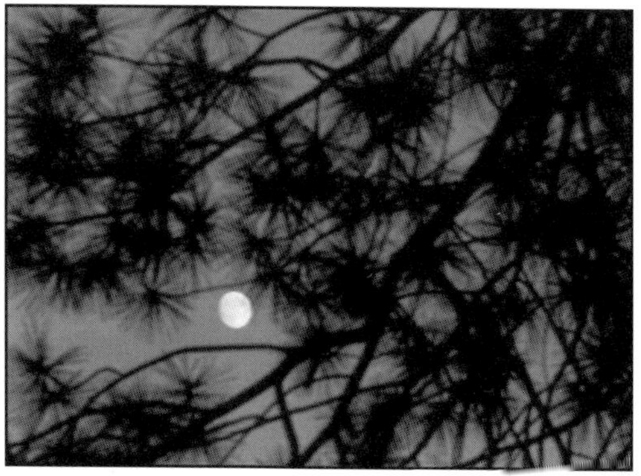

long. Exposures can be measured by means of a good light meter, especially one with spot-metering capabilities. However, you can also use a trial-and-error method by making a series of test exposures, writing the appropriate numbers down and determining, after processing the film, which exposures produce the best results. Use those as a reference for future shots.

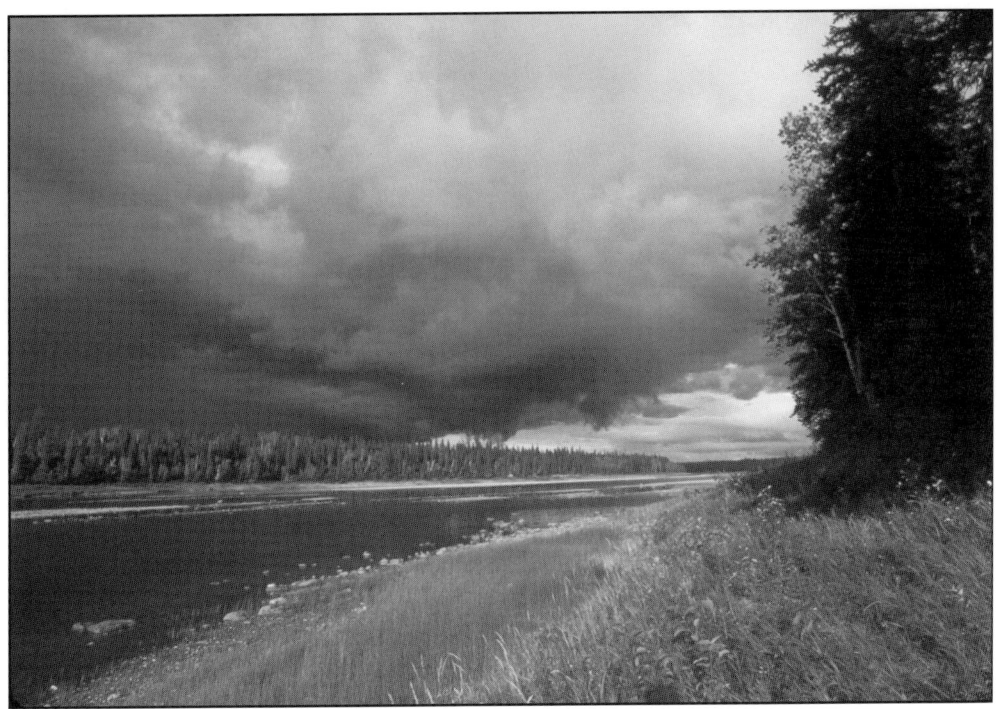

Most outdoor photography is done in dry weather, when there is no chance for rain to damage the sensitive equipment. However, bad-weather photography can produce dramatic pictures of dark ominous skies and rain-swept water surfaces, making the story of your wilderness trip much more realistic and true-to-life. The worse the weather, the more impact and mood your pictures will have. And the more unique they will be, because too few people attempt this kind of photography.

So, when slate-grey storm clouds threaten to gradually block out the sun, get your camera and prepare to make some fine pictures filled with atmosphere. Once appropriate precautions have been taken (see chapter Equipment), wet-weather photography can produce images worthy of your pride.

Rainbows, created from the union of sunlight and minuscule water drops of mist, are one of nature's most intriguing atmospheric displays. When the rainbow you want to photograph is too large for the frame, try tipping your camera over so that the horizon lies on a diagonal, giving you more room in the frame. With some luck you may be able to capture the complete rainbow. Two technical tips: to darken the sky and make the rainbow colours more vivid, you should underexpose somewhat and use a polarizer filter.

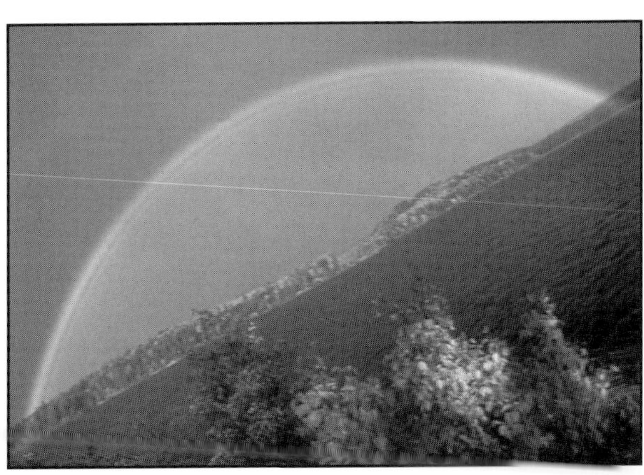

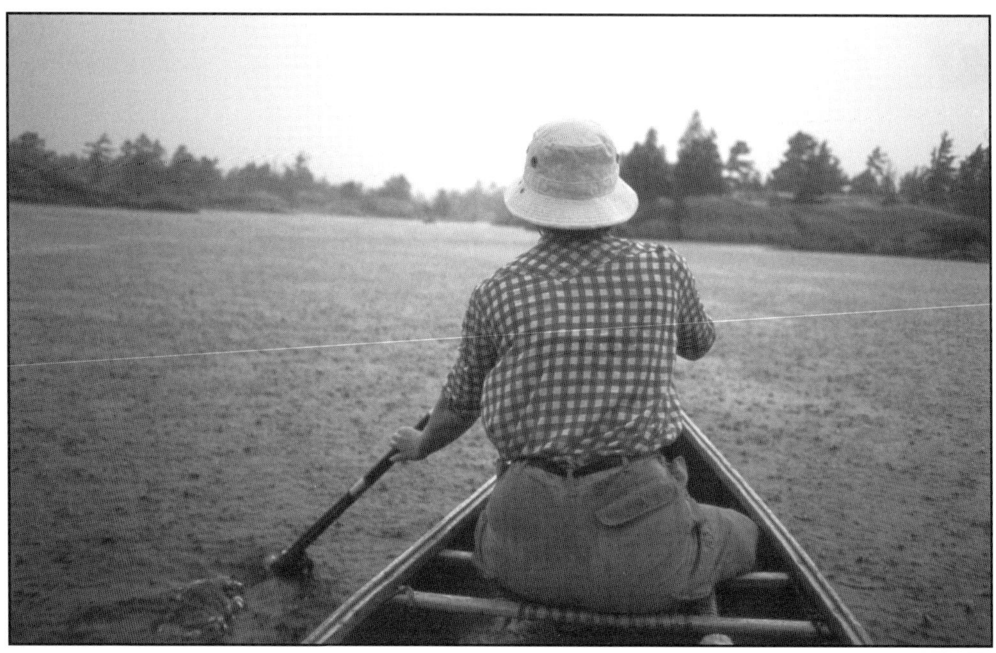

Making photos of people paddling in the rain is, in fact, quite simple, at least if you are willing to put up with the adverse weather conditions yourself, and if you have the right equipment. These two snapshots illustrate some special moments when a sudden rain shower had surprised us without our rain gear on (but it was such nice mid-summer weather when we left on our day trip!), quickly soaking us while carving uncounted little pits into the water surface. Although we were soon wet through and through, we hurriedly went ashore—as shown in the bottom picture—to get some shelter under a tarp, while the rain continued unabated.

As usually happens to us in situations like this, we adapted quickly and had lots of fun, using our waterproof point-and-shoot camera for some snapshots to record the events. (And who cares if the horizon is a bit crooked?)

Because of the heavily overcast sky, the light level was rather low, although the light itself had a pleasant soft quality without hard shadows. If you know beforehand that you are going to shoot in the rain, load your camera with high-speed film, say ISO 400. This will give a better chance for sharp pictures as you can shoot with a shorter exposure time. Better still, if you go on a trip where the weather is expected to be dark and wet much of the time, take a special water-proof or rainproof camera loaded with high-speed film along, just for rain shots.

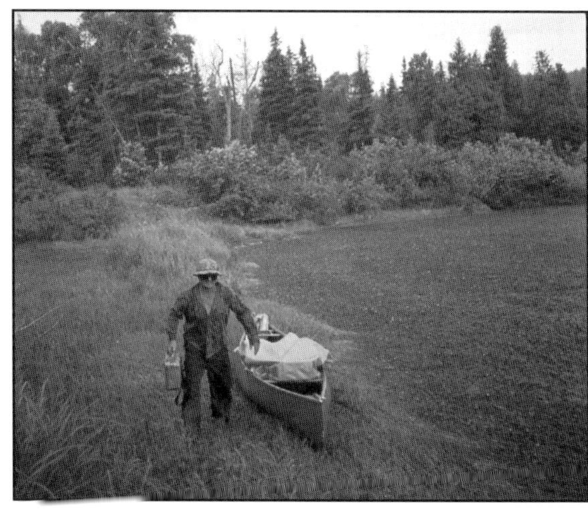

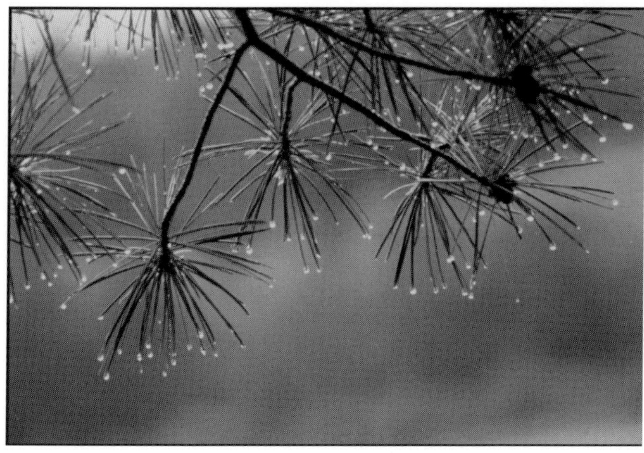

Finally, the rain is over and the wet world is waiting to be photographed. Now get out of your cosy tent, put your camera on the tripod and roam around the campsite, looking for many subjects that have been touched and transformed by the rain.

These pine needles, each with a single drop of water on its tip, create a fine picture against the blurred background. The very simple photograph would have been even better if the light area in the top-left corner had been avoided by moving the camera somewhat or by zooming in closer. It is important to frame your pictures correctly by paying attention to details, especially at the edges. If you work seriously to strengthen your photographic technique and your talent for seeing subject matter, you will surely be able to make photos like the close-up of the droplets shown in the section Colour.

The bottom picture is a nice portrait of a campsite after the rain. Everything is wet, the tent has a glossy sheen to its smooth finish, and the upside-down canoe has successfully protected the gear under it from the downpour. The tree branches close off the image at the top, eliminating much of the grey sky. This picture has a strong feeling of depth because of the haze hanging over the river in the background. It is photographs like these that make the story of your canoe trip come really alive.

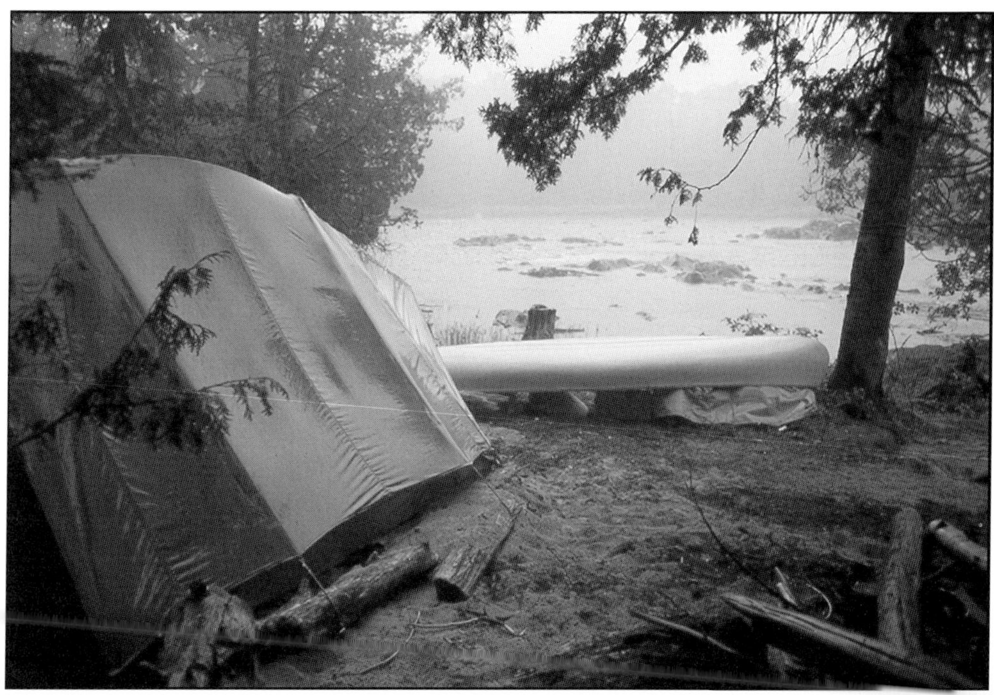

Your photography will improve dramatically by giving yourself assignments to make pictures of only one kind of subject matter at a time. Keep working at these tasks until you have learned to do them correctly. By concentrating on understanding and solving specific problems only, you challenge yourself to improve creativity and refine technical skills. Develop your visual awareness by really looking at light and what it does under special conditions; learn to feel at ease with a camera and other equipment before you actually need to use them in the field. If not successful at first, try again and again. You will be surprised how soon the quality of your photography will be strengthened.

Before you go on a long canoe trip in a remote area where support and repairs are not available, teach yourself how to deal with the adverse weather situations likely to be encountered. Having to learn how to make photos in the rain when already on the trip can be very disappointing. Better be prepared.

The photo below is the result of a task I had given myself to check the efficiency of rainproofing my camera by means of a plastic bag I had made. The self-assignment was to photograph people in inclement weather, which can be done almost anywhere, not only on a canoe trip. This shot was made at a canoe race on the Gull River near Minden, where I spent a weekend of almost constant drizzle and showers photographing paddlers as well as spectators, using my home-made contraption. I especially concentrated on close-up portraits like this one, shooting mostly at eye level and making sure that the background was uncluttered and out of focus.

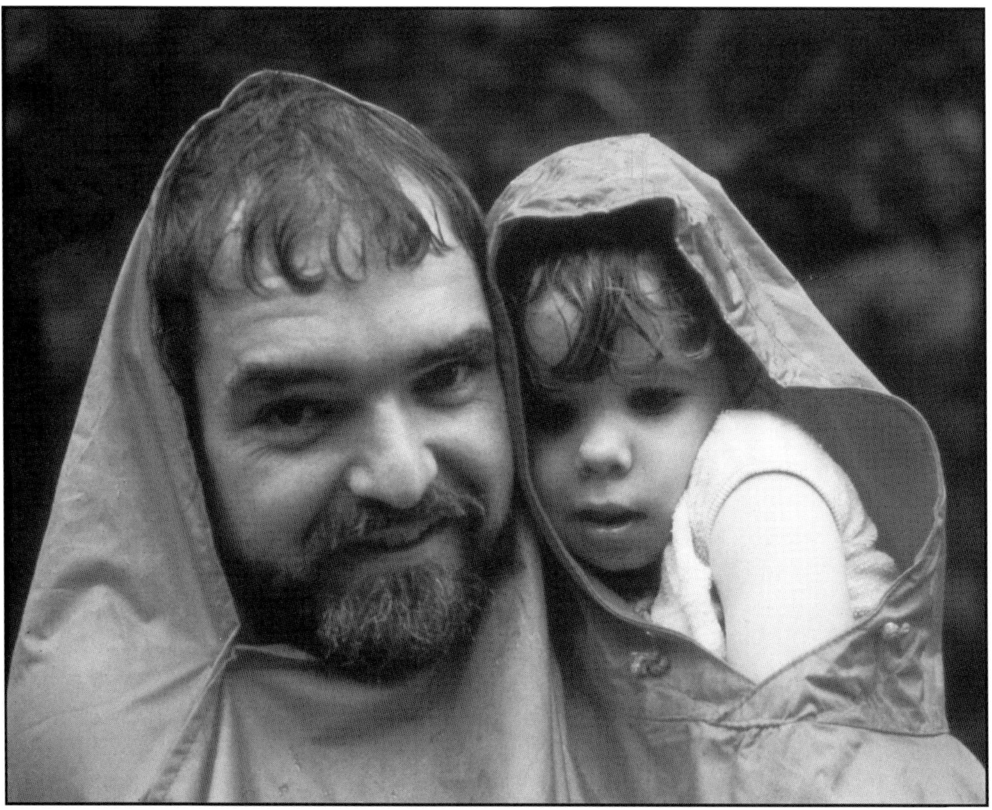

EQUIPMENT

To a large extent, paddling photography uses the same kind of equipment as general photography. Only in situations where the possibility for damage caused by water or other environmental hazards exists may specialized techniques like waterproofing be required. Because of the rapid development and wide assortment of photographic equipment available, specific makes and models will not be mentioned here. Tools and techniques will only be discussed in general terms, helping you find the right approach to solving any photographic problems and to becoming technically proficient. You can improve your paddling photography significantly by following the advice presented in this chapter. You, of course, can continue to learn more about photography by studying information from books, magazines, stores, repair shops, clubs, experts, courses…

CAMERAS–LENSES

The most popular choice for paddling photography is the extremely versatile 35 mm camera system. The similar-sized Advanced Photo System and digital camera systems are also well suited for use in the paddling environment. (To some degree, all kinds of suitably adapted cameras can be used, but the above systems are the most practical.) The cameras, lenses and numerous accessories available in these systems come in an impressive variety of makes, models, prices, specifications and quality. These are available from the extremely simple and inexpensive throw-away cameras to the highly sophisticated, dependable, durable and very expensive top-end professional cameras equipped with a huge number of features. There are quality APS cameras as small as business cards; such a tiny camera is convenient to have with you permanently on your trips.

A great advantage of the 35 mm system is that many of the cameras are easy to handle. Most of them have limited bulk and weight, and are very portable. The level of technical innovation is so high that many modern automatic cameras are good enough to make most of the technical decisions and do the required adjustments by themselves, without human intervention. For instance, numerous cameras can determine correct exposure in more than 90% of the cases. The photographer 'only' has to creatively select the subject and compose the picture, then push the button. Of course, subject selection and composition are central to your success as a photographer, whatever technical system you select.

When possible exposure to moisture and other hazards are not really a concern, 35 mm cameras can be used in paddling photography without special precautions. Only when making pictures in paddling environments that are potentially dangerous to the equipment, are specific measures and sometimes even specialized cameras required.

These situations are characterized by possible exposure to moisture (humidity, water), particles (dust, sand, rock flour, silt) and impact. Dozens of specialized cameras are available, ranging from extremely simple, weatherproof single-use cameras to professional waterproof models that can withstand almost any kind of water-related assault. Although they can take a limited amount of abuse, cameras are delicate instruments, especially the battery-powered electronic ones.

Lenses are more important for picture quality than camera bodies (as is film!), but are more vulnerable to outside influences. When exposed to hard shocks, for instance, glass lens elements may come loose from the mount, effectively destroying the lens. Treat them with extra care and keep them away from water and dust; they are very expensive to repair

Most photos in this book were taken with 35 mm single lens reflex cameras equipped with a variety of interchangeable lenses, ranging from a 20 mm wide-angle lens to a 75–300 mm telephoto zoom lens. (Because zoom lenses combine the capabilities of several single—or fixed—focal length lenses into one, they enable the making of photographs from a stationary position, such as on the shore or in the canoe, with the option of framing the photo for the best composition. Many zoom lenses are of very high optical quality.) My favourite lens for general use is a superb 24-120 mm zoom lens that covers the range of focal lengths often used in my kind of paddling photography.

A good many photos presented in the book were made with a fine quality, automatic, rangefinder point-and-shoot camera, equipped with a 35 mm lens, that I always try to carry with me on trips. This kind of compact camera is particularly good for quick grab shots, capturing the picture before the opportunity is gone. A couple of photos were made with a single-use point-and-shoot camera, which delivers prints of quite acceptable quality. These cheap throw-aways come with one roll of ISO 400 or 800 colour print film inside and can be recycled after processing. Some are even waterproof (immersible in water) or at least weatherproof (resistant to rain and spray).

To show the high quality possible with filmless digital techniques, several photos were made using a good megapixel digital camera. Digital equipment is extremely convenient and can be very helpful in demanding paddling environments, especially canoe tripping, if they are properly adapted. With this system and the appropriate tools, one can even transfer pictures from deep inside the wilderness directly to family and friends at home using satellite technology. Because digital cameras use a lot of power, it makes sense, on longer trips, to bring a solar-powered battery charger with you.

Finding the right camera for your needs is an important task; one that should be performed with care and dedication. If you spend some time studying the subject and discussing your plans with knowledgeable people, and trying out several cameras before buying, you will surely succeed in your search for the appropriate paddling photography equipment.

TIPS

- Bring only what you need in terms of equipment and film; too much slows you down and takes up precious space.
- Find out how many cameras there are in your group. Save weight and bulk by sharing equipment with each other.
- Take an extra camera with you as a back-up, if you are the only photographer, especially on long difficult trips.
- Encourage the young kids in your group to have their own uncomplicated camera.It will help them tremendously to learn to see.
- Insure your photographic equipment properly against damage and loss.
- Attach waterproof identity labels to your equipment and carrying cases.
- Study the camera instruction manual before the trip. Take it with you for reference.
- Become very familiar with the camera and other tools. Practise using them without looking. Learn to set the controls automatically and intuitively. Have your camera serviced regularly, certainly before and after a long, far-away trip.
- Put in new batteries before each trip of significant duration, and bring at least one extra set of fresh batteries of the correct size.
- Replace *all* batteries at the same time.
- Check the batteries and the contacts first, should the camera stop working
- Test AA batteries by means of a flashlight or in a special tester.
- Make sure the exposure meter is accurate; have it tested and adjusted before a trip.
- Keep the camera quickly accessible for action at all times, even when in the canoe.
- Check regularly for enough film in the camera; avoid disappointments when an interesting subject comes up.
- Make sure the film is winding correctly on the take-up spool.
- Anticipate any possibilities for damage to the lens; consider protecting its front surface by permanently attaching protective filters such as skylight, ultra violet or haze filters. Remember, however, these filters will increase flare and slightly reduce image quality.
- Experiment with polarizing filters: to intensify the colour of blue sky; to reduce reflections on sun-lit water surfaces and wet foliage; to increase colour saturation when photographing rainbows.
- Do not buy cheap filters for use on an expensive lens.
- Use a lens hood as much as possible to protect the lens and to reduce flare.
- Make sure that the lens hood and filters are of the correct size to avoid vignetting.
- Attach a strap to your camera to carry it around your neck for safety.
- Bring spare lens caps, both front and back, because those get lost easily.
- Have a small film leader retriever with you; very useful if you accidentally rewind the film into the cassette.
- Bring a blower brush and micro fibre cloth to clean lens and camera body.
- Bring a notebook or a small cassette recorder to make field notes of what you shoot and how you do it.

SUPPORT

In any kind of good photography, including paddling photography, sharpness is as important as correct exposure. Efficient support of the camera, either by hand or some other means, is therefore required.

Hand-holding a camera correctly has to be learned and practised; the method depends upon the kind of camera used and the subject being photographed. The best way to support a single lens reflex camera by hand is illustrated in this photograph, which also shows that looking through the gauze of a bug vest does not have to be a problem as long as the viewfinder is held close to the eye. The following steps should be practised until they become quite natural and automatic. If you follow these general recommendations and adapt them to your own situation, your hand-held photos will be the better for it.

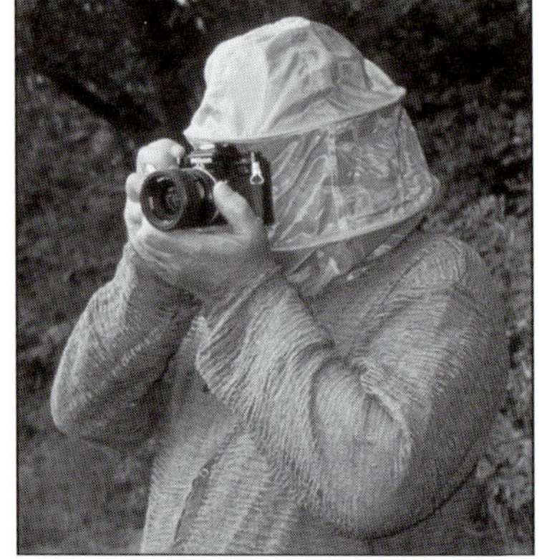

Brace yourself so that your position is firm and stable, not likely to sway or tremble even in a gusty wind. Hold the camera securely in your left hand so that the palm supports the camera body and the fingers are curled around the lens to manipulate its control rings. With your right hand, firmly grip the camera body and rest your index finger on the release button. Thumb and index finger are also used to manipulate other camera controls. Lightly press the back of the camera against your nose and forehead to provide extra support. Tuck your elbows against your body as much as feasible to keep your hands steady. Breath calmly; then hold your breath and gently push the button to take the photo. If done carefully, this technique will enable you to shoot acceptably sharp photos at exposure times of 1/15th of a second or longer. Hand-holding other types of camera, such as point-and-shoots, requires some adaptation of your holding technique because of the different body shapes, but the principle remains the same. In case of rangefinder point-and-shoot cameras, remember to keep your fingers and the camera strap away from the front of the lens and the built-in flash.

When simple hand-holding is not sufficient, another means of support must be found to ensure acceptably sharp pictures. Leaning yourself or, even better, the camera, against a tree or a rock wall or similar kind of sturdy support can be a big improvement. Even resting the camera on somebody's shoulder is worth trying. Sometimes a beanbag can help. This is a hand-sized cloth or nylon bag filled with beans, rice or a similar kind of granular material. Rest it on top of a supporting platform or structure and put the camera on it. A special photographic clamp equipped with a small ball head is also worth taking with you.

In most cases the best support is the tripod, but in order to use it you obviously must take one with you, which, admittedly, can be a nuisance on a trip. Using a tripod also enables you to improve focussing and composition because it forces you to slow down and reflect upon what you are doing. When positioning a tripod, make sure it is held in place securely and cannot be toppled over by wind or through carelessness. Even in a canoe a tripod can be used; it can make or break the quality of your photo.

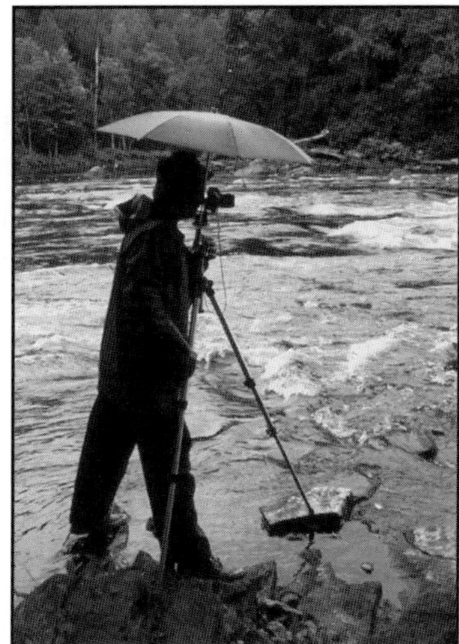

There are many models, sizes and weights of tripod available. Look some of them over and try them out before buying. The tripod to be taken on a canoe trip should, above all, be sturdy but also compact and functional. It should be as heavy as you are willing to carry. There are expensive carbon-fibre tripods available that are 30% lighter than similar ones made of aluminum. These are also less of a problem when the temperature is low and metal becomes dangerously cold to the touch. It is better to attach the camera to a ball head than a pan head; a ball head is convenient to use, takes up little room and is free from handles sticking out in several directions. Also, attach a sturdy quick-release bracket between camera and ball head; this will greatly improve the ease of securing the camera to the tripod and removing it again as quickly as possible. If you do not want to carry a tripod with you, try to construct an adequate emergency tripod by tying three canoe paddles together just below the grips, then putting a beanbag on the grips for camera support. You can also attach a clamp with a ball head to this makeshift support.

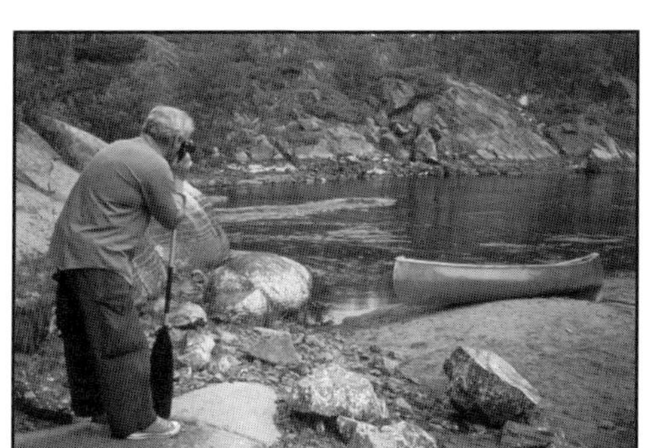

A simpler but sometimes quite effective support is the monopod, regularly used by professional sports photographers working with long telephoto lenses to make action shots. You can approximate the effect of a monopod by putting a paddle vertically on the ground and resting the camera on the grip.

PROTECTION

In paddling photography, two levels of protection exist: normal protection required by all equipment, and special protection in case of the difficult environment one may encounter in recreational paddling. Here we will only deal with the latter. Protection of film will be dealt with later.

When doing tripping photography, protection will be needed against heavy impact, temperature extremes and contaminants like water, humidity, moisture, sand, rock flour, dust and silt, often blown around by wind. Two types of this special protection must be applied: when transporting the equipment and when actually using it in adverse climatic conditions such as in a rain storm or when paddling whitewater.

Transporting equipment like cameras and tripods should be done in a way that offers them adequate protection. The familiar padded canvas or nylon bags used everywhere are quite acceptable in most cases but they are not really waterproof, only water repellent to some extent. Photographer vests equipped with numerous pockets are a very convenient way to transport photographic equipment on a shoot, but they do not provide much protection. A padded soft case used to conveniently carry a 35 mm point-and-shoot camera on portages is shown on page 139.

In the world of recreational paddling, the best protection against water and other environmental dangers is obtained by using specially designed cases, packs, bags and other containers. There are numerous different designs available in many sizes, made from flexible or hard material; some are better than others. Whatever their design and construction, they should have enough buoyancy to stay afloat in highly aerated whitewater.

The flexible containers are pouches or bags made from plastic, rubber, nylon, vinyl or other pliable material, fitted with roll closures, slide closures, watertight zippers, roll tops or fold tops. Some are inflatable to provide extra shock resistance and buoyancy. The small ones are particularly suited for use in sea kayaks. Nylon fanny packs worn around the waist and carried in front on one's lap while paddling are convenient because they ensure quick access. When water or spray is coming into the kayak or canoe, the little fanny pack can be quickly put in a large waterproof one placed on the bottom of your boat.

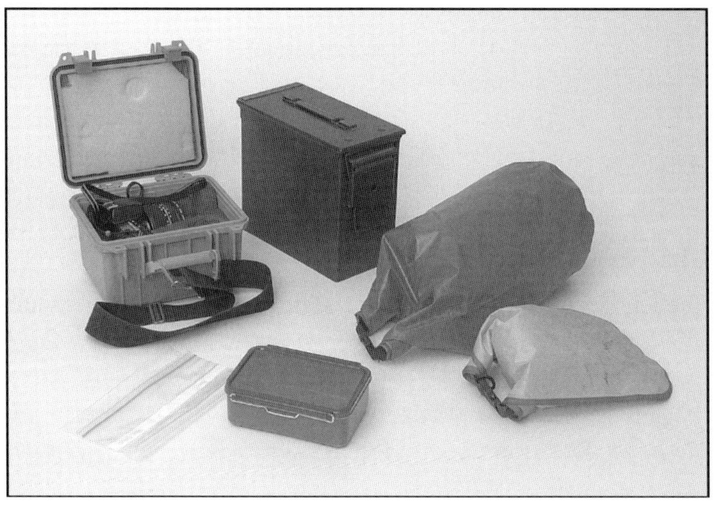

Undoubtedly, rigid hard cases give the best protection against impact; most of them are also dependably waterproof. Steel army surplus ammunition boxes used to be very popular because these are cheap, strong and easy to open and close. (They have sharp corners, though, that can damage the canoe as well as you.) Lining them with foam plastic makes their contents reasonably safe from shocks. You can also try to use a plastic bucket with a snap-on lid. These are cheap, roomy, provide easy access and give adequate protection to photographic equipment and other items that have to be kept safe and away from the water, such as car keys, money and papers. You can even use them as a stool or small table. Also, there are some watertight plastic fishing lure boxes available suitable for film, camera, lens or other small items.

However, when transporting equipment, the very best protection against shock and water, sand and other hazards is given by commercial, impact-resistant, submersible hard cases supplied with watertight neoprene/silicone O-rings. See the photo above. Be careful, though, several of the many models on the market are often hard to open with wet cold hands. Try them out first. Most of these hard cases have blocks of open-cell foam inside when you buy them. Replace these with close-cell foam (that you have to cut yourself to fit your equipment) so that water is less likely to be absorbed by the foam. If water has somehow penetrated inside one of these cases, thoroughly dry out both case and foam before putting camera and lenses inside, otherwise they will be damaged by the moisture when the lid is closed. Regularly check the O-ring to see if it is still intact and clean. Make sure the case's colour is a sunlight-reflecting white, grey or silver, or even a conspicuous orange; black absorbs too much heat from the sun. It is necessary to keep all containers, soft and hard, out of the sun as much as possible because too much heat will irreparably damage film and even cameras. A most suitable way to protect your camera in the canoe is inside one of those popular blue or green plastic canoe-tripping barrels with their easy-to-open lids. For convenient and quick access, the barrel should be placed vertically in the canoe within easy reach of the paddler/photographer.

When actually *using* the camera, different special protection measures come into play to keep it from being damaged by too much rain or splashing water. (A few drops on the outside usually do not cause real harm and can be easily wiped off.) A simple but quite effective solution to the problem is found by cutting off the bottom corners of a sturdy, four- or eight-litre heavy-duty, plastic refrigerator food bag, threading the camera strap through the holes and letting the bag hang down over the camera while wearing the camera strap around your neck. Pull the bag away from the lens when shooting. Another excellent method is to fashion an inexpensive rain- and splash-resistant housing from a pliable plastic bag by cutting holes in it for the lens and the viewfinder, securing it in place with elastic bands and adhesive tape. Leave room inside for the right hand to grab the camera with, while the left hand stays outside and holds the lens, controlling it through the flexible plastic. Always attach a protective filter and hood to the front of the lens. To some extent, even a plastic shower cap can be used in an emergency. A very convenient tool to have for protecting your camera from the rain, if there is not too much wind, is a small umbrella, preferably attached to the tripod.

There are commercial soft plastic bags available that provide an excellent rainproof and even waterproof housing for a regular camera. These have a hole in the front, covered by optical-quality glass, for the lens, and a glove attached for your right hand, enabling you to grip the camera and manipulate the controls. These are awkward, however, when you have to change film because the camera must be taken out first.

The ultimate solution to the problem of water damaging your camera is provided, of course, by using a special waterproof camera. Several models with different specifications and prices are on the market, from cheap throw-aways to expensive professional cameras. Some of these are somewhat difficult to use on dry land, though, as they are often bulkier than 'regular' cameras.

TIPS

- Protect tripod and ball head from sand, water and impact by carrying them in a special hard or soft tripod case, after wrapping the head in a plastic bag.
- When changing film or lens, protect the open camera with your body turned away

from the sun and the wind. If possible, do the change in a tent or a large, clean bag.
- When holding the camera in your hand while in a canoe, kayak or raft, secure it to your arm or body with a short strap.
- Put the protective cap on the lens when the camera is not in use.
- In an emergency, some splash resistance can be provided by applying adhesive tape to openings and small crevices of the camera.
- When walking, use a strap to carry your camera around your neck or from your shoulder.
- In the rain, carry your camera underneath your coat or jacket.
- Large garbage bags can protect packs from rain and sand.
- Try to keep your hands dry when operating the camera. They *must* be dry when opening the camera to change film.
- Do not leave your unprotected camera lying on the bottom of the canoe; it will get soaked and be trampled.
- Waterproofing is only as good as you make it, so be diligent.

MAINTENANCE AND REPAIR

Proper maintenance of your delicate photographic equipment is required to keep it in good dependable working order. At the end of each shooting day, normal maintenance means checking the outside of the camera for dirt and damage and giving it a thorough cleaning. Remove dust from inside the back of the camera each time a new film is loaded. Clean the inside of the camera, both front and back, by blowing away and brushing off dust and other particles that can badly scratch the film and damage the mechanism. Be careful not to touch the camera's delicate mirror, shutter and diaphragm. A shaving brush works well, but for cleaning the front of the lens, either a blower brush or a special lens brush that comes in its own protective container is more suitable. Several chemical bug repellants are not only greasy but they can also dissolve the plastic of your camera, making the camera stick to your hands and hair. Take precautions when you use these products.

Carefully remove fingerprints from the front of your lens by first blowing or brushing off the dust, then putting on a drop of lens cleaning liquid and finally using lens cleaning tissue to gently wipe off the smudges. Avoid using facial tissue or a handkerchief; these may leave scratches and dust. Only with a spotless lens can you hope to achieve maximum sharpness and brilliance of your images.

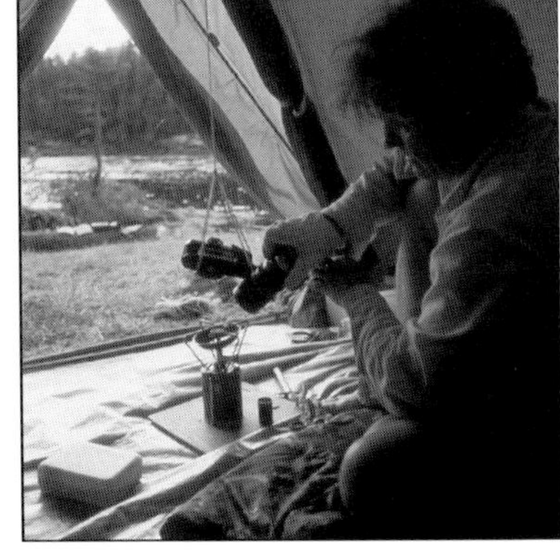

After a minor accident involving rain or splash water that has not penetrated inside, dry your hands before you wipe the outside of the camera with a clean cloth. You should always dry your hands first when changing film, lens or filter. Use a special soft chamois cloth to wipe water drops off the front of the lens, and use tissue to absorb condensation.

In case of a major accident, where both camera and film are soaked with water, there is only limited hope of saving them. One sometimes successful method is to dry out the camera in clean warm air, as shown in the photo on the previous page. On page 77 some information is given that may be of help in a such serious situations.

FILM

In paddling photography, there really are only two kinds of film: negative print film and positive slide film. (Some comments on filmless digital photography are presented below.) Special films such as Polaroid and infra red will not be discussed here.

Weight, bulk and cost of film are small compared to the rest of the outdoors gear, so take as much film as you can manage. How much film will be needed depends, of course, upon what you want to shoot. It is a good idea, before leaving for the trip, to go over your expected needs by preparing a shot list and estimating the number of films required. Then double that. Better to have left-over film when you return then missing important shots because of a lack of film. What I take with me on my trips depends on the length of the trip and the expected subjects, but in general I carry at least four roles of slide film per shooting day. If you just make photographs for yourself, not for publication, one roll of 24 images per day is a good start. Double that, if you feel confident. Remember, nothing beats the powerful magic of visual memories! The more pictures you have of your adventure, the more interesting your trip report will be.

There is not *one* film that can be used for everything, covering all situations you are likely to meet in the world of paddling. Within the more than 120 different 35 mm films available, many are of excellent quality that will enable you to make superb photographs. You can not go wrong if you use a film or films made by the reputable names in the business; just ask the people of your photo shop for advice. You may want to try out several films first, learn their characteristics and see if you like them, before deciding what to take.

On the trip, keep the films in their cassettes in the original canisters (most of them are waterproof) and mark these using a grease pen or waterproof ink with the roll number and the kind of film. Write the important shoot information in a notebook, referring to the roll number. For extra security, put the canisters in a separate waterproof box or bag, and keep this container cool and out of the sun. Heat and humidity are deadly enemies of photographic film.

Of all the film purchased in the world, about 97% is colour negative film, also called colour print film, that is used to make positive paper prints for viewing. Its very high quality and wide exposure latitude has made many professional photojournalists switch from slide film to high-speed print film (mainly ISO 400) for their work in newspaper photography. You cannot go wrong if you use that versatile film (or the slightly slower ISO 200) for your purposes too, including for paddling photography. Print film can be processed very quickly and conveniently by one-hour photo labs. The resulting prints, judiciously cropped, can be easily assembled in an album. For those with an artistic mind, black-and-white film can be used to create prints with an appealing quality, especially in case of abstract photography.

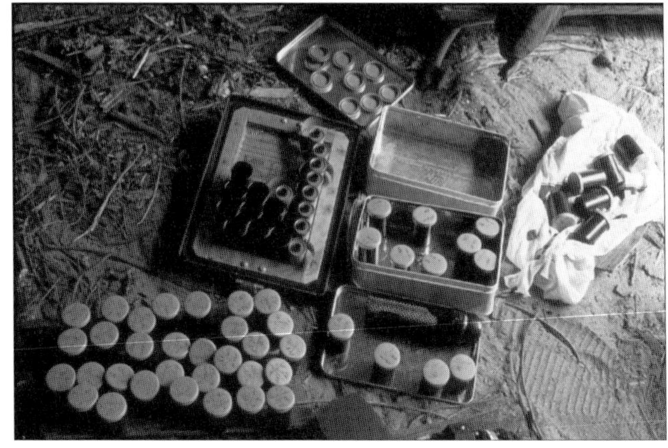

Although colour slide film has limited exposure latitude and is therefore more demanding, it generally produces finer-grained pictures of superior sharpness, colour fidelity and saturation. It is also cheaper than print film (after processing and printing) and the resulting slides are easier to file and take up less storage room. However, projecting them onto a screen is less convenient than looking through an album filled with prints. Because of its superb quality, most of the film used in the world of professional photography is slide (also called transparency) film. When slides are made into prints using standard photographic processes, the results can be disappointing. By scanning slides digitally with the help of a computer and then outputting them on a special printer, however, the prints are frequently of outstanding quality.

A good slide film speed for general use in a paddling environment is ISO 100, but you could also try to take some other slide film with you, for instance ISO 200 or ISO 400 for action photography. The photos in this book were mostly made on colour slide film ranging from ISO 64 to ISO 400 (primarily ISO 100), but some high-speed ISO 400 print film, colour as well as black-and-white, was also used.

Digital photography does not use film, but records the images on special media such as disks or cards, which require similar kind of care and protection from heat and humidity as does film.